Growth, Inequality and Social Development in India

Developmental Pathways to Poverty Reduction Series
Series Editor: Yusuf Bangura

Efforts to fight poverty cannot be separated from broader processes of economic growth and development. It is the premise of this series that variations in poverty outcomes are best understood through countries' development trajectories or structural change, as well as the interconnections of institutions, policies and practices in the social, economic and political spheres.

This series brings together contributions that engage with current policy debates on poverty reduction from a developmental and social policy perspective. As the international community approaches 2015, the Millennium Development Goals are a growing focus of attention, as is the shaping of the post-MDG agenda. Contributions to this series highlight a range of institutional, policy and political dimensions across the economy, society and polity that need to be taken into account for an inclusive and sustainable development agenda beyond 2015.

This series is being inaugurated in 2012 with six volumes emerging from research carried out under the auspices of the United Nations Research Institute for Social Development (UNRISD). The research examined 16 cases from the perspectives of development strategies and structural change; wealth and income inequality; social protection; social services; organized interests; and developmental state capacity.

The key findings of the research are reported in the UNRISD flagship report *Combating Poverty and Inequality: Structural Change, Social Policy and Politics*, and in the first six volumes of the present series.

UNRISD is grateful to the Swedish International Development Cooperation Agency (SIDA) for their financial support of this research, as well as the governments of Denmark, Finland, Mexico, Norway, South Africa, Sweden, Switzerland and the United Kingdom for providing core funding to UNRISD during the course of this work.

Titles include:

R. Nagaraj (*editor*)
GROWTH, INEQUALITY AND SOCIAL DEVELOPMENT IN INDIA
Is Inclusive Growth Possible?

Forthcoming titles are:

Khoo Bhoo Teik (*editor*)
POLICY REGIMES AND THE POLITICAL ECONOMY OF POVERTY REDUCTION IN MALAYSIA

Jeremy Seekings and Nicoli Nattrass
POLICY, POLITICS AND POVERTY IN SOUTH AFRICA

Onalenna Selolwane (*editor*)
POVERTY REDUCTION AND CHANGING POLICY REGIMES IN BOTSWANA

Juliana Martínez Franzoni and Diego Sanchez-Anochea (*editors*)
GOOD JOBS AND SOCIAL SERVICES: HOW COSTA RICA ACHIEVED THE ELUSIVE DOUBLE INCORPORATION

Yusuf Bangura (*editor*)
DEVELOPMENTAL PATHWAYS TO POVERTY REDUCTION

Developmental Pathways to Poverty Reduction Series
Series Standing Order ISBN 978–0–230–37088–3

You can receive future titles in this series as they are published by placing a standing order. Please contact your bookseller or, in case of difficulty, write to us at the address below with your name and address, the title of the series and the ISBN quoted above.

Customer Services Department, Macmillan Distribution Ltd, Houndmills, Basingstoke, Hampshire RG21 6XS, England

---

Growth, Inequality and Social Development in India

Is Inclusive Growth Possible?

Edited by

R. Nagaraj
Professor, Indira Gandhi Institute of Development Research, Mumbai, India

palgrave
macmillan

UNRISD
United Nations
Research Institute
for Social Development

First published 2012 by
PALGRAVE MACMILLAN

Palgrave Macmillan in the UK is an imprint of Macmillan Publishers Limited, registered in England, company number 785998, of Houndmills, Basingstoke, Hampshire RG21 6XS.

Palgrave Macmillan in the US is a division of St Martin's Press LLC, 175 Fifth Avenue, New York, NY 10010.

Palgrave Macmillan is the global academic imprint of the above companies and has companies and representatives throughout the world.

ISBN 978–1–137–00075–0

This book is printed on paper suitable for recycling and made from fully managed and sustained forest sources. Logging, pulping and manufacturing processes are expected to conform to the environmental regulations of the country of origin.

A catalogue record for this book is available from the British Library.

Library of Congress Cataloging-in-Publication Data
Growth, inequality and social development in India: is inclusive growth possible? / edited by Rayaprolu Nagaraj.
p. cm.
ISBN 978–1–137–00075–0
1. Poverty—Government policy—India. 2. Income distribution—India.
3. India—Economic conditions—1991– I. Nagaraj, R.
HC440.P6G76 2012
339.4'60954—dc23 2012011168

10 9 8 7 6 5 4 3 2 1
21 20 19 18 17 16 15 14 13 12

Printed and bound in Great Britain by
CPI Antony Rowe, Chippenham and Eastbourne

For
Manaswini
(*in memoriam*)

Contents

List of Figures, Tables and Maps

Figures

Tables

Maps

Preface and Acknowledgements

This volume, consisting of six chapters and an introduction, is part of a multi-country research programme on poverty reduction and policy regimes, under the auspices of the United Nations Research Institute for Social Development. The central question addressed in these studies is if there is an identifiable relationship between policy regimes and the record of poverty reduction in a country. More specifically, according to the initial research proposal, the project aimed to:

- Assess the contribution of contemporary approaches to poverty reduction, including the Millennium Development Goals (MDGs) and Poverty Reduction Strategy Papers (PRSPs);
- Identify key institutional, policy and political issues that are not being addressed in current poverty reduction strategies; and,
- Examine the contradictions, complementarities and synergies between different components of 'policy regimes', including social, labour market and macroeconomic policies, and political and regulatory institutions.

The project seeks to achieve the objectives following the approach of 'policy regimes'. In other words, it seeks to understand how different policy regimes have influenced the outcomes of poverty reduction. The underlying assumption of such an approach is that poverty reduction is not simply a positive function of economic growth; the macroeconomic environment, social policies and politics may also have significant bearing on the outcomes.

The project seeks to explain the value of such a proposition by detailed case studies of selected countries. The country studies are expected to illustrate how poverty reduction has been achieved under diverse economic conditions and social policy regimes, to debate the viewpoint that growth alone may explain poverty reduction, and to propose that a variety of policy regimes and institutional conditions can yield the desirable outcomes. The approach implicit in all the chapters in this book is broadly social democratic, where the authors perceive the advantages of selective, yet decisive state intervention in securing the social development goals and poverty reduction.

In a research effort like this one, accomplished over an extended time period, it is but natural for the editor to have accumulated considerable debts to many individuals. It was a pleasant surprise when Yusuf Bangura invited me to join him to coordinate the India component of the research programme, with the freedom to shape the details of the research questions and the choice of writers. He was extremely supportive of our efforts right through the project. I am deeply grateful to him for his guidance, advice and help in bringing our efforts to fruition.

I was indeed fortunate that most scholars I approached readily agreed to contribute to the volume. The workshop held in Mumbai to discuss the draft papers was an intense and fruitful effort – during which Yusuf Bangura went through the draft papers meticulously to offer copious comments and suggestions – that helped the writers to refine their arguments and revise their contributions. Despite the delays, the contributors were by and large supportive of my efforts, for which, I thank them all.

Atul Kohli was the source of intellectual sustenance all through; his advice on practical matters of running a project of this nature in its early stages was truly valuable. I am indebted to him for all the intense discussions and disputations I have had with him on most issues that have shaped the ideas dealt with in this volume.

P. S. Vijay Shankar has been a very helpful colleague in the project, and a source of considerable learning for me on the issues of health and social sector. I thank him immensely for poring over drafts of my chapters and critically commenting on them.

A. V. Jose and N. Krishnaji were kind enough to go through the entire manuscript to offer detailed written comments and suggestions, for which I express my gratitude to them. I also thank C. Rammanohar Reddy, a sounding board for many of my ideas, for his patient hearing and advice.

R. Nagaraj
Mumbai
March 2012

Notes on Contributors

Vivek Chibber is Professor of Sociology at New York University. He is author of *Locked in Place: State-Building and Late Industrialization in India* (Princeton: Princeton University Press, 2003), as well as many articles on development, Marxist theory, imperialism and US politics. He has completed a critique of post-colonial theory with the working title of *Post-Colonial Theory and the Specter of Capitalism*, to be published by Verso Books in 2012.

Atul Kohli is the David K. E. Bruce Professor of International Affairs and Professor of Politics and International Affairs at Princeton University. His principal research interests are in the areas of comparative political economy with a focus on developing countries. He is the author of *State-Directed Development: Political Power and Industrialization in the Global Periphery* (winner of the Charles Levine Award (2005) of the International Political Science Association); *Democracy and Discontent: India's Growing Crisis of Governability; The State and Poverty in India*; and the editor of six volumes: *The State and Development in the Third World; India's Democracy; State Power and Social Forces; Community Conflicts and the State in India; The Success of India's Democracy; States, Markets and Just Growth*. He has also published some fifty articles. His current research focuses on the topic of 'imperialism and the developing world'. He is the Chief Editor of World Politics. He has received grants and fellowships from the Social Science Research Council, Ford Foundation and Russell Sage Foundation. Ph.D. University of California, Berkeley.

R. Nagaraj is a professor at the Indira Gandhi Institute of Development Research, Mumbai. His research interests include industrialisation, economic growth and distribution and policy reforms. A selection of his papers are available in a book entitled, *Aspects of Economic Growth and Reforms in India* (Academic Foundation, 2006). His recent research papers include 'Industrial Performance, 1991–2008', in *India Development Report*, 2011 (Oxford University Press, 2011); 'Disinvestment and Privatisation in India: Assessment and Options', in Asian Development edited *Trade Policy, Industrial Performance and Private Sector Development in India* (Oxford University Press, 2008); 'Public Sector Performance since 1950: A Fresh Look' in Gopal Kadekodi and Brinda Vishwanathan edited *Agricultural Development, Rural Institutions and Economic Policy*

(Oxford University Press, 2009). He was a visiting professor at Princeton University during 2007 and 2008. He obtained a PhD from Jawaharlal Nehru University, New Delhi.

D. Rajasekhar is Professor and Head at the Centre for Decentralisation and Development, Institute for Social and Economic Change (ISEC), Bangalore. His areas of interest are decentralisation, micro-finance, social protection for the unorganised workers and rural development. He is currently engaged in a long-term research programme on 'Improving Institutions for Pro-Poor Growth', undertaken in collaboration with Oxford University and London School of Economics, UK.

Gita Sen is Professor of Public Policy at the Indian Institute of Management in Bangalore (IIMB), India, and Adjunct Professor of Global Health and Population at the Harvard School of Public Health, Harvard University. She received her MA from the Delhi School of Economics, and her PhD in Economics from Stanford University. Her recent work includes research and policy advocacy on the equity dimensions of health, the gender dimensions of population policies and the gender implications of globalisation and economic liberalisation. She is the author and editor of a number of articles and books including *Gender Equity in Health – the Shifting Frontiers of Evidence and Action* (Routledge, 2010); *Engendering International Health: the Challenge of Equity* (The MIT Press, 2002) and *Gender, Economic Growth and Poverty: Market Growth and State Planning in Asia and the Pacific* (APDC/Kali for Women, 1994).

Mihir Shah is a member, Planning Commission, Government of India since 2009, the youngest person ever to occupy this position. He is working on a new strategy for sustainable water resource management that he has been asked to draft by the Prime Minister. He is co-founder, Samaj Pragati Sahayog, one of India's largest grass-roots initiatives for water and livelihood security, working with its partners on a million acres of land across 72 of India's most backward districts. This work shows that watershed development combined with bio-diverse agriculture, other nature-based livelihoods and institution-centred micro-finance, can result in sustained higher incomes and empowered communities. A PhD in Economics from the Jawaharlal Nehru University, New Delhi, Shah combined 20 years of living and working at the grass roots in tribal central India, with academic research and policy advocacy. He played a key role in shaping the National Rural Employment Guarantee Act.

P. S. Vijay Shankar is a founder member of Samaj Pragati Sahayog (SPS), an NGO based in Dewas district of Madhya Pradesh. He got his MPhil from Jawaharlal Nehru University, New Delhi. He has lived and worked among the tribal communities of the Narmada valley for the last 20 years. His areas of interest are water resource management and sustainable agriculture. Vijay Shankar co-authored the book *India's Drylands: Tribal Societies and Development through Environmental Regeneration* (OUP, 1998). He has also co-authored papers titled 'Groundwater Demand Management at Local Scale in Rural Areas of India' (*Hydrogeology Journal*, 2004), 'Rural Credit in 20th Century India: Overview of History and Perspectives' (*Economic and Political Weekly*, 2007) and 'India's Groundwater Challenge and the Way Forward' (*Economic and Political Weekly*, 2011). He was Visiting Scholar at the Centre for Advanced Study of India (CASI), University of Pennsylvania, Philadelphia, USA.

M. H. Suryanarayana is a professor at the Indira Gandhi Institute of Development Research, Mumbai. He teaches introductory econometrics and works on empirical issues in development economics, with particular reference to poverty, human development, food security and the MDGs. He is also a visiting professor at the Maastricht Graduate School of Governance, Maastricht, Netherlands, where he teaches a course on 'Food Policy Analysis'. He recieved his PhD from the Indian Statistical Institute, Kolkata (1986). Since then he has worked, *inter alia*, as a Consultant to the Ministry of Industry, Government of India (1986–7), Visiting Fellow, Economic Growth Centre, Yale University, USA (1992–3), Senior Economic Advisor, International Poverty Centre, UNDP, Brasilia (2004–5), and also as an international consultant to the UNDP/World Bank on policy/outcome evaluations in Vietnam (2002), Nepal (2003 and 2005), Botswana (2007–8) and Brunei Darussalam (2010).

List of Abbreviations

APL	Above Poverty Line
ARWSP	Accelerated Rural Water Supply Programme
BPL	Below Poverty Line
CABE	Central Advisory Board on Education
CAG	Comptroller and Auditor General
CGHS	Central Government Health Service
CHC	Community Health Centre
CRSP	Central Rural Sanitation Programme
CSO	Central Statistical Organisation
DISE	District Information System on Education
DLHS	District Level Household Survey, Ministry of Health and Family Welfare, GoI
DPEP	District Primary Education Programme, Ministry of Human Resources, GoI
DWS	Drinking Water Supply
DWSS	Drinking Water Supply and Sanitation
EGS	Education Guarantee Scheme, Government of Madhya Pradesh
ESI	Employees State Insurance
FYP	Five Year Plans
GDP	Gross Domestic Product
GoI	Government of India
ICDS	Integrated Child Development Services
IEC	Information, Education and Communication
IMR	Infant Mortality Rate
JBY	Janashree Bhima Yojana
LIC	Life Insurance Corporation of India
MDG	Millennium Development Goals
MHRD	Ministry of Human Resources, GoI

MMR	Maternal Mortality Rate
MoHFW	Ministry of Health and Family Welfare, GoI
MoRD	Ministry of Rural Development, GoI
MP	Madhya Pradesh
MPCE	Monthly per Capita Consumer Expenditure
NAS	National Accounts Statistics
NCEUS	National Commission for Enterprises in the Unorganised Sector
NCEUS	National Commission on Enterprises in Unorganised Sector
NCL	National Commission on Labour
NCMH	National Commission on Macroeconomics and Health, Ministry of Health and Family Welfare, GoI
NEP	New Education Policy
NFHS	National Family Health Survey, Ministry of Health and Family Welfare, GoI
NHP	National Health Policy
NRHM	National Rural Health Mission, Ministry of Health and Family Welfare, GoI
NSS	National Sample Survey
NSSO	National Sample Survey Organisation, GoI
NUEPA	National University for Education Planning and Administration, New Delhi
NWDM	National Drinking Water Mission
NWP	National Water Policy
OBC	Other Backward Castes
PCI	Per Capita Income
PDS	Public Distribution System
PHC	Primary Health Centre
PRI	Panchayat Raj Institutions
PTR	Pupil-Teacher Ratio
RGNWDM	Rajiv Gandhi National Drinking Water Mission
SC	Scheduled Caste

SCR	Student-Classroom Ratio
SDP	State Domestic Product
SGRY	Sampoorna Grameena Rozgar Yojana
SGSY	Swarna Jayanti Gram Swarozgar Yojna
SHG	Self Help Group
SRP	Structural Reform Pilot Project
SSA	Sarva Shiksha Abhiyan ('Education for All'), Ministry of Human Resources, GoI
SSE	Social Sector Expenditure
ST	Scheduled Tribe
TSC	Total Sanitation Campaign
UEE	Universalisation of Elementary Education
UHIS	Universal Health Insurance Scheme
UNECLAC	United Nations Economic Commission for Latin America and the Caribbean
UP	Uttar Pradesh

1
Introduction

R. Nagaraj

1.1 An overview

Since the industrial revolution, the world has come to accept a steady rise in income per head as the 'natural' state of an economy. Following Kuznets's hypothesis – also known as the "inverted U" hypothesis – inequality is expected to rise initially and then fall with growing income levels. It is also believed that social development would improve in some proportion to the rise in per capita income; as the demand for social services increases; and as governments acquire a rising share of output as taxes, their ability to augment social services would go up.

In reality, however, none of these propositions can be taken for granted as 'natural' or 'automatic'. Recent experience shows that not many countries have witnessed uninterrupted growth for long periods. Growth reversals and stagnations are perhaps more common than perceived (Pritchett, 2000).[1] While the developed Western economies have followed Kuznets' inverted U hypothesis, evidence with respect to income distribution from developing countries is mixed at best (Kanbur, 2000). Similarly, the relationship between economic growth and poverty reduction is not unambiguous and proportional. The association between growth and social development is perhaps even more tenuous. Thus, empirically, one can discern a rich mosaic of relationships between these fundamental aspects of growth and development (Fields, 2001).

How then does one understand these patterns? As economic theory does not provide unique or unambiguous relationships among these variables, we often fall back on the 'stylised facts' in modern economic growth. Perhaps, there are social and economic institutions and policy environments that 'mediate' between economic growth, its distribution and their consequence for social development. The nature of the policy regimes, historical antecedents (or initial conditions) of modern economic growth, and a variety of institutional arrangements could influence the outcomes.

In liberal policy regimes where markets are the dominant mechanisms for allocating resources, social development and poverty reduction is perhaps relatively modest, compared to the experience in social democratic regimes where the state plays a much greater role in steering the economy. As Amartya Sen has shown, public action can be an important factor in better educational and health outcomes. He cites the example of the Indian state of Kerala, with low per capita income, which has a better social development record on account of public action than of many cities in the US with a large African American population. Similarly, democratic institutions and public action have prevented famines in post-independence India compared to China, which witnessed large-scale deaths due to famine in the early 1960s. More recently, health outcomes in the US are widely known to be inferior to western Europe, despite the US spending a much larger share of gross domestic product (GDP) on these services – an outcome clearly related to better and public provision in Europe.

In light of these, what have been the relationships between economic growth, policy regimes, poverty reduction and social development in India? What are the political and economic factors that might encourage (or hinder) the process of social development? How does India's development experience measure up in a comparative perspective?

This volume, consisting of six chapters, offers detailed answers to some of these questions. An overview of the issues addressed and the perspectives of their broad answers are included in the first part of this introduction; the second part briefly summarises the findings of the chapters.

1.2 India's development strategy and poverty reduction

India's economic development was centred on rapid industrialisation to produce capital and intermediate goods (or 'heavy' industry) to maximise long-term growth in a world that was deemed to offer limited scope for trade, and to sustain an independent development path in a politically polarised world in mid-twentieth century. With a low domestic saving rate, weak capital market and nascent indigenous entrepreneurship, the public sector assumed the role of the biggest entrepreneur to acquire the 'commanding heights' in a predominantly private sector economy. However, fiscal incentives and physical controls were devised to preserve and promote traditional labour-intensive methods (cottage industry) of producing consumer goods. And to feed the growing industrial labour force, a rising food supply was assumed to follow from improved farm productivity, secured by land reforms and public investment in irrigation and related services.

Given the heterogeneity, inequality and predominance of the traditional sector, maintaining macroeconomic stability has remained an abiding policy concern. Moreover, there is also a commitment to parliamentary democracy. It was initially believed that poverty and inequality would be addressed with the expanding opportunities in the modern sector, and that agrarian reforms would secure equity and efficiency in the rural economy as the state would be in a position to expand social services with rising public resources.

Statistically speaking, India (along with a few countries, including China) is an example of uninterrupted growth acceleration in the second half of the twentieth century (Hausmann, et al., 2005). Breaking from the colonial stagnation, India, on a trend basis, grew at 3.5 per cent per year during 1950–1980, and close to 6 per cent per year thereafter – with low and stable inflation, and modest balance-of-payment deficits (as a proportion of the domestic output).

Workforce transformation – the defining character of the 'modern economic growth' – that was stalled during much of the twentieth century, finally commenced in the 1980s, with a fall of about 15 percentage points in the workforce engaged in agriculture. But the output composition has moved rapidly in favour of services since 1990, without a corresponding shift of the workforce (as was the case historically). Thus, the economy has acquired a dual face: it is rural and agrarian with 68 per cent of the population living in villages, and with 56 per cent of the workforce still subsisting on agriculture (as in 2004–5); yet it is a services economy, contributing 55 per cent of the domestic output. The dichotomy implies growing inequality between town and country, as the services have created modest additional jobs.

India's quest for development could be seen as an effort to create a nation state and a national market out of a civilisation that is deeply stratified and heterogeneous in terms of caste, religion and regional affinities. Thus, its modest accomplishments perhaps represent work in progress. Yet, in comparison to its neighbours who attained political independence around the same time, the 'idea of India' – as a society and economy – has perhaps taken a deeper root with a distinct identity, aided and abetted by evolving democratic ethos and a homogenising popular culture.

Silencing many international critics, India has avoided some of the worst-case scenarios of development disasters. It has abolished famines, attained food self-sufficiency, and brought down the population growth rate without coercion. The state-led heavy industrialisation during the first three decades, followed by a gradual loosening of investment and output controls, has created diversified and flexible industrial and services sectors (with increasing openness to trade and finance) that seem capable of responding to market signals, giving rise to a domestic entrepreneurial class that is quickly internationalising its business. India has witnessed changes in its policy regimes, from the state-centric import substitution strategy to an increasingly market-driven one with export orientation.

After remaining stubbornly high at 50–60 per cent of the population, absolute poverty (headcount ratio measured in real money terms) has nearly halved in the last quarter of the twentieth century, with modestly rising consumption levels even among the bottom deciles – though its pace has apparently wavered lately. However, the reduction in poverty has not lessened the nutritional deficiency proportionately, or improved long-term health status, as widespread food deprivation persists, especially among women and children.

As Deaton and Dreze (2009) concluded after carefully sifting the available evidence:

> ... [o]verall levels of child under nutrition in India (including not only severe but also "moderate" undernourishment) are still very high, both in absolute terms as well as relative to other countries. Even today, close to half of all Indian children are underweight, and about half suffer from anaemia. These are appalling figures, which place India among the most "undernourished" countries in the world. ... In particular, child undernourishment is much higher in south Asia (48.5% underweight in 1999) than in sub-Saharan Africa (29.6% underweight in 2005) ... (Deaton and Dreze, 2009: 50)[2]

This is in sharp contrast to China, where with rising incomes, heights of children, both in rural and urban areas, have steadily gone up. Thus, contemporarily, India is perhaps an example of polarising growth with modest decline in absolute poverty.

1.3 Social development

At independence, in the mid-twentieth century, India's record in education, health and social deprivation was probably one of the world's poorest (Morris and McAlpine, 1982). Despite the notable progress, improvement remains modest compared to most of Asia and Latin America. As a proportion of its domestic output, public expenditure on health has remained slightly less than one per cent – perhaps one of the lowest among the developing economies.[3] Similarly, public expenditure on education has also remained at around 3.5 per cent of GDP. In spite of the growth acceleration noted earlier, public expenditure ratios on social development have not improved.

So, the modest social sector outcomes should not be a surprise. While the educational accomplishments are still passable, perhaps the most damning neglect is of public health – sanitation and drinking water. For instance, in 2008, only 22 per cent of the population had access to piped drinking water; in rural areas it was just 11 per cent (WHO and UNICEF, 2010). A nationwide survey about a decade ago had found: (1) only 55 per cent of households had access to drinking water within 100 metres of home; (2) only 40 per cent of households had access to public health facilities within one kilometre distance; (3) only 40 per cent of the villages were connected with 'pucca' (all-weather) roads; and, (4) only 80 per cent of households had access to government-owned or supported primary schools (Paul et al., 2004).

Arguably, poor sanitation and lack of clean drinking water could spread infectious diseases contributing to high levels of morbidity (illness), resulting in adverse health outcomes. Deaton and Dreze, cited above, have shown that poverty reduction (improved income and consumption growth) has not translated into improved long-term nutritional status, especially of women and children. Combining the foregoing propositions, one could hypothesise the following: the missing link between poverty reduction and the persistence of abysmal nutritional and health status is the pathetic state of public health facilities – the principal reason for widespread infectious diseases that affect not just the poor (who, of course, bear the brunt of it), but the rich as well. The proposition does not seem to have received the attention it seems to warrant.[4]

To understand why public health is neglected, one perhaps needs to understand the evolution of health policy. Historically, much of the improvements in health status in the developed economies came about as a result of expansion of sanitation, drainage and access to clean drinking water – all of which meant augmenting public goods and services. During the colonial times, these facilities were mostly restricted to army cantonments, railway colonies and the 'civil lines' (where the bureaucracy lived).

However, with the advent of antibiotics around the mid-twentieth century, Indian policymakers apparently opted for the curative means to treat infectious diseases instead of universalising access to public health by investing in sanitation and drinking water – as had happened in the developed countries in the early part of the century (Das Gupta, 2005). Hence, public health in India has come to be identified with setting up of public health centres for curative medicines and vaccination against specific disease. Compared to China (24.9%) or Sri Lanka (45.4%), India spends a meagre 17.3 per cent of its health budget on public health (National Health Policy, 2002). Further, with the spread of subsidised higher (medical) education, and lately with the proliferation of private and hospital care, public health has got marginalised.

The neglect of public health services – especially of sanitation, – even from a private household point of view remains a puzzle. The WHO and UNICEF report cited above has also noted that in 2008, 54 per cent of the population (638 million) and 69 per cent (579 million) in rural India resorted to open defecation. Surprisingly, even in an agriculturally well-off state like Haryana, according to the 2001 decennial census, 52 per cent of rural households had television sets and 76 per cent had radio sets, but only 29 per cent had private toilets (Gupta and Pal, 2008). Why is sanitation not a problem? Certainly, it cannot be due to lack of awareness. One suspects, it has to do with curative orientation of the health services and its impact on the popular belief in the virtues of consuming medicines to cure most illnesses.

How does one reconcile the abysmal record in public health with, say, India's achievements in skill-intensive manufacturing and services, or in atomic energy and space technology? The simple answer is, perhaps, the elitist approach to development: emphasis on higher education and curative medicine against primary and vocational education, and against preventive and public health.

What accounts for the elitism? Prima facie, it can be the national priorities to create qualified scientific and technical manpower to meet the plan requirements.[5] As curative health was emphasised earlier on, a need for qualified doctors and nurses to run hospitals is understandable. So India has managed to produce including the world's largest number of engineers, world-class software professionals, and run international quality hospitals, all of which have surely contributed to the boom in services (including medical services), and human capital. This, in turn, has yielded the world's largest inflow of international remittances (factor income in balance of payment). Yet, the neglect of public health has not spared the well-to-do from infectious diseases like malaria or dengue.

There could, however, be deeper social reasons for the elitism. At the risk of drawing hasty generalisations, it is arguable that in the deeply ingrained ethos of the caste-based society, if education is mainly meant for the upper castes (as Myron Weiner argued), the menial jobs, the obverse of it, are meant to be performed only by specific caste groups at the bottom of the social pyramid.[6,7] Despite modernisation, social beliefs about the duties and responsibilities of the lower castes nevertheless persist. Therefore, under-investment in sanitation probably reflects social apathy and policy neglect towards the services that these caste groups perform. Alternatively, one could perhaps attribute the problem to ineffective public administration at the lower levels of government (as Atul Kohli argues in this volume, see Chapter 7).

The results of the neglect are abundantly evident in the failure to meet the millennium development goals (MDGs) (Table 1.1). For instance, as against the target of under-five mortality of 41 by 2015, achievement as in 2003 was 99.1; the MDG target for the population with access to sanitation in rural areas is 72 per cent, the achievement in 2005 was just 32.5 per cent. Going by the trends reported in the table, the chances of meeting the goals seem remote.

1.4 Social protection

Universal social security was introduced in the first half of the twentieth century in mature market economies where the concept of welfare state took root. It is also associated with the Great Depression, when for the first time the advanced market economies faced a generalised recession. In fact, universal social security is a widely accepted sign of a rich and industrialised economy with high labour productivity.

In operational terms universal social security has also meant tight immigration control and a progressive taxation system. Usually, universal social protection comes after meeting the requirement of social services and economic infrastructure. East Asian economies that have joined the ranks of the developed countries have introduced the universal social protection only recently.

As developing economies, by definition, do not have these prerequisites, what, then, is the scope for social security? How will it be financed? East Asia seems to offer a model where with rapid employment-oriented growth, workers' contribution were invested by public institutions to provide safety nets. Alternatively, in many small export-oriented economies like Costa Rica, growing public revenues are used to provide social protection to insulate workers from the vagaries of the world market.

Table 1.1 India's achievements in meeting MDG goals as in the mid-2000s

Indicator	Year	Value	Year	Value	MDG Target Value
Proportion of population below poverty line (%)	1990	37.5	2004–05	27.5	18.75
Proportion of underweight children	1992	51.5	2005–06	46	27.4
Literacy rate of 15–24 years olds (%)	1990–91	64.3	2001	76.4	100.0
Ratio of girls to boys in primary education	1990–91	0.71	2004–05	0.88	1
Ratio of girls to boys in secondary education	1990–91	0.50	2004–05	0.71	1
Under five mortality rate (per 1000 live births)	1988–92	125	1999–03	99.1	41
Infant mortality rate (per 1000 live births)	1990	80	2005–06	58	27
Maternal mortality ratio (per 100,000 live births)	1991	437	2001–03	301	109
Population with sustainable access to an improved water source, rural (%)	1990	55	2001	82	80.5
Population with sustainable access to an improved water source, urban (%)	1990	81	2001	87	94
Population with access to sanitation, urban (%)	1990	44	2001	63	72
Population with access to sanitation, rural (%)	1991	9.46	2005	32.4	72
Deaths due to malaria per 100,000	1994	0.13	2006	0.14	–
Deaths due to TB per 100,000	1990	44	2005	29	–
Deaths due to HIV/AIDS	2000	471	2004	1114	–

Source: CSO (2009).

In contrast, social protection in India is dualistic, as is the rest of the economy. Those employed in the organised sector (consisting mostly of the public sector, private corporate sector and recognised educational institutions) – constituting about eight per cent of the workforce – have a well-developed social protection system. About 15 per cent of the workforce, including about 7 per cent consisting of specific social groups, currently has some social security in India (NCEUS, 2006). Broadly, social protection for the organised workers includes the following:

1. Defined benefit pension for government employees, gratuity and health facilities for life and maternity leave with pay (of late, paternity benefit too).
2. For those employed in the factory sector (units employing ten or more workers using electricity) a provident fund with mandatory matching contribution from employers, gratuity and paid maternity leave for women, and so on. These benefits usually expand with factory size.
3. In specific industries that are outside the organised sector, like beedi (traditional cigarette), legally mandated modest social protection schemes are provided.

Why is social protection restricted to the organised sector? It represents a high productive and high wage sector where such benefits could be justified on considerations of efficiency wages to provide incentives for qualified, skilled and experienced workers. Moreover promotion of social protection for the organised sector, which is largely unionised, is encouraged by various conventions of the International Labour Organisation (ILO) to which India is a signatory.

There are however voluntary (largely public-sector-provided) life and health insurance schemes, long-term saving instruments with government mandated interest rates offered through the post office that are open to all citizens. A new defined contribution pension scheme with investment in financial markets – on the lines of 401 K plan in the US – is just about to be introduced.

There are state level schemes for socially vulnerable groups, such as widows, who get modest pensions to essentially mitigate the loss of the breadwinner. A few state governments also provide pensions to economically vulnerable groups, such as fishermen.

The modest extension of social security for sections of unorganised workers probably represents the outcome of workers' struggles and political responses in a democracy. Some of these originated as components of national and regional anti-poverty programmes. However, in an underdeveloped administrative system that lacks identification of all its citizens, implementing such schemes is difficult, often inviting considerable corruption and delay.

1.5 Inequality

Accelerating economic growth, with modest effect on reducing absolute poverty and an elitist social development strategy, has had a cumulative effect in widening economic inequalities, however measured. This is so regardless of the policy regime in place (and its political rhetoric), though the liberal reforms seem to have accentuated the inequalities. In a comparative perspective, however, economic inequality in India is moderate – lying somewhere between the more equal East Asia and the highly unequal Latin America. But considering that economic inequalities are embedded in highly stratified societies, their combined effect is likely to be immense.

Surely, economic growth and the constitutionally mandated social protection for scheduled castes and scheduled tribes have opened up avenues for economic mobility. The spread of democratic ethos and a variety of social movements have created a greater semblance of social equality, at least in the public sphere. Abolition of the zamindari system (landlordism) has lessened the traditional forms of social hierarchy to bring about progressive social change.

Yet, unlike in East Asia where modern education was an equalising force, it perhaps has had the opposite effect in India due to its elitist orientation. Bardhan (2007), citing evidence from the World Development Report, 2006, has argued that educational inequality in India is worse than that in Latin America.

How does one understand the growing economic inequality? India, in effect, has followed a 'top-down' approach to development that has sought to first create capital and intermediate goods industries (which conventionally came at the end of it), involving a high level of technical sophistication. Though land reforms got rid of absentee landlords (unlike in Pakistan), the land was not redistributed to peasents (as was the case in Japan or Korea), which could have boosted equity and land productivity. Modest agricultural performance created a wage goods constraint, throttling the pace of industrialisation, exerting pressure on the balance of payment periodically and limiting the size of the domestic market for manufactures. Faced with a severe food crisis in the mid-1960s, the urgency of augmenting food production acquired priority (to avoid international embarrassment and to retain an independent foreign policy) over its distribution, thus, perhaps, forfeiting the potential benefits of equitable growth through land reforms.

To understand the foregoing account, it could be hypothesised that India's development policy accorded a higher priority to the creation of the nation state, a national market and the promotion of its socio-cultural identity, with an abiding commitment to democracy. Improving citizens' capabilities and welfare were often subsumed and have remained secondary to these overriding considerations.

Is there a social or political force that could work for the poor and the disadvantaged? Political democracy, perhaps. Not withstanding its well-known shortcomings, deepening democracy and the open society are apparently the forces that could diffuse development, albeit very slowly, creating opportunities for mobility, and loosening the traditional social and economic barriers. In a comparative perspective, India's economic achievements are surely modest – especially in contrast to China – but they are accomplished with a greater participation, with a better record of human freedoms and with relatively limited social costs. Social and political movements, civil society initiatives and a fairly progressive judiciary (often in response to public interest litigations) in an open society seem to be exerting pressures from below. Political parties, however elitist in their practice, are compelled to reckon with such pressures, as elected representatives cannot any more take their electorate for granted on the basis of caste, religion, or local ties. The recent enactment of the National Rural Employment Guarantee Act (NREGA) and the Right to Information Act (RTI) are perhaps a testimony to the progressive change that seems feasible, albeit slowly.

1.6 Political economy

Admittedly democracy works within the confines of the class configuration of the political forces. So, to understand the possibilities and limitations of deepening democracy, one has to comprehend the political and economic forces at work. There are broadly three strands of thought on this issue.

Applying neoclassical economic reasoning, India's modest achievements, say, in comparison to the East Asian success stories, is explained in terms of the rent-seeking behaviour of the organised interest groups such as politicians, bureaucrats and the organised working class that have immensely benefited from the controls on output and investments, at the expense of unorganised workers and private entrepreneurs, whose market-based initiatives are throttled by the regulatory regime (Srinivasan, 1985). At the other end of the theoretical spectrum are the neo-Marxist explanations that emphasise the dominance of international financial interests, thwarting the state from pursuing an independent development path (Patnaik, 1995).[8]

Between these two analytical constructs, there are many class-theoretic explanations, perhaps the most prominent being that of Bardhan (1984 and 1998). It argues that the inability of the dominant classes of big business and rich farmers to sort out their collective action problems, to step up public investments and plug huge subsidies, limits the state's action to augment economic growth.

Chapters in this volume seem closer to the third perspective, which could be broadly called a social democratic position.

1.7 Summary of the contributions

Development strategies

In light of the foregoing we now briefly highlight the main findings of the volume. Chapter 2 offers a bird's-eye view of India's development experience since independence. It is a case of growth acceleration in the twentieth century, starting from a low level and with enormous economic and social inequalities. The experience has been one with practically no growth in per capita income in the first half of the century under colonial rule to growth acceleration by the turn of the century to over four per cent per year.

The chapter describes India as an agrarian economy in a stable macroeconomic setting and with a low and declining inflation in the second half of the twentieth century. The chapter asks the following questions:

1. Are there clearly delineable policy regimes with distinctly identifiable economic outcomes?
2. Is there a discernible relationship between policy regimes and outcomes in terms of economic growth, poverty reduction and social development?
3. Where does India stand now in its policy orientation, and what does it portend for social development in general and poverty alleviation in particular?

The chapter delineates three policy regimes. The first, 1950–1965, was a period of planning and import substitution. The second regime covers the years between the mid-1960s and 1980, a period of growth with redistribution when poverty alleviation made an entry into the policy discourse. The years after 1980, representing the third policy regime, is associated with a growing role for market forces in economic decision-making. The pace of policy reform gathered momentum after 1991 in the changed global political context, and when the country faced a serious balance-of-payment crisis. But India is a case of gradual change, compared to dramatic shifts in Latin America.

India's gradualism has contributed to a cumulative improvement in output performance and a modest decline in absolute poverty more recently, but with an undeniable rise in inequality over the entire period. While the domestic output is lately dominated by the services sector and their exports, it is as yet an agrarian and rural economy as 55 per cent of the workforce draws its livelihood from agriculture and 68 per cent of the workforce resides in villages. Such a dichotomy between the output and labour market outcomes imply growing inequalities. India's record of social development is modest, though it exports high-tech services that reflect advanced higher educational attainment.

The official estimates of poverty began to decline since the second half of the 1970s, from roughly half of the population to about a quarter, over the last three decades. There are serious disputes on this claim, however. Poverty in monetary terms has declined, but not in terms of nutritional deficiency. Malnutrition of children and widespread destitution are evident everywhere. Further, the pace of poverty reduction is slower after the reforms.

Regardless of the policy regime, economic inequality has increased in many dimensions – across the states of India, between rural and urban areas, between organised and unorganised sectors, and between capital income and wage income.

While India's economic growth is getting increasingly respectable, its attainments in social development remain modest – to put it mildly. With one-third of the population and half of women illiterate, India has a long way to catch up with East Asia and China to meet the MDG targets. Despite much rhetoric in the liberalised policy regime, there is little to show in terms of enhanced public commitment to achieve these goals.

However, the modest accomplishments, seen against the background of a politically inclusive democracy, seem tolerable. Given the highly iniquitous economy and society, it is hard to expect radically progressive outcomes. However, deepening democracy has improved political equality, demanding a share in the economic pie and access to minimal social services.

M. H. Suryanarayana addresses the issues of economic inequality in Chapter 3. The chapter surveys the trends in inequality in the distribution of operational holding of agricultural land as a proxy for its ownership distribution, and in consumption inequality as a proxy for income inequality. The study discerns an increase in inequality of land ownership, regardless of the policy regime, although the average size of the operational holding has declined on account of population growth and sub-division of family holdings.

Though poverty and inequality are the two most widely studied topics, Suryanarayana avers that there are serious shortcomings in the official data that make it hard to draw definitive conclusions. He finds three sets of problems with the data. First, the most widely used data set to examine inequality are designed to estimate average consumption, not its distribution. So, by definition, it is incorrect to draw inferences about changes in consumption distribution using the NSS data.

Second, until recently, the data were available in tabulated form that restricted the computation of many indicators. Third, the NSS methodology was designed for a semi-monetised rural economy, where household consumption would often include payment of wages in kind, in terms of cooked meals by the landlord for the farm servants. However, with the decline of wage payment in kind, and the practice of keeping permanent farm servants (with the casualisation of the workforce), reduction in average household consumption may not reflect lowering of consumption, but changes in the organisation of the rural economy. Thus, Suryanarayana is cautious in drawing inference on the long-term trends in inequality. Notwithstanding these caveats, the chapter makes the following observations:

1. There was no increase in average consumption or inequality in consumption between 1960 and 1977–78. However, average per capita consumption went down during the first half of the 1960s, and was recovered over the next decade or so.
2. There was a marginal improvement in average consumption and reduction in inequality from 1977–78 to 1993–94.
3. Average consumption across all deciles continues to rise between 1993–4 and 2004–5, both in rural and urban India. But inequality in consumption has increased. So, this seems like a Pareto improvement, but with a wide initial gap in per capita consumption.

These trends indicate that the 1980s were probably a better period of reduction in poverty and inequality, while after the reforms of 1991 the inequalities widened despite continued reduction in poverty.

These findings seem consistent with the broad trends reported in the previous chapter. It seems reasonable to infer that the problems of poverty and inequality are so deeply embedded in the structure of the economy and society that they do not seem to easily respond to the changes in policy orientation as the alternative policy regimes have barely affected employment growth and labour market performance.

Social policy and poverty reduction

Reviewing the various approaches internationally, Chapter 4 by Gita Sen and D. Rajasekhar (Sen and Sekhar hereafter) advocates a rights-based approach as the ideal way to promote social protection. It is defined as pension or provident fund, health and maternity care, compensation for work-related accidents and gratuity, provided by employers; they are available in India mainly for workers in the organised sector. Efforts to extend these to the unorganised sector have remained modest.

Expanding the scope of social security to include all welfare measures provided by the state, Sen and Sekhar show that since the early 1970s, there have been many targeted employment and anti-poverty programmes for the unorganised sector. These include self-employment programmes, wage employment programmes and a public distribution system (PDS) to supply subsidised food grains. The PDS that was mostly restricted to urban areas became universal in the 1980s, and the items of food included under it were also expanded. Some state governments, especially in south India, have initiated modest insurance schemes for socially vulnerable groups such as widows and fishermen, as part of the anti-poverty programmes.

However, with the onset of the economic reforms in the 1990s, there was a contraction in anti-poverty programmes, and the universal PDS was restricted to only those with income below the poverty line (BPL). Yet, growing concerns are expressed for universal social security and health insurance to meet the increasing economic insecurity caused by the change in the policy regime. In the present decade, faced with poor agriculture and growing agrarian distress, an ambitious rural employment guarantee scheme has been launched that assures 100-days of productive employment in a year.

Sen and Sekhar document newer initiatives for the unorganised sector workers such as the group insurance scheme, and a universal health insurance scheme with subsidised premium payment. Though numerous, the combined effect of the various initiatives does not add up to very much, as their scale remains modest.

The authors rightly comment that after decades of neglect, there appears to be a flood of fresh initiatives: 'a hundred flowers appear to be blooming; how long this will last remains to be seen' (p. 35).

Commending the recent effort to set up the national commission for unorganised sector enterprises, the chapter concludes with a plea for a rights-based universal social protection and assistance as entitlement.

In Chapter 5, P. S. Vijay Shankar and Mihir Shah (Shankar and Shah, hereafter) focus on three social services, namely, drinking water and sanitation, health services and primary education. The chapter describes how the approaches to these services have changed over different policy regimes. During the planning period, the emphasis was on public provision of the services, under the community development programme; later it was seen as part of the basic needs programme; and, in the reform era, there is a clear shift toward private provisioning with a demand-based approach.

The study does not find significant changes in public expenditure on these services: about 1 per cent and 3.5 per cent of GDP on health and education, respectively. What is clearly discernible is a gradual – creeping, perhaps more appropriately – improvement in access to these services over the last half century; with better provision in urban areas compared to rural; and better in southern states than the rest of the country. However, there are worse outcomes among scheduled castes and scheduled tribes compared to the rest of the society. The diversity in outcomes is enormous and perhaps widening across states, and more so across the districts.

According to the first Five-Year plan document, only six per cent of India's towns, accounting for nearly half of the urban population, had access to protected water supply. Half a century later, official reports state that 96 per cent of urban India and 92 per cent villages had access to safe drinking water. But the reality may be quite different, with widespread reports of shortage of drinking water. Similarly, official data report that households with sanitation were as low as 1 per cent and 27 per cent in 1981, in rural and urban areas, respectively. These have gone up to 21 per cent and 61 per cent respectively in 2001.

At the time of independence, emphasis was on universal free access to all social services. But as the focus of health policies shifted to family planning, population control gained primacy over all other health-related policies. However, the coercive practices during the political emergency (1975–77) discredited the official effort so thoroughly that for a long time there was little political courage to seriously redesign the health policies. It was only in the mid-1990s that government come out with a "target-free" reproductive health approach to health policy.

Compared to drinking water, sanitation and health services, the record in providing access to primary education appears somewhat better, with near total gross enrolment of children in the school-going age. However, due to high dropout rates, the literacy rate is about two-thirds of the population in 2001, and only half for women, with a slow and steady inching up of the rates, without any notable difference across the policy regimes. However, the quality of education imparted is abysmal as the outcome indicators show poor results.

Shankar and Shah find enormous interregional variation in the provision of social services with Kerala being the best-known positive outlier. The authors also document distinctive achievements in Tamil Nadu and Himachal Pradesh, which have recently witnessed a sharp improvement in literacy.

After the liberalisation in 1991, there is a definite trend towards privatisation in the supply of these services, neglect of public systems, increasing levy of user charges, and abandonment of the principle of universal access.

Politics of poverty reduction

Addressing the politics of policy regimes, Vivek Chibber, in Chapter 6, looks at how organised interests groups such as industrial labour and domestic capitalist classes have shaped the policies towards poverty alleviation and social policy more broadly. He finds that the capitalist class is mainly interested in growth policies, not in social policy or poverty alleviation. It was interested in land reforms insofar as it created domestic demand for industrial goods. Even after the economic reforms, the focus continues to be on growth.

The chapter divides the post-independence period into three policy regimes, coinciding with Nehru's regime, Indira Gandhi's regime and the regime of economic liberalisation starting with Rajiv Gandhi. Such a periodisation roughly coincides with what is outlined in Chapter 2. Chibber argues that during the Nehru era, there was little concern for social policy or poverty reduction. Welfare provisions in labour laws for the organised sector workers were diluted under pressure from the capitalists on whose support Nehru relied for achieving the goals of planned economic development. Similarly, in the agrarian sector, the new class of rich peasants on whose support Nehru depended to feed the growing mass of urban industrial workers thwarted radical land reforms.

While India achieved respectable economic growth during Nehru's premiership, it did not reduce poverty. Unequal distribution of the benefits of growth was reflected in the rising left wing mobilisation of poor peasants under the Naxalite movement. Indira Gandhi responded to the challenge by coming to power on a slogan of Garibi Hatao (Abolish Poverty) in 1971. She also undertook a radical decision to abolish privy purses of the erstwhile princely states, and nationalised the commercial banks. Such a left-ward shift was also driven by her aim to wrest the control of the Congress Party from the old-timers.

With near total control over the banking system, Indira Gandhi's regime was in a position to extend bank credit for agriculture, rural development, and small enterprises to enhance productive employment, and hence, alleviate poverty. Such a policy boosted India's agricultural production and reduced import dependence. To improve the access to food grains, the PDS was expanded, leading to a decline in poverty with a lag, though many of the populist polices of Indira Gandhi adversely affected industrial growth.

Chibber says pithily 'that India was never not pro-rich' (p. 185). But after the reforms, the façade of equity in economic policy was seriously diluted. This is best evidenced by the sharp decline in wage share on organised manufacturing, decline in organised sector employment and the number of lockouts by employers overtaking the number of strikes by workers. The pro-rich stance is evident in continuation of subsidies for the rural rich. Chibber also quotes evidence to suggest that public spending on social services had declined marginally in the 1990s in response to the changed policies.

In sum, Chibber portrays a picture of Indian social policy as being weak, given the deeply class-based nature of politics and society. Labour, and more generally, the labouring poor have little political strength to compel the dominant classes to spend more on welfare measures. This was true right from independence, and perhaps has become more pronounced in the liberalised era. Reforms of industrial policies reflect the growing clout of newer entrepreneurial groups, which were largely kept out of the older patronage system under the licence raj. Chibber's chapter is a clear exposition of the roles of big business and organised trade unions in shaping the development policies.

But what do we know about the somewhat less organised but numerically strong groups such as farmer groups, organisations of petty producers such as retail traders, truck owners, and region/product-specific manufacturers such as power loom owners? In other words, the chapter has not addressed the role of 'intermediate regimes', an analytical category coined by Micheal Kalecki to describe the loose coalition of classes that lies between big business and the industrial working class. What can probably be said of them is that they have demonstrated their ability to paralyse the economy, refuse to pay taxes, or accept rises in user charges – all of which have contributed to fiscal crisis. Referring to Schumpeter's piece on the fiscal crisis of the state, Chakravarty (1986) had raised very pertinent questions about the role of such groups in restraining public expenditure.[9] So, perhaps this is an area that requires further research in order to fully understand the contribution of production-based interest groups in shaping development strategies and social policies.

In Chapter 7, Atul Kohli argues that the capacity of the Indian state to promote poverty alleviation has been limited, though the deepening of democracy seems to be constantly testing the limits of it. The Indian state can enhance poverty alleviation by improving the performance of lower levels of the bureaucracy and making public infrastructure investment.

Kohli finds India's state capacity to be somewhere between that of East Asia and Africa. Successful East Asian economies undertook land reforms and followed a path of labour-intensive industrialisation that yielded growth with equity. In contrast, India did not seriously implement land reforms; in the fractious democracy that India is, economic growth has been modest up to 1980, but improved thereafter with a greater alliance of interests between domestic capital and the state, but such an alliance brought about greater inequality though absolute poverty has declined. Why is India's state capacity limited? Kohli contends that this is on account of the state's 'multi-class social base, a not so well organised ruling party, and a bureaucracy that is professional at the apex but not so in the periphery'.

Offering an overview of the changes (p. 197) in the nature of the Indian state, the chapter describes the Congress Party as a party of propertied classes though it had openings for other social forces as well. It was an umbrella organisation claiming to represent all sections of Indian society. Economic policy roughly up to 1980 sought to appeal to a variety of interest groups; leading the authors to label the Indian state as a 'soft state'. However, after the 1980s, there is a gradual narrowing of the gap between the domestic capitalist class and the Congress, leading to a greater focus on growth, and a neglect of the concerns of organised workers and the poor generally. This has delivered faster growth, modest decline in poverty that necessarily follows from it, but at the expense of increasing inequalities.

However, there is enormous variation across regions. States with better bureaucratic capacity and social democratic politics have performed better than the rest – Kerala and West Bengal being the best examples, and the Hindi heartland being the worst cases. What accounts for the variations in state capacity? Both Kerala and West Bengal had land reforms that brought about some semblance of equality and social mobility for the poor. Similarly, southern states that have generally performed better have witnessed various backward class movements that curbed the economic and social power of the upper castes (Brahmins mainly), and offered greater scope for lower castes to acquire educational and public facilities.

How does Kohli explain the superior economic performance of the western Indian states of Maharashtra and Gujarat that are economically the most powerful, though they may not socially be so? Kohli explains it by referring to political decentralisation below the state level (local governments). In both these states, powerful local caste groups – Marathas in Maharashtra and Patels in Gujarat – benefited from the well-functioning panchayats and they also made use of the cooperative movement to further their collective economic cause.

Does the Indian state have the capacity to bring about rapid poverty reduction and social development? In so far as rapid growth reduces poverty, there would be some measure of poverty reduction in India, but it would be accompanied by growing inequality. Given the low and shrinking capacity of the state on account of its narrowing class base, it is hard to expect improved social development outcomes in the foreseeable future.

Kohli argues that deeper reasons for the outcomes in social development are political. Given the class structure and growing alliance of the ruling classes and the dominant political parties, the scope for radical redistributive policies is shrinking. While the top echelons of the bureaucracy maintain high standards of efficiency, the lower levels of it lack the capacity to deliver decent administration, though deepening democracy seems to test the limits of the class alliance.

Kohli's thesis that states ruled by communists have been better at delivering poverty reduction because of their history of land reforms may be correct only partially. While West Bengal has reduced poverty from a high base, its average levels are as yet higher than many south Indian states. Moreover, West Bengal's record in social development is distinctly poorer than not only the southern Indian states, but also that of the national average (Maharatna, 2007). If so, the relationship between political orientations, state capacity and development outcomes probably needs further investigation.

Kohli's thesis prompts us to ask further questions. For instance, why is it that the state that could effectively carry out democratic elections with increasing sophistication and rigour, or carry out the world's largest census effectively decade after decade, is not be able to deliver anti-poverty measures effectively? Within the education field, why does the state fail to deliver effective primary education, but can design and conduct foolproof entrance examinations for Indian Institutes of

Technology (IITs) and Indian Institutes of Management (IIMs) over four decades to create world-class engineers and managers? The simple answer is that it is perhaps not the lack of capacity, but the lack of inclination, given the class nature of the state apparatus.

1.8 Conclusions

What is the message that emanates out of this volume? India is probably a unique case of a large, heterogeneous country with deepening democracy and a nation state that is still in the making. From an extremely low level, the economy has witnessed a modest improvement in living standards – abolishing famines, making a dent into absolute poverty and improvements in social development. It is an economy and society of contrasts and extremes, where – as often said – any statement about its progress and the opposite are equally true. Perhaps, its greatest achievement is that an ancient civilisation is modernising itself slowly yet peacefully, and democratically.

Yet, the achievements appear modest in a comparative perspective. Economic growth, regardless of the policy regime, has been iniquitous, though social and political changes have brought about a semblence of inclusiveness. Looking at it another way, India is a case of a gradual, if glacial change, where social stability and political freedom have proven to have a greater value.

Inquiring into the politics of poverty reduction contributions in this volume shows the underlying class nature of the polity and economy that offer deeper explanations for the development record. They underline the limitations of a purely economic view of policymaking, demonstrating how the deepening democracy seems to offer a ray of hope for the poor and helpless.

Notes

1. Very few countries have experienced consistently high growth rates over periods of several decades. The more typical pattern is that countries experience phases of growth, stagnation, or decline of varying length (Pritchett 2000). Examples of countries that have sustained long-term growth during the second half of the twentieth century are Botswana, China, India, Indonesia, Korea and Mauritius (Hausmann et al., 2005).
2. India's richest state, Maharashtra, which has per capita income 43 per cent higher than the national (unweighted) average, ranks tenth in nutritional status among 17 major states in 2008, with some of the worst cases

of malnutrition deaths reported from the tribal tracts close to Mumbai (Bombay), the national financial capital (Pitre et al., 2008).

3. However, as the total expenditure on health services is about five per cent of GDP in recent years, households are effectively bearing the bulk of the medical expenses out of their pocket (Yip and Mahal, 2009).
4. 'India suffers from a staggering toll of ill-health from communicable diseases, largely resulting from poor environmental conditions. Outbreaks of diseases such as dengue, diarrhoea, hepatitis and even cholera are common place, affecting all from the richest to the poorest. Half of India's children are stunted, and the fact that 25 per cent of those in the highest wealth quintile are similarly affected reflects the burden of morbidity even among the affluent. The World Health Organisation (WHO) estimates that *half of malnutrition is attributable not to lack of food but to infections arising from poor sanitation*' (Das Gupta et al., 2010: 46) (emphasis added).
5. As Sukhmoy Chakravarty said, ... [T]he fact that India has seen a proliferations of of the unrecognized industrial sector which is an almost complete tax haven. Furthermore, while agriculture has prospered in many states, ..., there is hardly any attempt to raise resources through direct taxation. What is more, both the unorganized industrial sector and prosperous agriculture receive significant subsidies, such as fertilizer, power and irrigation ...' (Chakravarty, 1986: 87).
6. Weiner contended, 'At the core of these beliefs are the Indian view of the social order, notions concerning the respective roles of upper and lower strata, the role of education as a means of maintaining differentiation among social classes, and concerns that "excessive" and "inappropriate" education for the poor would disrupt existing social arrangements' (Weiner, 1991: 5).
7. As Arthur Lewis argued, 'The doctrine that manual work should be done only by people of low social status is well entrenched in all those communities where considerations of caste or social prestige bulk large. Often the fundamental explanation is overpopulation. In overpopulated countries the tradition is established that there is a moral duty on the part of the better-off to provide as much employment as they can for the not-so-well-off, and hence, if people of higher status are seen doing manual work they lose respect – not only because that they are lowering their caste, but also because their refusal to give the work to someone else shows either that they are mean and heartless, or else they are not-so-well-off as they would like it to be thought. Such traditions are very appropriate to static over populated communities; but they do not mix well with the philosophy of individualism and self-help with which more dynamic societies are associated' (Lewis, 1955: 45).
8. '[T]he current phase of capitalism is marked by the rise to dominance of financial or rentier interests, and the fluidity of finance across national boundaries. This has the effect of undermining the control area of nation states, of making all agendas of state intervention for improving the living conditions of the people appear vacuous, of precipitating stagnation and unemployment even in the metropolitan countries, and of prising open the third world economies for penetration not only of metropolitan goods, but even more importantly of metropolitan finance. This economic milieu, however, has the effect of producing greater unity in the advanced capitalist world (where there is talk even of supra-national states, as in Europe), but,

as a dialectical counterpart of this, greater disunity in the third world, with tendencies towards separatism, divisiveness and disintegration acquiring prominence. The question which naturally arises is: are we now doomed to this fate for ever? Or can we overcome this fate?' (Patnaik, 1995: 2052).

9. '... [t]he fact that India has seen a proliferation of the unorganized industrial sector which is an almost complete tax haven. Furthermore, while agriculture has prospered in many states, ... there is hardly any attempt to raise resources through direct taxation. What is more, both the unorganized industrial sector and prosperous agriculture receive significant subsidies, such as fertilizer, power and irrigation ...' (Chakravarty, 1986: 77).

References

Bardhan (2007): 'Poverty and Inequality in China and India', *Economic and Political Weekly*, Vol. 42 September 22: 3849–52.

Bardhan (1984 and 1998): *The Political Economy of Development in India*, Delhi: Oxford University Press, (first and the second editions).

Chakravarty, Sukhamoy (1987): 'Development Strategies in the Asian Countries', in Louis Emmerij (ed.) *Development Policies and the Crisis of the 1980s*, Paris: OECD, 78–95.

Chakravarty, Sukhamoy (1986): *Development Planning: The Indian Experience*, Oxford: Clarendon Press.

CSO (2009): *Millennium Development Goals: India Country Report 2007*, New Delhi: Government of India.

Das Gupta, Monica (2005): 'Public Health in India: Dangerous Neglect', *Economic and Political Weekly*, Vol. 40: 5159–65.

Das Gupta, Monica, B. R. Desikachari, Rajendra Sukhla, T. V. Somanthan and K. K. Datta (2010): 'How Might India's Public Health Systems Be Strengthened? Lessons from Tamil Nadu', *Economic and Political Weekly*, Vol. 45, No. 10, March 6.

Deaton, Angus and Dreze, Jean (2009): 'Food and Nutrition in India: Facts and Interpretations', *Economic and Political Weekly*, Vol. 44, No. 7, February 14–20: 42–65.

Fields, Gary S. (2001): *Distribution and Development: A New Look at the Developing World*, MIT Press: Cambridge, MA.

Gupta, Vikas and Pal, Mahi (2008): 'Community Sanitation Campaign: A Study in Haryana', *Economic and Political Weekly*, Vol. 43, No. 33, August 16: 20–23.

Hausmann, Ricardo, Lant Pritchett and Dani Rodrik (2005): 'Growth Accelerations', *Journal of Economic Growth*, Vol. 10, No. 4: 303–29.

Kanbur, Ravi (2000): 'Income Distribution and Development', in A. B. Atkinson and F. Bourguignon (eds) *Handbook of Income Distribution: Volume 1*, Elsevier Science B. V.

Lewis, W. Arthur (1955): *Theory of Economic Growth*, London: Allen and Unwin.

Maharatna, Arup (2007): 'Population, Economy and Society in West Bengal since the 1970s', *Journal of Development Studies*, Vol. 43, No. 8, November: 1381–422.

Morris, Morris David and McAlpine, Michelle (1982): *Measuring the Conditions of India's Poor: The Physical Quality of Life Index*, New Delhi: Promilla and Co.
MOH (2002): *National Health Policy, 2002*, Ministry of Health, New Delhi: Government of India.
NCEUS (2006): *Social Security for Unorganised Workers: Report*, Government of India.
Paul, Samuel, Suresh Balakrishnan, K. Gopakumar, Sita Sekhar and M. Vivekananda (2004): 'State of India's Public Services: Benchmarks for the States', *Economic and Political Weekly*, Vol. 39, February 28: 920–33.
Patnaik, Prabhat (1995): 'Nation-State in the Era of "Globalisation"', *Economic and Political Weekly*, Vol. 30, No. 33, August 19: 2049–53.
Pitre, Amrita et al. (2009): *Nutritional Crisis in Maharashtra*, report prepared by SATHI for Maharashtra Health Equality and Rights Watch, http://www.sathicehat.org/uploads/CurrentProjects/Nutritional_Crisis_in_Maharashtra_Report.pdf.
Pritchett, Lant (2000): 'Understanding Patterns of Economic Growth: Searching for Hills among Plateaus, Mountains, and Plains', *World Bank Economic Review*, Vol. 14, No. 2: 220–50.
Sen, Amartya (1999): *Development as Freedom*, New Delhi: Oxford University Press.
Srinivasan, T. N. (1985): 'Neo-classical Political Economy, State and Economic Development', *Asian Development Review*, Vol. 3, No. 2: 38–58.
Weiner, Myron (1991): *The Child and the State in India*, Delhi: Oxford University Press.
WHO and UNICEF (2010): *Progress on Sanitation and Drinking Water: 2010 Update*, Geneva: World Health Organisation.
Yip, Winnie and Mahal, Ajay (2008): 'The Health Care Systems of China and India: Performance and Future Challenges', *Health Affairs*, Vol. 27, No. 4: 921–32.

2
Development Strategies and Poverty Reduction

R. Nagaraj

2.1 Introduction

With per capita income of US$1,124 at the current exchange rate in 2009 (Government of India, 2010), India is the world's eleventh largest economy in nominal GDP, and the fourth largest in terms of purchasing power parity (IMF, 2009). With 1.1 billion people accounting for one-sixth of the world population, India's ranking in per capita income stands at 142nd; its ranking in the human development index is 119th among 169 countries in the Human Development Report, 2010 (United Nations Development Programme, 2010). As with most large countries, India remains a domestic oriented economy with exports of goods and services constituting 26.2 per cent of GDP in 2009–10 (RBI, 2010).

India's constitutional democracy has three tiers: a strong central government, 28 states, and the local bodies consisting of Panchayats in rural areas and municipalities (or corporations) in urban areas. The Constitution has a social policy of positive discrimination in favour of the scheduled castes and scheduled tribes (SCs/STs) in their access to public employment and education to ameliorate centuries-old socially sanctioned disadvantages and deep-rooted discrimination. The Constitution also has 'directive principles' that mandate (not guarantee) the state to provide school education, health and protection for the socially vulnerable and the weak.

The chapter seeks to address the following questions regarding the post-independence development experience (1950 onwards):

1. Are there clearly delineable policy regimes with distinctly identifiable economic outcomes?

2. Is there a discernible relationship between policy regimes and their outcomes in terms of economic growth, poverty reduction and social development?
3. Where does India stand now in its policy orientation and what does it portend for social development in general, and poverty alleviation in particular?

Excluding the introduction and the conclusions, the study consists of five sections. Section 2.2 briefly describes the 'initial conditions', in terms of output, investment and exports; and the structure and performance of the labour market. Section 2.3 delineates three broad policy regimes and their evolution. Sections 2.4 and 2.5 examine India's record in poverty alleviation and social development and try to discern if there is a relationship between the outcomes and the policy regimes. In section 2.6, we suggest that India is currently at crossroads, the policy regime that it chooses could probably determine whether it moves closer to the path of growth with equity, or, gets caught in an increasingly polarised economy and society.

2.2 Economic record

India in 1950

In 1950, India's population was about 360 million, over 70 per cent of which lived in villages producing over half of the domestic output, mostly dependent on subsistence agriculture, with a high level of inequality in the ownership and operation of land. Though economic inequality was lower in a comparative perspective, considering the practices of social and cultural exclusion, overall inequality in Indian society could be considered quite extreme.

The economy's 'modern' sector consisted of plantation agriculture producing export crops like tea and coffee, and a few port-based enclaves of large-scale manufactures in the cities of Calcutta (Kolkata), Bombay (Mumbai) and Madras (Chennai) producing mostly cotton and jute goods for export; besides the railways, defence and civil services. The first half of the twentieth century witnessed practically little growth in per capita income, though there were islands of prosperity with the spread of irrigation, export-oriented plantation and of modern industry.

India was practically at the bottom of economic and social indicators of development. Morris D. Morris's estimate of physical quality of life index (PQLI) – a simple average of index of literacy, life expectancy at age one and infant mortality rate – stood at 14 in 1950, against 89 for the US (Morris, 1979). Among the 70 mostly developing nations for which Morris has provided estimates, only Afghanistan, Gambia and Central African Republic stood equal to, or lower than, India.

Economic Performance, 1950–2010

Between 1951 and 2010, on a trend basis, the domestic output has grown annually at 4.6 per cent (2.4 per cent in per capita income) (Table 2.1)[1]. It is as yet an agrarian economy with about 55 per cent of the workforce subsisting on agriculture in 2004–5, producing about 20 per cent of the domestic output, with the services or the tertiary sector accounting for a little over one-half of the domestic output (Figure 2.1). With a steady decline in agriculture's share of the domestic output, but without a corresponding transformation of the workforce (as was the case in the presently developed economies), output per head between agriculture (rural) and non-agricultural (urban) sectors has diverged, contributing to growing economic disparities between town and country.

India's growth is mostly financed internally, with the domestic saving rate going up from about nine per cent of the output in 1950–1 to 38 per cent in 2007–8; external resources contributing in the range of one to three per cent of GDP. Until recently, much of it came from multilateral and bilateral sources with modest reliance on international capital markets. The household sector that includes unincorporated businesses, accounts for the bulk of the domestic saving, while the public sector saving is close to negative (as reflected in the deficit on the government's revenue account), because of growing subsidies, low prices and inadequate recovery of user charges in public utilities and services (Nagaraj, 2006).

India is an inflation-averse economy: measured by the implicit GDP deflator, the average annual inflation rate over nearly six decades is 7.4 per cent. Price rise is a politically sensitive barometer that has unseated several governments, as nine-tenths of the workforce is employed in the unorganised sector with no indexation of their income. Similarly, India placed a premium on external financial stability, with the current account balance seldom exceeding three and half per cent of the domestic output (Figure 2.2). However, as with most growing economies, it has faced periodic balance-of-payment crises: in 1957–8, 1965–6, 1973–4, 1979–80, and 1991–2. Though India's external debt in 2010 is US$261 billion, servicing it has not been an onerous burden for most years; for instance, of late it accounts for only 19 per cent of GDP, and the debt service accounts for 5.5 per cent of its

Table 2.1 Long-term growth rates of Indian economy and its principal sectors, 1951 to 2010

	(Per cent per year)						
	1951–66	1967–80	1981–91	1992–2010	1951–80	1981–2010	1951–2010
1. Agriculture	2.5	2.4	3.1	2.7	2.2	3.0	2.6
2. Industry	6.9	4.2	7.0	7.0	5.4	6.4	5.5
2.1 Manufacturing	6.9	4.8	7.4	7.1	5.3	6.4	5.5
3. Services	4.9	4.5	7.0	8.5	4.6	7.6	5.8
GDP	**4.0**	**3.6**	**5.6**	**6.8**	**3.6**	**6.0**	**4.6**
GDP per capita	**1.7**	**1.2**	**3.0**	**5.0**	**1.4**	**4.0**	**2.4**

Source: *National Accounts Statistics*, various issues.
Note: Agriculture includes allied activities such as forestry, fishery, dairying; industry includes (1) mining, (2) manufacturing, (3) electricity, gas and water and (iv) construction; and, services include (i) trade, hotel and restaurants, (ii) transport, storage and communications, (iii) banking and insurance, real estate, dwelling and business services and (iv) community, social and personal services.

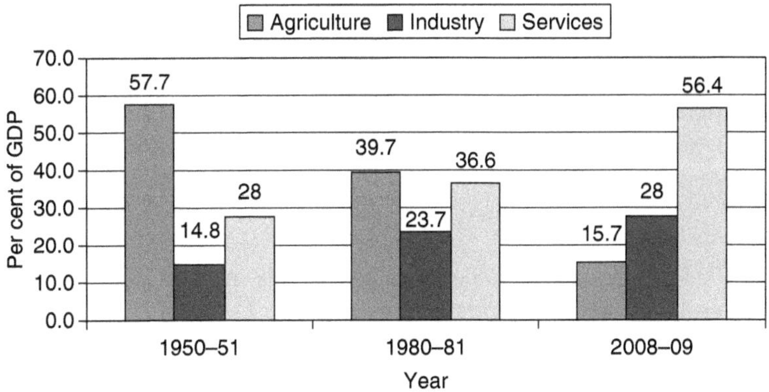

Figure 2.1 Composition of output, 1950–1 to 2008–9
Source: *National Accounts Statistics*, various issues.

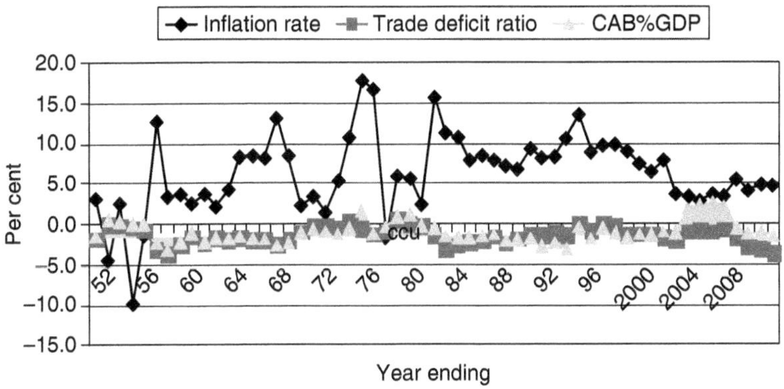

Figure 2.2 Inflation and external balance, 1951–2 to 2009–10
Source: *National Accounts Statistics*, and *Economic Survey*, various issues.

exports. Apparently, India has the distinction of having never defaulted or rescheduled its external debt repayment, making it a poor yet proud international borrower.

India's macroeconomic record and industrial capability stands somewhere between East Asia and Latin America. Her achievements in social development are distinctly inferior (except perhaps in higher and technical education), though starting from far adverse 'initial conditions' (as noted above).

Public expenditure on health and education has remained around 1 per cent and 3.5 per cent of domestic output respectively for a long time. Over one-half of the educational budget is apparently spent on higher education – a hugely subsidised service that has mostly benefited the elite and urban population. This is well-reflected in the persistence of illiteracy, poor school and vocational educational training on the one hand, and excess supply of college graduates (and more recently, in the export of high valued services), on the other.

Indian labour market

In 2004–5, the labour force consisted of 458 million persons, growing annually at about one per cent; with 11 million unemployed (Government of India, 2007). Slightly less than three-fifths of the workforce is employed in agriculture, residing in rural areas and producing one-fifth of the domestic product. Cultivators form about two-thirds of the rural workforce; the remaining are agriculture workers. The share of employment in the industrial sector (mining, manufacturing, construction and utilities) is around 19 per cent, producing about 27 per cent of the domestic output (Table 2.2).[2]

The worker-population ratio has remained stable at around 40 per cent, with about 28 per cent for women (probably an underestimate). India is home to the largest number of child labour, though the proportion of children working has steadily declined, with rising school enrolment.

Table 2.2 Sectoral distribution of labour force, 1951 to 2004–5

(Per cent)

Year	Agriculture	Industry	Services
1951	72.4	10.6	17.0
1961	71.9	11.7	16.4
1971	72.0	11.5	16.5
1981	68.8	13.5	17.7
1983	68.0	15.2	16.8
1987–88	64.2	17.8	18.1
1993–94	63.3	16.7	20.1
1999–00	59.8	18.0	22.2
2004–05	56.4	18.8	24.8

Note: Data for the years 1951 to 1981 are from the decennial population census, and the remaining years from NSS five-yearly sample surveys on employment and unemployment. The data over the census years as well between the census and NSS estimates are not strictly comparable. However, they are adequate to show the broad pattern of change. Some rows may not add up to a little more than 100 on account of rounding off error.
Source: Anant et al. (2006), Sundaram (2007).

Nevertheless, it is still pretty large in absolute numbers – 8.6 million in 2004–5 representing 6.2 per cent of children in the age group of 5 to 14 – often producing goods for export.

India is less urban than the average of Asia: in 2004–5, only 29 per cent of its workforce is urban, mostly residing in the metropolitan cities. Long-term migration rates are low (relative to developing countries); rural-urban migration is largely to the metropolitan cities – moderating and declining urban wage growth, as well as causing considerable open (and disguised) unemployment, swelling the size of the urban informal sector.

Institutionally, the labour market consists of three sectors: at one end of it is the rural labour force, mostly in agriculture; and at the other end is the organised labour in urban areas employing eight per cent of the workforce consisting of educated, skilled and experienced workers, producing about two-fifths of the domestic output. Between these two lies the informal (unorganised) sector that is mostly urban, employed in industry and services, representing the growing segment of the labour market (at the expense of the other two sectors).

In 2004–5, the unemployment rate – measured by the 'usual status' depending on whether a person was employed at all during the last one year – was 3.1 per cent (Government of India, 2007). The low unemployment level – a spurious measure of 'full employment' – suggests that few can afford to be unemployed in a poor country with no other source of livelihood. As is known, much of the problem in underdeveloped countries is not of open unemployment, but of severe underemployment or disguised unemployment.

2.3 Policy regimes

India has a history of economic and political discourse on the poverty of its people. Perhaps the earliest scholarly discussion goes back to the writings of Dadabhai Naoroji in the second half of nineteenth century that provided the intellectual basis for the anti-colonial movement. In 1938, the National Planning Committee headed by Jawaharlal Nehru (assisted by K. T. Shah) examined all aspects of economic policy for the impending political independence. The 'Bombay Plan', an initiative of the nascent capitalist class, also dealt with the same issue.

The main themes of these writings were: to remove poverty and social backwardness, and the need for an independent and autonomous development strategy that would put the levers of economic policymaking in the hands of Indian nationals. They also argued for a large role for the state as a means to acquire the desired independence in the economic sphere. While economic growth was deemed necessary, it was considered inadequate without significant changes in the ownership of means of production. Since land is the most important productive asset in an agrarian economy, economic growth was considered to be dependent on reforming its ownership and operation. Hence, radical agrarian reforms were seen as a necessity for long-term economic development.

1950–65: The planning era

The main challenge the economy faced, as discussed in the development literature, was to raise the capital stock per head. The solution was to augment domestic supply, restrict and reorient domestic demand, to get on to a path of increasing domestic saving and investment to secure sustained increase in output per head. While acute poverty and widespread deprivation were widely acknowledged, they were primarily sought to be addressed by expanding domestic output. However, there was an considerable awareness of how more equal income distribution was not only desirable, but also valuable for greater efficiency and growth.

The initial one and half decade or so of planning, coterminus with the first three five-year plans (1951–65), form a reasonably coherent policy regime when the state assumed the central role in promoting economic development, and the economy was reoriented towards the domestic market. The primary objective during this period was to raise the rate of economic growth, following an import substituting industrialisation model. During the Second Plan in the mid-1950s, efforts were made to channel a sizable share of the investments into metal and machinery manufacturing ('heavy industry', for short) to secure dynamic comparative advantage, given India's abundant natural resources of ores and coal. Lack of these capabilities was perceived as the binding constraint on accelerating the long-term output growth.

To meet the employment objective, however, the plan sought to encourage cottage industries and curtail machine-made consumer goods, using a variety of fiscal and physical measures. Such a strategy also meant a (almost deliberate) withdrawal from the international trade in textiles, where India had carved a significant presence. Promotion of the traditional methods of production was consistent with Gandhian views, although economic rationality of such initiatives remained contentious.

During this period, land reforms were high on the policy agenda, coupled with the expansion of irrigation potential of large dams to augment agricultural output and to meet the expected demand for foodgrains and industrial raw material from the 'modern' sector. Perhaps, an equally urgent need was to make up for the lost irrigated tracts after the partition of the sub-continent. In the rural economy, these were supplemented by community development programmes (based on the Balwantrai Mehta committee report), which sought to modernise agriculture and provide modern services, including public health and education, and thus, to meet the Constitution's Directive Principles. The attempt was predicated on the creation of the third tier of Indian democracy, namely, the panchayati raj institution to ensure administrative accountability by the elected representatives. These efforts were supplemented by expansion of cooperative credit institutions to finance agricultural growth.

During this period (1950–65), the economy grew annually at about 4.0 per cent, with agriculture at 2.5 per cent and industry at about 7 per cent – representing a significant departure from the colonial period, a fairly respectable record by the contemporary standards.[3] Substantial import substitution in metal and machinery manufacturing was accomplished, leading India to become perhaps one of the competitive producers of steel by the late 1960s.

However, with fast industrial growth relative to agriculture, demand for food outstripped the domestic supply, exerting an upward pressure on prices that were kept in check with food aid from the US. But the matter came to a head in the mid-1960s with two successive crop failures (in 1965 and 1966), and external (non-economic) shocks that put an end to this phase of development. Industry was saddled with excess capacity in machine building and underutilised technical manpower (an outcome of large-scale investment in higher education) as planned public investment did not materialise.

1966–80: Period of shocks and crises

With foodgrains emerging as the binding constraint in an increasingly hostile international political environment, import substitution shifted to agriculture by accepting the 'green revolution' technology of high yielding variety seeds, and chemical fertilisers in locations of assured irrigation. It was an unequal development path in terms of class and region, but considered a national necessity, given the immediate goal of food self-sufficiency. As often happens in policymaking, considerations of economic growth took precedence over its distribution. This was, in principle, justifiable since the green revolution technology was scale neutral; what was required was to expand the access to irrigation and timely credit that would diffuse the technology among smaller farmers. In due course, foodgrain policy and supporting institutions evolved to offer sustained incentives for augmenting food production and its distribution.

With the decline in public investment in infrastructure and food constraint, industrial growth slowed down after the mid-1960s. As substantial import substitution was accomplished, there existed an option to move ahead with export-oriented industrialisation, as Korea and Taiwan did around that time. The wisdom of such a strategic shift, in terms of the economics and politics of the period, remains debatable. Instead, prompted by domestic and external political factors, the policy shifted towards securing a better distribution of growth by promoting regional development, small-scale industries, curbing industrial monopolies and regulating foreign-owned enterprises. Policymaking in the industrial sphere, therefore, became discretionary and specific.[4]

The oil shocks in the 1970s diverted attention towards exploiting the newly discovered (though modest) domestic hydrocarbon resources in Bombay High, and to augment domestic production of fertilizers to insulate the food economy from input shortages. This was a period of domestic and external (economic and non-economic) shocks, shortening the time horizons of policymakers. Industry suffered, as its growth rate nearly halved to about four and half per cent during 1966–80 – known in the Indian discourse as a period of 'relative stagnation' (Table 2.1). Moreover, there was a shared perception of falling behind rapidly industrialising East Asia.

The green revolution ensured food security, proving many international sceptics wrong. However, it was more of a 'wheat revolution' that helped maintain foodgrain output. As wheat is mostly grown in the north-western parts of the country, it led to a regional imbalance in production, straining the infrastructure in food grain movement and its distribution. As food consumption across the states was largely determined by food production regionally, the technology-based solution to augment agricultural output perhaps accentuated the poverty of the poorer states. Lack of technological improvements in oilseeds and pulses (main sources of fat and protein in much of vegetarian south Asia) dented the claim of food self-sufficiency.

1980 – Onwards: Creeping liberalisation

As the oil crisis ended, with the return of political stability at the centre, economic policymaking saw a distinct shift. The focus was now on efficiency in import substitution, a greater desire for foreign technology and capital to modernise industry, and a gradual dismantling of the restrictions on output, investments and imports. Public investment was stepped up in infrastructure in the 1980s, an integrated rural development programme (IRDP) was initiated as the main instrument for poverty alleviation by amalgamating various target-group oriented programmes (more about it later). This is a period of creeping liberalisation with a steadily growing role for markets.

India's annual growth rate accelerated to about 5.5 per cent in the 1980s, with industry regaining the status of the leading sector, overcoming the prolonged period of relative stagnation (1965–80). India's economic growth picked up momentum at a time when much of the developing world – especially Latin America – was mired in debt and inflation. However, a balance-of-payment crisis in 1991 punctured the growth process. Whether it was caused by exogenous or endogenous factors is debatable. Further, it remains a moot point whether import liberalisation or the cumulative effects of import substitution caused the crisis. (Joshi and Little, 1994; Nayyar, 1995).

Attributing the crisis to the ills of the latter, the newly elected minority government sought to accelerate the reforms by accepting an orthodox policy agenda that perhaps went well beyond the requirements for stabilising the external disequilibrium. There was a serious effort to withdraw the state from many economic spheres, in the belief that private (including foreign) initiative would fill the void quickly and efficiently. While the pace of the policy shift appeared swift by India's past standards, it was perhaps modest when compared to Russia and Eastern Europe.

The balance-of-payment crisis was resolved quickly. An industrial boom ensued for four years (1992–6), followed by a deceleration that persisted until 2003. While the protagonists advocated speeding up to 'complete the reforms agenda', sceptics questioned their premises, based on the comparative experience. But the slowdown in industry was compensated by a surprising boom of services in information technology followed by IT-enabled services, shoring up India's balance of payment – perhaps an interesting case of an unintended consequence of the reforms amid a technological revolution.

This has led to an acceleration of economic growth after the liberal reforms in 1991. But it has hurt the agricultural sector leading to what is now widely accepted as an agrarian distress (more later). Severe reduction in public investment – most of which is in infrastructure – seems to have adversely affected both agricultural and industrial growth, denting the prospects of exporting labour-intensive manufactures (Figure 2.3).

Economic growth has revived on a stronger note since 2002–3, with some suggesting that India is on to a higher growth path of 7–8 per cent per year. What accounts for the resurgent growth is yet to be seriously analysed. Perhaps it represents a construction-led boom in

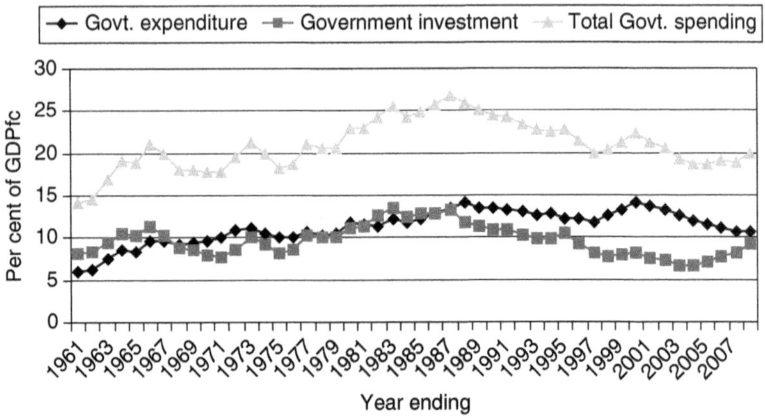

Figure 2.3 Public spending as % of GDP, 1961–2008
Source: *National Accounts Statistics*, various issues.

manufacturing, lubricated by easy credit at low interest rates and a cyclical surge in exports (Nagaraj, 2008).

There has been a further change after 2004 with inclusive growth as a new phase of development, although it is, perhaps, too soon to be sure about it.

2.4 Economic inequality and poverty

In the early years of independence (1950–65), land reforms were expected to generate more equitable distribution of income, and hence, social development. Land reforms consisted of four distinct components: (1) elimination of intermediary tenancy (abolition of the Zamindari system), (2) land redistribution, (3) tenancy reforms, and (4) land consolidation. As land is a state subject in the Constitution, the pace of these reforms varied across the country.

In practice, land reforms were reasonably effective in abolishing intermediary tenancy, implying the elimination of absentee landlordism. But very little land got redistributed, as there were gaping loopholes in the laws (Joshi, 1975). Contrary to the intent of the policy, land ownership probably got accentuated as landowners evicted tenants to resume self-cultivation by engaging agricultural labour. Evidently, the share of agricultural labour in the rural workforce increased from 17 per cent in 1961 to 26.3 per cent in 1971, and has remained there (Figure 2.4).

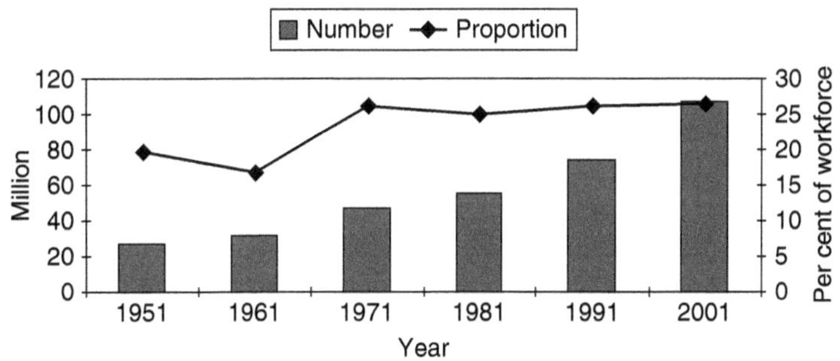

Figure 2.4 Agriculture labour: number and as proportion of total workers, 1951 to 2001
Source: *Statistical Abstract of India*, and *Indian Labour Statistics*, various issues.

By the early 1960s, dissatisfaction with the poor progress in land reform had begun to surface.[5] Though nationally land reforms had lost steam, Kerala and West Bengal (and to a modest extent, Karnataka in the 1970s) persisted with them with varying intensity and success.[6]

There is evidence to suggest that even in the first decade after independence, economic inequality increased. Analysing the distribution of consumption (as a proxy for income), P. C. Mahalanobis came to the following conclusion:

> From the information and analysis given ... it seems likely that there was some improvement in the levels of living and an increase in opportunity in many directions for most people of India during the first decade of planning (1951–61). The rate of growth of consumption was still low. Benefits arising from growth also seemed to have accrued, in a large proportion, to the richer sections of the people. In consequence, disparities between the rich and the poor did not generally decrease, but increased in many respects (Mahalanobis, 1975: 1168–9).

Faced with the inability to alter inequality, the Planning Commission in 1962 sought to shift the focus on removing absolute poverty defined as the minimum consumption basket to satisfy the nutritional requirement for a normally healthy person (also known as income poverty). This was estimated to be Rs 20 per person per month in 1960–1 in rural India. According to this measure, about half of the population was poor.

Though pioneering in its analytical effort and policy initiative, the Planning Commission did not come up with radical measures to implement the policy, given the political opposition to mobilising the resources. More fundamentally, the study raised the classic trade-off between equity and growth, via the problem of incentives in a market economy. To quote the report:

> It [poverty] must be eradicated both on humanitarian grounds and as well as an essential condition for orderly progress. No programme or policy, which fails to alleviate the conditions of the poor appreciably, can hope for the necessary measure of public co-operation and political support in a mature democracy. *The central concern of our planning has to be the removal of poverty as early as possible.* The stage has now come when we should sharply focus our efforts on providing an assured minimum income to every citizen of the country within a reasonable period of time. Progressively this minimum itself would be raised as development goes apace (emphasis added).

But it went on to add:

> The minimum that can be guaranteed is limited by the size of the total product and the extent of redistribution, which is feasible. ... Redistribution on this scale, however, is operationally meaningless unless revolutionary changes in property rights and scale and structure of wages and compensation are contemplated. To raise the standards of living of the vast masses of the people, output therefore would have to be increased very considerably (Srinivasan and Bardhan, 1974: 13–14).

Moreover, the anti-poverty initiative could not be taken up in the face of the series of shocks and the food crisis around the mid-1960s, as well as the policy shift that ensued.

As noted earlier, although India did succeed in overcoming the food crisis with the help of the new seed–fertiliser–irrigation package, it also gave rise to concerns over the accentuating inequalities as the gains of such a growth process were (expectedly) unequally distributed. This is best exemplified by the stagnation of agricultural wages in the 1960s (Jose, 1974). In politics, this found expression in the rise of the left-wing extremism of the Naxalbari movement in rural Bengal towards the late 1960s that soon spread far and wide, rattling the political establishment.

Indira Gandhi sought to face these concerns by coming up with the programme of 'Garibi Hatao' (Abolish Poverty) in the early 1970s. It provided an opportunity for the policy of 'growth with equity', that sought to give a shape to the vision of the 1962 Planning Commission document. The Fifth Five-Year Plan (1972–7) sought to analyse the implications of meeting the minimum consumption requirement on domestic production and its implications for saving and investment. Such an initiative was more generally consistent with the dissatisfaction of the 'growth first' strategy.[7]

But many of these planning exercises could not be translated into an actionable programme for lack of credible policy instruments. However, the planners sought to augment public provision of services under the 'minimum needs programme', and expanding the access to food under the public distribution system (PDS).

In practical terms, these concerns of equity and poverty reduction were addressed by a variety of 'target-oriented development programmes' intended to increase the productivity of small and marginal farmers to diffuse the seed–fertiliser–water technology, and to provide self-employment opportunities in the non-farm sector. Regardless of the nomenclature, the logic of these efforts was quite simple: as the existing distribution of assets could not be disturbed for political reasons, the way out is to provide bank credit to the poor to enable them to acquire a productive asset whose yield could potentially enable them to overcome poverty (Chakravarty, 1990). Often these loans came with a subsidy by the state governments to improve the profitability of the proposed self-employment activities. Such a strategy appeared credible after the nationalisation of 14 major commercial banks in 1969 as the state secured control over domestic credit.

For those who were too poor to acquire an asset (or a skill), employment generation programmes were also initiated, though they remained modest. Later, these initiatives were combined to create the Integrated Rural Development Programme (IRDP), the principal vehicle for poverty alleviation (Figure 2.5).

Success of such an effort depends on correctly identifying the beneficiaries, and monitoring the loans and their prompt repayment. But the IRDP got discredited pretty soon, as it was poorly implemented, and the loans turned sticky, since a large proportion of them were made on political considerations. In other words, the IRDP became the proverbial leaky bucket of redistribution with only a small share of the benefits reaching the intended social segment.

Self-employment programmes, therefore, were replaced by wage employment programme in the 1990s – called the Jawahar Rozgar Yojana – and modelled after the Maharashtra employment guarantee scheme.[8]

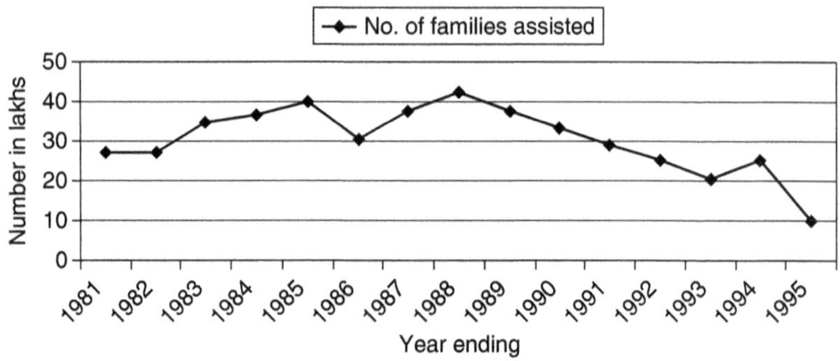

Figure 2.5 Number of families assisted by IRDP, 1981 to 1995
Source: *Economic Survey*, various issues.

But since public expenditure contracted as a proportion of domestic output with the initiation of the liberal reforms, the employment generation efforts failed to make a difference.

Further, the policy of universal distribution of food grains as a means of food security was replaced with targeted programmes meant only for the poor to reduce food subsidies. There was an apprehension that such a policy shift could have adversely affected the poor, on account of mistageting.

By the turn of the century, there was a growing concern over poor agriculture growth and agrarian distress – as evidenced by a dramatic rise in farmers' suicides and rapid spread of left-wing extremism in eastern India (Map 2.1).[9] In response, the notion of employment guarantee for the rural poor took root. The concerns of organisational weaknesses of such an effort are met by the institutionalisation of panchayats and the Right to Information Act.

Outcome of anti-poverty efforts

Though seemingly straightforward, counting the poor has been a contentious issue, on account of many statistical considerations: (1) representativeness of the sample, (2) comparability of sampling procedures over the years, and (3) deflators used to adjust for inflation that varies across regions, income classes and varying consumption baskets. By the official statistics, based on a uniform methodology, income poverty began to decline from about 50 per cent of the population in 1977–8 to about 27 per cent in 2004–5 (Figure 2.6). This also meant a decline in the absolute number of poor from about 330 million (Government of

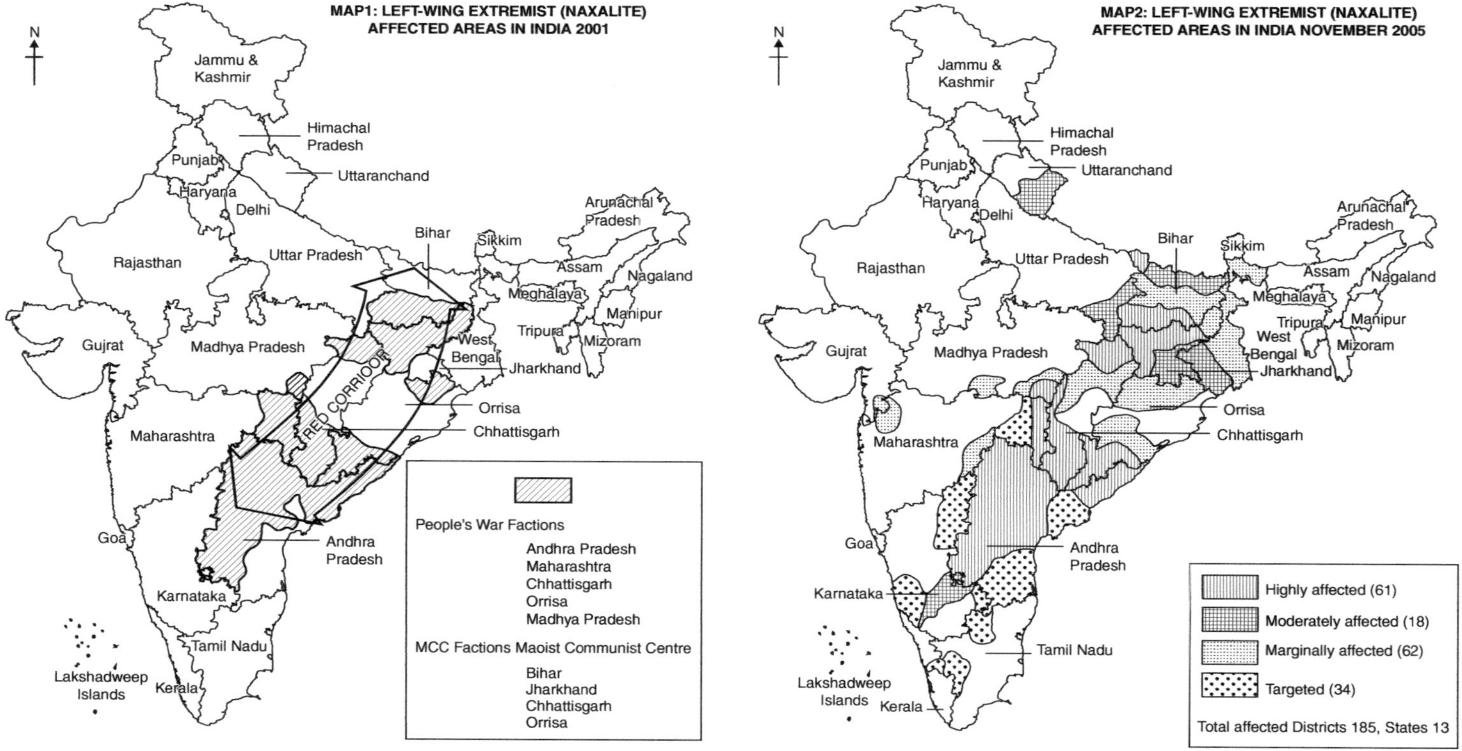

Map 2.1 Spread of left-wing extremism between 2001 and 2005
Source: Chakravarty (2008).

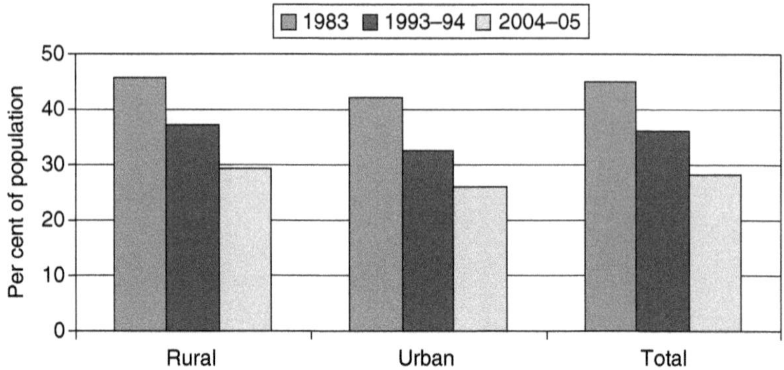

Figure 2.6 Headcount ratio of poverty, 1983 to 2004–5
Source: *Economic Survey*, various issues.

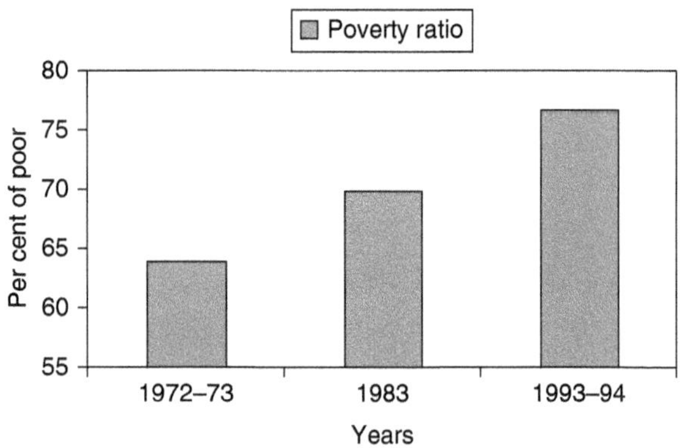

Figure 2.7 Nutrition poverty, 1972–3 to 1993–4
Source: Nagaraj (2000).

India, 2007). But the rate of decline in poverty was faster in the 1980s, compared to the 1990s and beyond, suggesting a setback after the initiation of the liberal reforms (Mahendra Dev and Ravi, 2007).

However, there is an enormous dispute about the estimated trends, and more contentiously, the reasons for the decline. A contrarian view is one based on nutritional poverty – a measure that reads caloric value consumption ignoring the monetary equivalent and its adjustment for inflation – that shows an increase in poverty between the 1970s and the 1990s (Figure 2.7). Appropriateness of the nutritional poverty measures is a contentious proposition, as one gets bizarre results at the disaggregated level. For instance, Punjab, the nation's granary, shows high nutritional poverty, but low-income poverty. Nevertheless, Suryanarayana's (2000) careful estimates, for the period 1950–1 to 1993–4, using a more refined methodology also admits a decline in poverty, but to a much limited extent.

The decline in income poverty is highly uneven across the states. Is poverty reduction positively associated with economic growth, as expected in the conventional economic reasoning? Probably not. While the poverty decline is discernible since the second half of the 1970s, economic growth accelerated only after 1980. The association becomes ambiguous at the state level as no statistically valid relationship is discernible between growth in per capita output and declining poverty. For example, in the recent years, economic growth is robust in the southern and western Indian states, while the bulk of poverty is concentrated in the eastern and northern Indian states. Therefore, the observed inverse relation between economic growth and poverty at the national level may be spurious. However, there exists a statistically valid correlation between growth in value added in agriculture and decline in poverty across the major states. With the deceleration in agricultural output in physical terms since the 1990s, it seems reasonable to expect a slowdown in poverty reduction.

In sum, there has indeed been a decline in income poverty over the last three decades, but its spread and speed are open to dispute. Further, there is little doubt that deprivation in food and nutrition persists and is widespread, but they are not captured in the poverty estimates (Deaton and Dreze, 2009).

While the trends in poverty reduction remain disputed, modest progress in many physical indicators of well-being and deprivation are discernible (Mehrotra, 2006). While we have a reasonable idea of the extent of the decline in poverty, we know much less about income inequality, as data on income for over 90 per cent of the workforce that is employed in the unorganised sector is not available. However, measures across various institutional categories suggest a discernible increase in four types of economic inequality since the 1980s:

1. Between rural and urban per capita income (Figure 2.8),
2. Between the per capita net state domestic product (NSDP) across the major states (Figure 2.9),
3. Between the per capita income in the organised and unorganised sectors (Figure 2.10) and
4. Decline in wages and a rise in profit before tax as proportions of gross value added in the private corporate sector (Figure 2.11).

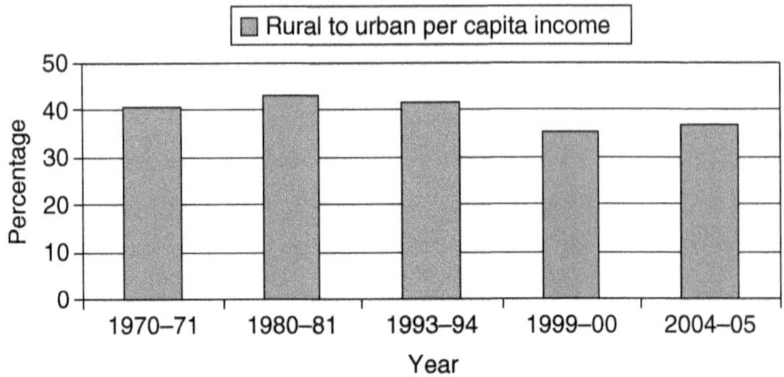

Figure 2.8 Rural to urban per capita NDP, 1970–1 to 2004–5
Source: *National Accounts Statistics*, various issues.

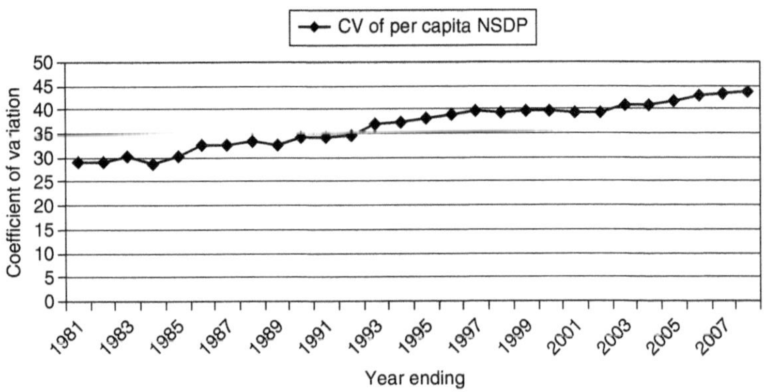

Figure 2.9 Coefficient of variation of per capita NSDP, 1980–1 to 2007–8
Source: EPWRF (2009), and Central Statistical organisation web site: www.mospi.nic.in
Note: Data for the years from 1980–81 to 1993–94 is based on the series with the base year 1980–81; from 1994–95 to 1999–2000 is based on the with the base year 1993–94; and from 2000–01 to 2007–08 is based on the series with the base year 1999–2000. The three segments are merged to depict at a continuous series.

To summarise the arguments of this section, during the first policy regime (1950–65), relative poverty or inequality was to be addressed by land reforms. As the euphoria of the radical redistribution evaporated by the mid-1960s, the focus shifted to reducing absolute poverty that perhaps got accentuated partly on account of macroeconomic instability and inflation. But the 1970s witnessed the emergence of poverty alleviation as a political agenda, which got translated into expansion of bank credit to augment agricultural productivity of small farms and non-farm self-employment activities and (to a much limited

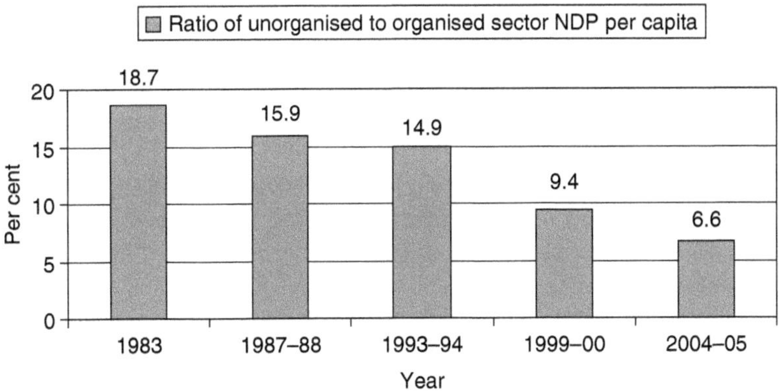

Figure 2.10 Ratio of unorganised to organised sector NDP per capita, 1983 to 2004–5

Source: *National Accounts Statistics*, various issues.

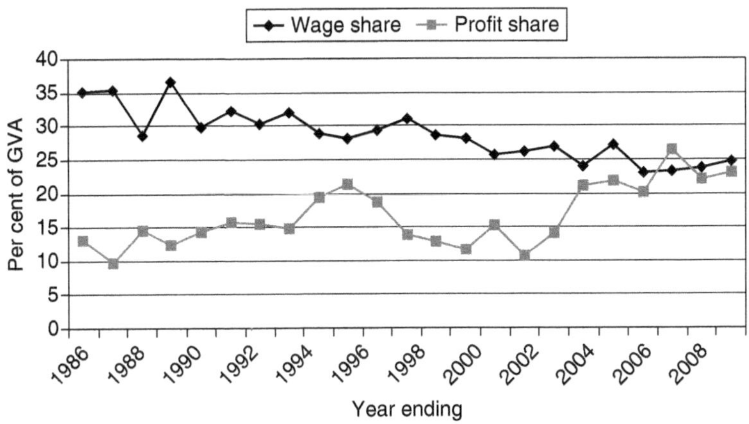

Figure 2.11 Wage and profit shares in private corporate sector, 1985–6 to 2007–8

Source: *Reserve Bank of India Bulletin*, various issues.

Note: The Figure above represents share of remuneration and profit before tax in gross value added in non-financial private corporate sector.

extent) wage employment for the asset-less rural poor. The results of these efforts were discernible since the late 1970s, though the extent of poverty decline remains contentious. However, the liberal reforms seem to have slowed the pace of poverty reduction.

Lessons of the Indian experience

On a closer reflection the trickle-down approach to poverty reduction does not seem to work, or perhaps works too slowly to be socially and politically acceptable; nor does the rhetoric of land reforms seem effective in a political democracy. Growth with poverty reduction seems possible if public investment augments provision of public goods and infrastructure, and agricultural development strengthens small farmers and rural diversification, as the experience of the 1980s seem to suggest.

Identifying poverty with nutrition and its monetary equivalent seems to have inherent limitations. It is perhaps better measured by health and educational outcomes and access to public services. This leads us to look at social policy.

2.5 Social policy

Social policy derives from the notions of the welfare state that gained acceptance in the developed economies in the post-war period. These considerations were quite different from the challenges faced in an ex-colonial nation such as India, where the primacy of creating the nation state in a heterogeneous society, addressing deep-rooted social divisions and discrimination, sowing the seed of growth in a stagnant economy and fighting mass poverty and deprivation (perhaps in the same order of importance), took precedence. These were sought to be resolved within a framework of political democracy.

Therefore, the social policy that has evolved in India seems to have three components: (1) positive discrimination in favour of SCs/STs to address centuries of social inequality, (2) public provisioning of basic facilities such as education, health, drinking water, sanitation and electricity and (3) social security.

Perhaps the most notable aspect of the social policy, as mentioned earlier, is the constitutionally mandated reservation for SCs and STs in higher education and public service. The size and scope of such an affirmative action has now expanded to include 'other backward classes', and in some states religious minorities as well, though these extensions remain politically contentious.

The 'modern' sector – mainly consisting of government (including its enterprises), and the private corporate sector, currently constituting eight per cent of the workforce producing about 40 per cent of the domestic output – has access to (substantially) publicly provided housing, education and health facilities, and provident fund and pension schemes for social security, modelled after the post-war welfare state in the advanced countries. Most of the legislations dealing with the labour market and social protection are concerned with the organised sector.

Why are these provisions restricted to the modern sector? The modern sector represents capital and skill-intensive activities with high labour productivity that permits payment of higher wage and social benefits.[10] Public sector jobs are mostly based on open competitions and competitive examinations to screen for quality. Initially, there was perhaps optimism that with economic progress, the modern sector would expand to absorb the unorganised sector as the stock of surplus labour gets exhausted (as suggested in the dual economy models).

However, there could be other reasons as well. Being a founding member of the International Labour Organization (ILO), India accepted, at least in principle, some of its enlightened guidelines of social welfare and protection. The state was also committed to being an ideal employer by setting the standard for the private sector to follow. Such provisions were also considered as necessary incentives for promoting education and skill development. Questions regarding the financial sustainability of these generous social provisions – a serious issue currently – were seldom raised, as the state was perceived to have the power to impose taxes and the administrative capability to collect them.

In the rural areas, initially the provision of social services was implemented as part of the community development programmes, discussed earlier. For this purpose, each district was divided into several community development blocks, assigned to an administrator called block development officer.[11] This was to be complemented by elected local self-government bodies, known as panchayati raj institutions. Inadequate supply of trained manpower – teachers, doctors and nurses – reportedly constrained the expansion of social services. Therefore, the planning laid considerable emphasis on higher education, at the expense of primary and secondary education, to meet the normative requirement of skilled manpower (together with addressing the requirement for industrialisation).

However, given the rigid rural social structure, economic inequality and the close nexus between the bureaucracy and richer segments of the society (mostly belonging to the higher castes), the fruits of community development and other official assistance did not percolate to the lower classes and poorer segments. In other words, as upper castes who wielded economic and social power in villages were also predominant in the administration, the institutional reforms were sabotaged and the resources meant for community development were cornered by the rural rich, by-passing the masses.

Though local self-government institutions form one of the Directive Principles, (until recently) regular elections for them were not constitutionally binding, but were left to the discretion of the state governments. It is widely believed that the states that persisted with more regular elections and devolution of responsibilities to the local bodies – like Maharashtra and Gujarat – have a better record of economic and social development (Singh, 1994).

With economic growth accelerating, the 1980s witnessed an increase in expenditure on social sectors (Burgess and Stern, 1993). With the initiation of stabilisation and structural reforms in 1991, social expenditures were cut, but were soon restored as the economy recovered by the mid-1990s, in response to growing public criticism (Nagaraj, 1997). There has also been an effort to redirect a greater share of public resources for primary education and to make higher education increasingly self-financed. However, with the recent surge in demand for technical education in response to export of IT and IT-enabled services, it is unclear if there has been a material shift in resource allocation towards primary education.

As mentioned earlier, measured by PQLI, India was nearly at the bottom of the league table in social development in 1950.[12] By 1970, it had risen higher than West Africa and the Persian Gulf countries (Morris and McAlpine, 1982). By 2001, the PQLI rose to 61, a level that Kerala had attained three decades earlier (Figure 2.12). In 2006, India ranked 49th

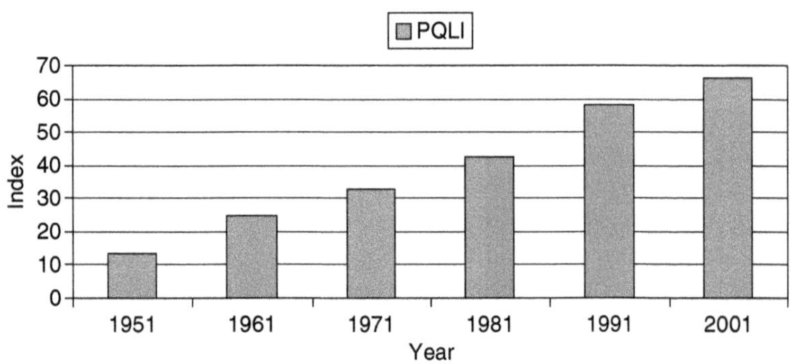

Figure 2.12 Physical quality of life index, 1951 to 2001
Source: *Statistical Abstract of India*, various issues.

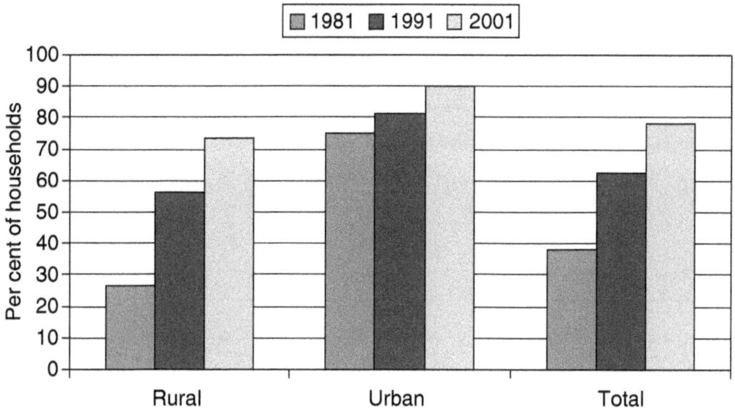

Figure 2.13 Access to safe drinking water, 1981 to 2001
Source: *Economic Survey*, various issues.

in under-five child mortality, the rate has declined from 115 in 1990 to 78 in 2006; infant mortality has declined from 82 to 57 in the same period (UNICEF, 2008).

Similarly, access to clean drinking water has reportedly improved over the decades, but still about 20 per cent of population does not get it (Figure 2.13).[13] There has undoubtedly been some progress, but it seems far from satisfactory. Currently, unlike in the 1950s, it is not the lack of skilled personnel or inadequate resources that seems to be constraining social development, but perhaps poor utilisation of the available funds and organisational deficiencies.

As Figure 2.14 shows, in 2001, about one-third of India's population was still illiterate; the proportion is higher for women. This tells us nothing about educational outcomes, which are probably abysmal.[14] Infant mortality at birth is one of the highest in the world, comparable or worse than those of sub-Saharan Africa (Dreze and Sen, 1995)[15] While there are enormous variations across the states, the national record nevertheless shows a slow but gradual improvement that seems invariant with respect to policy regime or the pace of economic growth.

While the reservation policy has secured modest upward mobility for the SCs/STs, a sizable proportion of the reserved jobs apparently remain vacant for lack of qualified persons. This is a further reiteration of the failure to pay attention to school education.

In sum, the development outcomes described above are clearly the results of the choices made. India invested heavily in higher education,

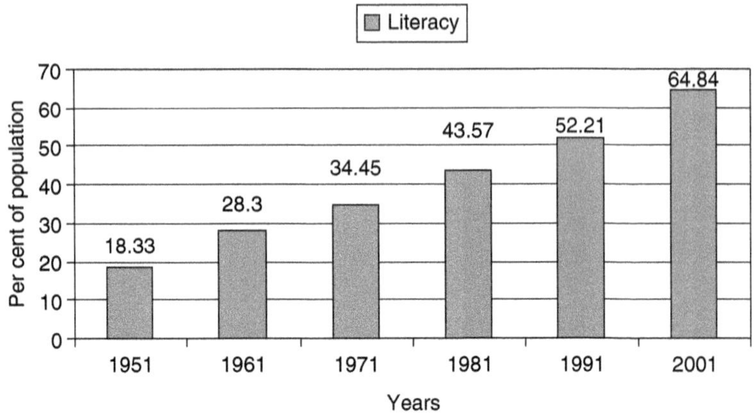

Figure 2.14 Literacy rate in India, 1951 to 2001
Source: *Statistical Abstract of India*, various issues.

so it has yielded a rich crop of highly qualified engineers and doctors. It was a strategic design, as noted earlier, considered necessary to meet the requirements of rapid industrialisation. But as the economy did not expand at the warranted rate, and/or its resources did not grow as envisaged in the initial plans, public resources did not expand adequately to fully utilise the available human capital.

There are a few well-known exceptions, however. Kerala, a relatively small and homogenous state in southern India, has bucked the national trend by allocating a greater share of its public revenue on school education, has excelled in literacy and health, becoming a much-cited model in the development literature. But as its economy lagged behind the national average to absorb the educated workforce, it found an outlet for their skills in the Persian Gulf region, and supplying nurses worldwide.[16]

Social security

Social security is largely restricted to the organised sector (Table 2.3); a more detailed list of the benefits for the blue collared workers is listed Table 2.4. The unorganised sector is restricted to socially vulnerable groups like destitute widows or the physically handicapped. The earliest effort in this direction was the old-age pension introduced in Uttar Pradesh in 1957. In 1985, the personal accident insurance scheme covered under the IRDP was introduced. It promised a lump sum payment of Rs 3,000 in case of the death of the breadwinner of the family if he was in the age group of 18 to 60 (Guhan, 1993).

Table 2.3 Protective social security entitlements available for the organised sector

Type of benefit	Government and quasi-government employees	Industrial workers in the organised sector
1. Medical care	Free treatment in government hospitals Reimbursement of costs of drugs	Free treatment and reimbursement for drugs under employees' state insurance scheme (ESI)
2. Sickness benefit	Medical leave on full pay	Sickness leave on pay under ESI
3. Maternity benefit	Maternity leave on full pay	Maternity benefits under Maternity Relief Act
4. Unemployment benefit	Does not arise	Retrenchment benefit under labour laws.
5. Employment injury benefit	Ex gratia relief	Provided under Workmen's Compensation Act
6. Invalidity benefit	Ex gratia relief	Provided under Workmen's Compensation Act.
7. Old age benefit	Pension or contributory provident fund	Employees' provident fund (EPF)
8. Survivor benefit	Lump sum payment on death while in service financed with state subsidy; family pension on death of retired employee	Deposit-linked insurance under EPF

Source: Guhan (1993).

A recent report by the National Commission for Enterprises in the Unorganised Sector (Chairman: Arjun Sengupta) summarised the current status of social security:

> India is yet to evolve a comprehensive national social security policy for its entire working population. Currently, social security entitlements such as provident fund, gratuity, health cover, etc, that are legally binding are available for a majority of formal workers in the organised sector. Formal social security arrangements in the unorganised sector are confined to a small minority of workers and assume the form of Welfare Funds for selected categories of workers sponsored by the Central Government and a few State governments. ..., [T]hese schemes as well as those initiated by a number of voluntary organisations do not cover more than 5 to 6 per cent of the workers in the informal economy.[17]

Table 2.4 Principal social security for industrial workers

Laws	Objectives	Coverage	Eligibility	Benefits	
Workmen's Compensation Act, 1923	To provide compensation for workers in cases of industrial accidents and occupational diseases resulting in disablement or death.	Persons employed in factories, mines, plantations, the railways, and others mentioned in schedule II of the Act.	The benefits are payable for work-related injuries to workers or dependents not covered by the ESI Act.	Compensation for Death: Permanent, total disablement: Temporary disablement:	Min.—Max. (rupees) 50,000—228,000 60,000—274,000 Fifty percent of wages for a maximum period of five years
Employee's State Insurance Act, 1948	To provide health care and cash benefits in cases of sickness, maternity, and employment injury.	Factories/establishments to which the law is made applicable by the Government.	Employees drawing wages not exceeding Rs. 3,000/- per month.	Compensation for: Death/Permanent, total disablement: Temporary disablement:	Seventy percent of the wage payable as monthly pension. Seventy percent of the wage payable for disability period.
Employee's Provident Funds and Miscellaneous Provisions Act, 1952	To provide for (a) Compulsory Provident Fund; (b) Pension; and (c) Deposit Linked Insurance.	Factories or establishments employing 20 or more employees (in scheduled industries); other establishments notified by the Central Government.	Employees drawing pay not exceeding Rs. 5,000/- per month.	Provident fund: at the rate of 8.33 percent or 10 percent, whichever is applicable. Apart from terminal disbursement nonrefundable withdrawals for: *Life insurance policies; *House building, and so on.	
Maternity Benefit Act, 1961	To provide for maternity protection before and after childbirth.	Factories, mines, plantations, commercial and other establishments to which the law is extended.	There is no wage limit for coverage provided the woman is not covered by the ESI Act.	Payment of actual absence up to 12 weeks' average daily wages, minimum wage or Rs 10.	
Payment of Gratuity Act, 1972	To provide for payment of gratuity on ceasing to hold office.	Factories, mines, oil fields, plantations, railways, companies, shops, and other establishments to which the law is extended.	Five years continuous service is required for payment of gratuity.	Fifteen days' wages for every completed year of service or part thereof in excess of six months, subject to a maximum of Rs. 100,000/-. The seasonal employees are entitled to gratuity at a rate of seven days' wages for each season.	

Guhan's pithy observation made two decades ago are valid even today:

> There are several inadequacies and shortcomings in this medley of arrangements [of social security]. First it is clear that the coverage of benefits is concentrated to a high degree in the organised public and private sectors. Of employment ... public employees are served the best, or rather have ensured that they are best served, with free or highly subsidised medical care, leave on full pay for sickness and maternity, insurance for death while in service, pension and gratuity on retirement and life pension for survivors. They also receive subsidised housing and other perquisites and are not vulnerable to contingent unemployment. Industrial workers in the organised sector are less well placed but have recourse to a structure of legislations which in principle take care of medical, sickness, maternity, disability, employment injury, old age and survivor benefits. ... labour legislations relating to social security are unsatisfactory in many respects, but at least a framework does exist and it can be improved. *While this is the case with white-collar and blue-collar workers, the collar-less workers and the self-employed in the unorganised sector, who constitute nearly 90 per cent of earners, get virtually no benefit from social insurance or social assistance. The system is thus patently regressive* (Guhan, 1992a: 288) (emphasis added).

However, some states, like Tamil Nadu, expanded social welfare activities for targeted groups not as part of a social policy, but as measures to ameliorate visible deprivation of the vulnerable social groups (Guhan, 1992 b). They represent perhaps populist measures in a personality-driven competitive democracy. Despite their known limitations and leakages, the cumulative effect of such efforts have apparently borne improved social development outcomes, but may not count much in reducing poverty or economic inequality.

With the shrinking size of the organised sector since the mid-1990s, as a result of widespread lay-offs and greater openness to trade and investment, there has emerged a growing voice for universal social security to cushion against increasingly market determined outcomes. This raises the question of why some state governments have succeeded in using their limited fiscal capacity for social development, while others have not. In other words, state capacity at the sub-national level needs to be examined.

2.6 Where do we go from here?

What are the main threads of the foregoing stylised narrative? India's story is one of growth acceleration and macroeconomic stability in the second half of the twentieth century, with the creation of a homogeneous domestic market.[18] That inequality in wealth and income has not prevented India from moving from a stationary colonial economy to accelerated growth after 1980, perhaps represents what Albert Hirschman (1971) termed as 'possiblism'. Yet, the growth has polarised the economy, as the trickle-down process is modest at best.

Income poverty has declined over the last three decades – at least in the aggregate – suggesting gains (albeit modest) for the absolute poor. The state has acquired modest administrative capacity and substantial buffer stocks to ensure food security, yet widespread and visible deprivation and malnutrition persist.

Poverty began to reduce in the latter half of the 1970s prior to the acceleration of output growth, but its pace has apparently decelerated since the 1990s after the initiation of the liberal reforms. Thus, the 1980s was probably a better period of growth and poverty reduction on account of the focus on agriculture, rural development and public investment in infrastructure and a growing role for markets in industry and trade. The trends in wages reported in Table 2.5 buttress such a view. It shows that real wages for most categories of workers rose faster between 1983 and 1993–4, compared to the period between 1994–5 and 2004–5. Moreover, for most regular workers and urban women the growth rate of wages was equal to, or higher than, the growth in per capita domestic product in this period.

Public policy has moved from addressing relative poverty in the 1950s by the promise of institutional reforms to amelioration of absolute poverty in the 1970s and beyond. Initially, poverty was addressed by seeking to improve productivity of small farms and promote self-employment in rural areas, but gradually moved on to focus wage employment since the 1990s and to employment guarantee in rural India more recently. The policy evolution seems to represent what is most feasible from the most desirable. In social development, the policy has moved from publicly-owned and managed education and health care in the 1950s (mostly for the organised sector), to a growing emphasis on primary education and universal health care and social security.

History informs us that there is probably no example of successful land reforms in peacetime by a popular democracy. So, the failure of land reforms seems to be on the expected lines. India now seems closer

Table 2.5 Growth in real wages

	Compound growth rates	
	1983 to 1993–94	**1993–94 to 2004–05**
	Regular paid workers	
Rural male	4.7	3.3
Rural female	3.4	3.2
Urban male	3.4	2.4
Urban female	4.0	1.8
	Casual worker	
Rural male	2.5	2.7
Rural female	3.1	2.6
Urban male	2.0	1.3
Urban female	3.7	1.5
GDP per capita	**3.4**	**4.0**

Note: Computed based on Unni and Ravindran's (2007) figures using the relevant NSS estimates.

to what Dandekar and Rath (1971) advocated over three decades ago for augmenting a wage employment programme. Organisationally, India is probably better placed now to implement a nation-wide wage employment programme to create public works, with elected local self-governments in place, and the Right to Information Act as an instrument to potentially keep the misuse of public funds under check.

How does one understand this 'movement' or 'progression' in the policy discourse? It probably represents the limits to poverty alleviation and social development given the highly unequal class structure of the society, yet the deepening of democracy perhaps tests the limits of it repeatedly.[19] This also seems to be reflected in the growing conflict over the need for fiscal prudence in an increasingly open economy on the one hand, and the demands of the democratic polity for greater resources for alleviating poverty and social deprivation on the other. But the conflict, in theory, may be a false one, if it is realised that an educated and healthy workforce is necessary to take advantage of the 'demographic dividend', and that the domestic market offers a cushion in an increasingly uncertain economic environment.

As poverty persists and inequality has increased, despite the faster growth, political discourse has now shifted to 'inclusive growth' – that is, growth with equity in the idiom of an earlier period – implying the need for conscious state action to ensure wider distribution of the gains of growth. However, one is not sure if this is as yet reflected in credible shifts in the budgetary allocations. The main instrument to achieve this seems to be the employment guarantee scheme, noted earlier.

2.7 Conclusions

This chapter has sought to identify distinct policy regimes in post-independent India, relating them to economic growth, poverty reduction and social development; and speculated what they portend for the future. India has witnessed a gradual acceleration of economic growth over nearly six decades, with services emerging as the leading sector constituting over half of the domestic output. As it is not accompanied by a proportionate shift in the workforce composition, the economy remains predominantly agrarian, with widening inequality between town and country. India's growth is mostly domestically financed, with modest inflation and reasonable macroeconomic stability. However, India's record in reducing absolute poverty and social development remains modest.

We have identified broadly three distinct policy regimes. During the first period (1950–65) economic policy focused on 'heavy' industrialisation, and removal of relative poverty (or economic inequality) by radical land reforms. While the record of industrial progress was respectable, inequality was hardly touched, given the class structure of the society. By the early 1960s, however, the policy focus shifted to addressing absolute poverty.

The idea found expression about a decade later, when the policy shifted to agriculture and poverty reduction more generally in the 1970s. But, again, radical redistribution was ruled out on political considerations. Instead, poverty alleviation mainly meant supply of subsidised bank credit for small farmers to augment land productivity, creating non-agricultural employment, and modest wage employment programmes with payment partly made in food.

These efforts culminated in the formation of the integrated rural development programme that grew in size in the 1980s, even as gradual liberalisation was set in motion in industry and trade. These were complemented by expansion of the public distribution system to ensure universal access to food at controlled prices. As growth accelerated with industry regaining its status as the leading sector, the 1980s also witnessed a growing concern for expanding health and education.

As the pace of economic reforms accelerated in the 1990s, the rural development effort was discredited on account of huge leakages and mounting bad loans, jeopardising the financial standing of the banking sector. Wage employment programmes replaced self-employment initiatives in the 1990s, but resources for it were cut back sharply as part of the liberal economic policy regime. In an increasingly open economy, the 1990s witnessed concerns to expand social security to the unorganised sector, probably influenced by the experience in states like Tamil Nadu and Kerala.

What are the outcomes of the poverty-allieviation efforts? Income poverty (in terms of headcount ratio) has declined, though the extent of it remains debatable. Nutrition poverty has probably not come down. While widespread famines have been banished, food deprivation and malnutrition persist. Droughts on account of crop failure continue to occur, which are addressed by emergency works programmes and food supply. Despite the progress, the social development record is modest in a comparative perspective. Economic inequalities have been growing, especially since 1980 when growth accelerated. Proposals for universal social security or for the disadvantaged social groups on a national scale are still rudimentary, though they seem to have taken root in a few states.

Agriculture growth seems to have been adversely affected since the 1990s, giving rise to concerns of agrarian distress, best exemplified by the phenomenal rise in Maoist violence engulfing nearly one-third of the districts in the country, and a growing number of suicides by farmers. The National Employment Guarantee Scheme was enacted in 2004, signalling a prospect of change in the policy regime. Prospects for such an ambitious scheme appear better now, as elected panchayats (local self government institutions) are broadly in place and the Right to Information Act, in principle, provides a powerful instrument to check misuse of funds at the local level.

Despite much rhetoric, the principal goal of the development strategy has always remained accelerating output growth with reasonable macroeconomic stability. As redistribution of existing property or a progressive system of income tax was ruled out on political considerations, what is left, in effect, is a pious belief of economic growth trickling down to the poor to 'lift all the boats'.

Is there an identifiable relationship between policy regime and poverty reduction? If the stylised account of this study is reasonably accurate, then it is difficult to be categorical about it. One could hypothesise that the 1980s were perhaps a better period of rapid growth and equity with modest decline in poverty, and with growing emphasis on social development. In terms of development strategy, this decade can be associated with the state's role of focusing more on infrastructure and rural development. This is also the period when wage growth improved for a sizable segment of the workforce above the growth rate of per capita domestic output.

One can also discern a gradual evolution of policy from redistributing land and changes in property relations to promotion of wage employment with attendant food security. Such a pragmatic evolution is made possible with growing food self-sufficiency, empowerment with mandated elections to local bodies and enactment of the right to information. But the realisation of the potential is constrained by fiscal conservativism, a self-imposed restraint under the liberal regime.

India now seems poised at a crossroads. It can either base its growth on poverty alleviation and social development to move towards a path of equitable growth, or it can pursue a path of liberal reforms that may improve growth but could further polarise the economy.

Notes

1. Unless otherwise mentioned, all growth rates in this chapter are at constant prices, estimated applying a log-linear trend equation.
2. For brevity, sources of many statistics and evidence cited in the text are not reported. For details see Anant, Hasan, Mohapatra, Nagaraj and Sasikumar (2006).
3. So impressive were these outcomes that W. W. Rostow said India was on a planned path to take off stage:

   The two outstanding contemporary cases of economies attempting purposefully to take off are India and communist China, both operating under national plans. ... The Indian Planning Commission estimated investment as 5% of NNP in the initial year of the plan, 1950–1. Using a 3/1 marginal capital-output ratio, they envisaged a marginal savings rate of 20% for the First Five Year Plan, a 50% rate thereafter, down to 1968-9, when the average proportion of income invested would level off at 20% of NNP. ... Indian effort may well be remembered in economic history as the first take-off defined *ex ante* in national product terms. (Rostow, 1960: 291)

4. Protagonists of planning have often justified discretionary controls a means of rational use of scarce resources. But, perniciousness of many of them became too evident to any reasonable observer. For instance, K. N. Raj's following scathing indictment should be an eye-opener for even the most ardent believer in planning the corruption that these controls entailed:

   For the industrial licensing system, as it grew over a period of nearly three decades, had accumulated much fat and filth. It had ceased to perform effectively most of the functions it was designed for earlier; had become a major source of political and bureaucratic corruption; and was being used by powerful vested interests (well-placed in New Delhi in thinly-disguised embassies of their own) to throttle competition from potential rivals (less influential) within the country, and increase their monopolistic (or oligopolistic) power even in industries in which there were no economies of scale to justify the growth of such enterprises. ... Given the balance of political and economic forces in the country very little could be done to bring about radical improvements, in these forms of direct administrative controls; and, in my view, it was wiser, therefore, to rather abandon the dishonesty and hypocrisy of it all than maintain pretences (which deceived no one, except perhaps some armchair radicals and created needless delays and inefficiencies all around) (Raj, 1985: 25–6).

5. Though land reforms had a marginal impact on inequality, it probably had a greater political effect in getting rid of absentee landlordism. Looking at Pakistan where landlordism still has considerable sway on political power, what India has achieved cannot perhaps be underestimated.
6. Raj and Tharakan (1981) on Kerala land reforms, and D Bandopadhyaya (2003) for West Bengal.
7. Mahabubul Haq's *Poverty Curtain* (1976) well-reflected this sentiment among development agencies.
8. Maharashtra Employment Guarantee Scheme (EGS) was initiated after a severe drought (or near famine) conditions in rural Maharashtra in 1973–74. It was a self-selected scheme offering market- determined wage rate guaranteeing a certain days of employment within a ten-kilometre radius of the location of the person for creation of productive assets. It was financed by a tax on urban salaried employees. Despite many limitations, the scheme is widely considered as one of the successful wage employment programmes in the developing world.
9. There is a growing literature on this problem. *See*, for instance, Mishra (2006).
10. The dualism persists not just due to the labour market regulations, as popularly believed but also on account of the dualism and discontinuities in technologies and organisation of production (Myint, 1985).
11. Balwant Rai Mehta Committee report, 1957, was a pioneering effort to visualise how the rural society was to be modernised and how local self-government should be made responsible for this task.
12. Charles Battalheim (1969) said: 'When British rule came to an end, India's public health situation was poor. The mortality rate was one of the highest in the world – 27.4 per cent in 1941–51 – and major epidemics were frequent. The population's working capacity was considerably reduced. In such conditions, the new Indian government should have made an effort to improve conditions of sanitation and hygiene. But just before the First Plan, annual expenditure on medicine, health services and sanitation was no more than 300 million rupees, which is less than one rupee per inhabitant' (Battalheim, 1969: 318–19).
13. This figure could be seriously overestimated as it refers only to 'access' without any indication of whether the water is piped or not; or whether the water is potable.

14. Reporting evidence on educational attainment in developing countries, Filmer, Hasan and Pritchett (2006) said the following about India:

    A baseline survey of 3rd to 5th graders in five districts of Andhra Pradesh, a middle performing Indian state, found that only 12 per cent of students could do single digit subtraction and that 46 per cent could not, when shown a picture of six balls and three kites, answer how many kites were in the picture.

    A recent survey of learning in India found that of students in government schools in grades 6–8, who are students who have completed the lower primary cycle and hence, met the MDG, 31 per cent could not read a simple story, 29 per cent could not do two-digit subtraction – both of which should have been mastered by grade 2 in the Indian curriculum.

    (Filmer, Hasan and Pritchett, 2006: 5–6)

15. While factually correct, it is perhaps necessary to appreciate that 50 years ago India was worse than sub-Saharan Africa, and India had one of worst records in PQLI.
16. The 'Kerala model' is an example of a more equitable development outcome, but perhaps with limited entrepreneurial capabilities. Some other parts of India (Andhra and Karnataka, for example) have yielded unequal economic outcomes, but have given rise to a new breed of successful entrepreneurs, in information technology, biotechnology and even in construction.
17. (http://www.nceus.gov.in/Final_Edited_Social_Security_Repor.htm#chap1).
18. Lant Pritchett's careful documentation of economic growth in the twentieth century shows that the world is full of examples of the growth reversals. In his account, India along with China, stand out as the few examples of accelerating growth (Pritchett, 2000).
19. Yet, a look at the performance at the state level seems to offer a silver lining. While Kerala's exceptionalism is widely acknowledged, some other states have recorded significant achievements under very different policies and political circumstances. For instances, Tamil Nadu's 'populist policies' seem to have delivered the desired health and educational outcomes, Himachal Pradesh's emphasis on economic infrastructure also seems to have improved educational attainments.

References

Agarwal, Ramgopal and Zafar Dad Khan (2002): *Labour Market and Social Insurance Policy in India: A Case of Losing on Both Competitiveness and Caring*, Washington DC: World Bank.

Anant, T. C. A., R. Hasan, P. Mohapatra, R. Nagaraj, and S. K. Sasikumar (2006): 'Labour Markets in India: Issues and Perspectives', in Jesus Felipe and Rana Hasan (eds), *Labour Markets in Asia: Issues and Perspectives*, Manila: Palgrave Macmillan, for Asian Development Bank.

Bandyopadhyay, D. (2003): 'Land Reforms and Agriculture: The West Bengal Experience', *Economic and Political Weekly*, Vol. 38, No. 9, March 1: 879–84.

Battalheim, Charles (1969): *India Independent*, New York: Monthly Review Press.

Burgess, Robin and Nicholas Stern (1993): *Tax Reforms in India*, DEP 45, Development Economics Research Programme, London School of Economics.

Chakravarty, Sukhamoy (1990): Development Strategies for Growth with Equity: The South Asian Experience, *Asian Development Review*, Vol. 8: 133–59.

Chakravarty, Sudeep (2008): *Travels in Naxalite Country*, Delhi: Penguin Book.

Dandekar, V. M. and Neelkanth Rath (1971): 'Poverty in India', *Economic and Political Weekly*, Vol. 6, No. 2 and 3, Jan 2 and 9: 28–48; 106–46.

Deaton, Angus and Jean Dreze (2009): 'Food and Nutrition in India: Facts and Interpretations', *Economic and Political Weekly*, Vol. 44, No. 2, February 14: 42–65.

Dreze, Jean and Amartya Sen (1995): *Indian Development: Selected Regional Perspectives*, Oxford: Clarendon Press.

EPWRF (2009): *Domestic Product of States of India – 1960–61 to 2006–07: Second Updated Edition*, Mumbai: Economic and Political Weekly Research Foundation.

Filmer, Doen, Amer Hasan and Lant Pritchett (2006): *A Millennium Learning Goal: Measuring Real Progress in Education*, Centre for Global Development, WP No. 97, November.

Guhan, S. (1993): 'Social Security for the Poor in the Unorganised Sector: A Feasible Blueprint for India', in Kirit S. Parikh and R. Sudarshan (eds), *Human Development and Structural Adjustment*, Chennai: Macmillan, 203–37.

Guhan, S. (1992a): 'Social Security in India: Looking One Step Ahead', in Barbara Harris, S. Guhan and R. H. Cassen (eds), *Poverty in India: Research and Policy*, Delhi: Oxford University Press, 282–98.

Guhan, S. (1992 b): 'Social Security Initiatives in Tamil Nadu in 1989', in S. Subramanian (ed.) *Themes in Development Economics*, Delhi: Oxford University Press, 242–83.

Government of India (2007): *Economic Survey, 2006–07*, New Delhi, Ministry of Finance.

Government of India (2010): *Economic Survey, 2009–10*, New Delhi, Ministry of Finance.

Haq, Mahabubul, (1976): *The Poverty Curtain: Choices for the Third World*, New York: Columbia University Press.

Hirschman, Albert O. (1971): *A Bias for Hope: Essays in Development and Latin America*, New Haven: Yale University Press.

IMF (2009): *International Financial Statistics*, Washington DC: International Monetary Fund.

Jose, A. V. (1974): 'Trends in Real Wage Rates of Agricultural Labourers', *Economic and Political Weekly*, Review of Agriculture, Vol. 9, No. 13, March 30.

Joshi, P. C. (1975): *Land Reforms in India: Trends and Perspectives*, Delhi: Allied Publishers.

Joshi, Vijay and I. M. D. Little (1994): *India: Macroeconomics and Political Economy, 1964–91*, Washington DC: World Bank.

Mahalanobis, P. C. (1975): 'Consumption and Welfare', in P. N. Chopra (ed.) *Economic Structure and Activities, The Gazetteer of India*, Vol. 3, New Delhi: Ministry of Education and Social Welfare, Government of India, 1160–70.

Mahendra Dev, S. and C. Ravi (2007): 'Poverty and Inequality: All-India and States, 1983–2005', *Economic and Political Weekly*, Vol. 41, No. 6: 509–21.

Mehrotra, Santosh (2006): 'Child Malnutrition and Gender Discrimination in South Asia', *Economic and Political Weekly*, Vol. 41 No. 10, March 11: 912–18.

Mishra, Srijit (2006): 'Farmers' Suicide in Maharashtra', *Economic and Political Weekly*, Vol. 41 No. 16 April 22: 1538–45.
Morris D. Morris (1979): *Measuring the Condition of the World's Poor: The Physical Quality of Life Index*, New York: Pergaman Press.
Morris, D. Morris and Michelle B. McAlpin (1982): *Measuring the Condition of India's Poor*, New Delhi: Promilla and Co., Publishers.
Myint, H. (1985): 'Organisational Dualism and Economic Development', *Asian Economic Review*, Vol. 3, No. 1.
Nagaraj, R. (2008): 'Recent Economic Growth: A Closer Look', *Economic and Political Weekly*, Vol. 43, No. 15, April 12: 55–61.
Nagaraj, R. (2006): 'Public Sector Performance since 1950: A Fresh Look', *Economic and Political Weekly*, Vol. 41, No. 31, June 24: 2551–57.
Nagaraj, R. (2000): 'Indian Economy since 1980: Virtuous Growth or Polarisation?', *Economic and Political Weekly*, Vol. 35, No. 32, August 5–11: 2831–8.
Nagaraj, R. (1997): 'What has Happened Since 1991? Assessment of India's Economic Reforms', *Economic and Political Weekly*, Vol. 32, Nos 44–45, November 8–14: 2869–79.
Nayyar, Deepak (1995): *Economic Liberalisation in India: Analytics, Experience and Lessons*, Kolkata: Orient Longman.
Pritchett, Lant (2000): 'Understanding Economic Growth: Searching for Hills among Plateaus, Mountains and Plains', *World Bank Economic Review* Vol. 14, No. 2: 221–50.
Raj, K. N. and Micheal Tharakan (1981): 'Agrarian Reforms in Kerala and its Impact on Rural Economy: A Preliminary Assessment' in A. Ghose (ed.), *Agrarian Reforms in Contemporary Developing Countries*, London: Croom Helm.
Raj, K. N. (1985): *New Economic Policy*, V. T. Krishnamachari Memorial Lecture, Institute of Economic Growth, Delhi: Oxford University Press.
RBI (2010): *Handbook of Statistics on Indian Economy*, www.RBI.org.in. Mumbai: Reserve Bank of India,.
Rostow, W. W. (1960): *The Process of Economic Growth* (second edition), London: Oxford at the Clarendon Press.
Singh, Hoshiar (1994): 'Constitutional Base for Panchayati Raj in India: The 73rd Amendment Act', *Asian Survey*, Vol. 34, No. 9 September: 818–27.
Srinivasan, T. N. and Pranab Bardhan, (ed.) (1974): *Poverty and Income Distribution in India*, Kolkota: Statistical Publishing Society.
Sundaram, K. (2007): 'Employment and Poverty in India, 2000–2005', *Economic and Political Weekly*, Vol. 42, No. 30, July 28: 3121–31.
Suryanarayana, M. H. (2000): 'How Real is the Secular Decline in Poverty?', *Economic and Political Weekly*, Vol. 35, No. 25, June 17: 2129–40.
Unni, Jeemol and G. Ravindran, (2007): 'Growth of Employment (1993–94 to 2004–05): Illusion of Inclusiveness?', *Economic and Political Weekly*, Vol. 42, No. 3, January 20: 196–99.
United Nations Development Programme (2010): *Human Development Report, 2010*, New York: Oxford University Press.
UNICEF (2008): *The State of the World's Children Report, 2008*, United Nations.

3
Economic Development and Inequalities

M. H. Suryanarayana

3.1 Introduction

The extent of economic inequality in its different dimensions is one parameter that has an effective bearing on (1) the choice of policies and strategies; and (2) the very development process, both form and spread, in a democratic society. Some pertinent questions from an economic perspective would be:

What is the nature and extent of economic inequality? What are its policy imperatives in a welfare state?
What would be the secular behaviour of wealth and income distribution during the development process?
How far would this pattern differ in a context marked by state intervention, as given by the Indian experience, in pursuit of 'growth with distributive justice'?
What would be their implications for economic inequalities and human development?

While the set of questions listed above are quite important by themselves from a welfare policy perspective, a careful outcome evaluation would call for a verification of the premises underlying choice of policies as well as the data generation process itself with reference to the following question:

> How reliable are the estimates as true measures of the data generation process in the context of economic development and how meaningful are the interpretations and inferences?

As regards the first two questions, much has been written about Kuznets's 'inverted-U hypothesis' from theoretical as well as empirical perspectives. Its empirical verification has been carried out in terms of time-series as well as cross-sectional information in the international context. Similar attempts have been made for developing countries such as India too, little realising that the hypothesis pertains to secular behaviour of distribution in the context of economic development with reference to variations in per capita income encompassing a wide range. In other words, there is little scope for verifying the Kuznets's hypothesis in situations like the one obtaining in India where the range of variation in income has been quite limited.[1] All the more so since an avowed objective of economic development policy in India has been to promote welfare and levels of living by reducing concentration of wealth and income, and their redistribution by institutional reforms as well as fiscal instruments like taxes and subsidies (Directive Principles of State Policy, Indian Constitution).[2]

However, it is not possible to carry out an empirical enquiry for India even from the limited perspective of evaluating the effectiveness of redistributive programmes since we do not have estimates of income distribution for India. The available limited estimates of income distribution are a couple of surveys conducted by the National Council for Applied Economic Research, which pertain to a few time points in the 1960s and 1970s. They are subject to the limitation that the estimates are not comparable in terms of concepts and statistical reliability parameters. Hence, experts have carried out studies with reference to the National Sample Survey (NSS) estimates of household consumption distribution in India, of course, with due appreciation of the relevance of consumption as a proxy for permanent income and acknowledgement of its statistical limitation of underestimation due to savings/dis-saving at either ends of the distribution plane. Hence, it may appear that corrections warranted by economic–theoretical and statistical considerations would go a long way in providing insights into the changes in income distribution in India. However, this is not true for reasons like data inadequacies in a changing institutional set-up.

Subject to this type of data constraints, this chapter focuses on the following issues:

- What are the different policy strategies pursued to reduce concentration of wealth and income during different phases of the Indian development process?
- How valid and consistent are such policy choices?

- What are the data constraints on distributional outcome evaluation?
- How far have the chosen strategies been successful in terms of the limited authenticated outcome measures?

The chapter is organised as follows: Section 3.2 highlights some of the major policy strategies pursued during different phases of the post-independence development era. Section 3.3 assesses policy choices, and verifies outcomes in terms of empirical profiles corresponding to different phases. The final section sums up the discussions and their implications.

3.2 Conceptualisation growth and development in the Indian Plan

'Growth with redistribution' has been the explicitly stated objective of development planning in India right from its inception. While 'economic growth' is measured in conventional terms like 'rate of growth of per capita gross national product', redistribution is conceptualised in terms of a reduction in inequality. However, the relative policy emphasis on these dual objectives and strategies adopted varied across successive five-year plans depending upon the emerging constraints, policy priorities and imperatives, and most important, information availability and its effective use. In spite of all these widely publicised policy goals and declarations, it should be admitted that there was little by way of conceptualisation of the operational part of the plan policies and programmes.

Indian post-Independence economic development era can broadly be divided into three phases: Phase I saw the initiation of the development process (1950–65); Phase II provided for a modern agricultural growth strategy (1966–80) along with an explicit programme for poverty alleviation; Phase III witnessed neo-liberal reforms for 'structural adjustment with a human face'. It is a 'Human Face' that called for periodic policy proclamations and programmes of targeted safety nets for the poor, with ample theoretical rationale, but little empirical understanding of the facts and realities. A brief description of these phases, their policy profiles and evaluations, both ex ante and ex post, are presented in the followings sections.

Classical growth phase (1950–65): Policy profile

This phase saw the initiation of the development efforts after the fashion of classical approach, which focused on issues relating to 'capital accumulation under conditions of structural backwardness' (Chakravarty, 1987: 27). There was a mature understanding and appreciation of the institutional and resource constraints on the growth as well as redistributive pursuits in the initial phases. Given the limited size of the cake, the Indian planners were quite conscious of the adverse implications of any attempt to radically transform asset distribution for savings, capital formation, and hence, output. It is this concern and the need to raise the real savings rate that called for some 'tolerance towards income inequality' and 'primacy to a faster rate of growth in the capital goods sector' (ibid 1987: 10–12). The first three five-year plans were based on a classical Lewis-growth framework (Lewis, 1954), which sought to industrialise the economy in terms of surplus, labour as well as food, from the agricultural sector. The 'Perspective of Development: 1961–76' explicitly acknowledged that the size of the cake set limits on the extent of feasible redistribution and the minimum, which could be guaranteed (Perspective Planning Division, 1962: 13–14).

At the same time, the Perspective made it quite explicit that (1) poverty eradication should be the central concern of planning in India; (2) every citizen should be assured of a minimum income within a reasonable period of time; and (3) the minimum itself should be revised upwards with economic progress (ibid: 13). However, till this day Indian planners have not bothered to raise this minimum, not to speak of revising it to take into account ongoing structural changes in the economy.

As regards the scope for income redistribution in the development context, the Perspective was quite conscious of the constraints, and hence, was realistic in admitting that the distribution of income in the upper 80 per cent of the population in 1975 would be any different from the pattern that existed then (ibid: 16).

The growth strategy focused on public investment in infrastructure, agriculture and industrial development. Of course, institutional reforms were carried out to redistribute physical endowment of resources, fiscal instruments to redistribute income and subsidies in cash and kind to improve distribution of levels of living.

Redistribution strategies: Land reforms

At the inception of the development era, the Indian economy was predominantly agricultural, which employed three-fourths of the workforce and contributed as much to value added. Land distribution was skewed. Land is the primary input in agriculture. A major cause of deprivation in overpopulated India has been landlessness. The land tenure system was feudalistic with little incentive for productive effort and enterprise. Land redistribution in favour of the landless would enhance national income at the macro level and reduce deprivation at the micro household level for two reasons: (1) By endowing landless households with major means of production in agriculture, new opportunities for employment and income would be created; and (2) as per the well known inverse size–productivity postulate, smaller holdings are cultivated more efficiently involving larger additions to national value added than larger farms. For these reasons, land reform is looked upon as a policy option to catalyse growth, employment and income redistribution, and hence, reduce deprivation in India. In keeping with this perspective, the policy focus right from the First Five-year Plan has been on comprehensive agrarian reforms.

Land reforms, as undertaken in India, have essentially aimed at improving the terms of access to land for the deprived. Broadly, they have taken the following forms: (1) land redistribution by imposing ceilings on size of landholdings; (2) tenancy reform through legislation for defining terms of contract and their registration; (3) legislation for eliminating absentee landlordism and intermediaries and (4) laws for consolidation of landholdings. However, the programme lacked an integrated focus and framework since the Indian Constitution empowered the states to undertake land reforms.[3] Further, for reasons like high man–land ratio, political constraints and incentive problems, the scope for land redistribution was quite limited; its major contribution has been towards improving terms and security of tenure. The First Five-Year Plan acknowledged the limited scope for land redistribution and the adverse implications of too low a ceiling for investment and growth in agricultural output. Hence, it explored options for limiting concentration of landholdings, and hence, income distribution by imposing ceilings on them. For instance, a ceiling for land used for personal cultivation was defined with reference to the size of a 'family holding', that is, one wherein a household size of five could earn a net income of Rs 1200 per annum. This ceiling, however, did not cover that portion of the land rented out, which, in some sense, restricted the scope for redistribution. However, thanks to the constitutional provision, the ceiling set on holding of land differed across states both in form and level (Appu, 1972).

In addition, ceiling limits could be relaxed on account of too many factors like poor quality of land, plantations, orchards and animal husbandry, with the result that legislation on land ceiling did not have any real impact on the extent of inequality in land distribution. The experiments with land ceilings and provisions for their relaxation, in form as well as limit, continued till the mid-1970s.

Outcomes: Land distribution

It appears that in spite of the policies and programmes for progressive changes in the agrarian scenario, the final outcome on distribution of ownership and operational holdings that has emerged by now is thanks largely to excessive demographic pressure on an inelastic land endowment (GOI, 2006a). Its salient features are as follows:

Due to demographic pressure, sub-division and fragmentation of holdings led to not only a decline in concentration of holdings, but also increasing landlessness. The average area owned per household (including landless households) in rural India has declined from 1.78 ha in 1961–62 to 0.73 ha in 2003; if the landless households are excluded, the estimates turn out to be 2.01 ha and 0.81 ha, respectively. The extent of inequality in household landownership in rural India as measured by the Gini ratio has virtually been stable around 0.73.

The average land area owned per urban household (including landless households) is small (0.130 ha). It is 0.252 ha, if the landless households are excluded. The extent of landlessness has varied over time and across states. At present about 10 per cent of the rural households in the country as a whole is landless.

Nearly 80 per cent of the rural households in the country own land that is less than or equal to one hectare, and most of it is used as homestead. Thus, only a small fraction of the rural household has the endowment of land for use in productive enterprises and earns non-labour income. For the majority of rural households, labour is the only source of income to meet livelihood requirements.

Increasing landlessness and marginalisation is a major factor that has been responsible for the transformation of the rural labour market in size as well as form, that is, terms of contract involving casualisation and uncertainty with respect to economic security.

From the perspective of income distribution, and hence, economic deprivation in the rural sector, it is important to examine distribution of not only ownership holdings but also operational holdings. This is because while the term 'ownership holding' refers to the total land area owned by a household, operational holding means a techno-economic unit operated for agricultural production, and hence, is the set of all types of land (owned/ leased in/under possession) at its disposal. Some major features related to issues on income distribution are as follows (GoI, 2006b):

1. Consistent with the increase in population, the number of operational holdings increased from 51 million in 1960–1 to 101 million in 2002–3. The growth in the number of operational holdings accelerated during the first three decades and decelerated during the last decade of the previous millennium. There has been a decline in fragmentation of holdings; the number of parcels per holding declined from 5.7 ha in 1960–1 to 2.3 ha in 2002–03.
2. The average area operated per holding in rural India has declined from 2.63 ha in 1960–1 to 1.06 ha in 2002–3. There has been a progressive shift towards self-cultivation as reflected in the decline in the proportion of tenant-operated holdings from about 25 per cent in 1970–1 to ten per cent in 2002–3. Most important, the share of operational holdings with partly or wholly leased-in land declined from 23.52 per cent in 1960–1 to 9.9 per cent in 2002–3. Corresponding estimates of share of area leased-in declined from 10.70 per cent to 6.5 per cent.
3. The extent of inequality in the size distribution of operational holdings has increased from 0.583 ha in 1960–1 to 0.586 ha in 1970–1, 0.629 ha in 1980–1 and 0.641 ha in 1990–1.

Thus, land owned per household as well as land operated per unit has declined over time. But land is the major factor of production in the primary sector. At the same time, the share of the primary sector (including the predominant agriculture) in total gross domestic product has declined from about 60 per cent to about a quarter during the post-independence period (GoI, 2007a: S-5). This would imply a proportionately larger weight for capital and labour as income sources and hence, in determining the shape of personal income distribution.

Policies for the industrial/urban sector

As regards the non-agricultural sector, the policy has largely been preventive in approach and focused on controlling concentration of assets and wealth by means of physical regulation of the economy, predominant role for the public sector, reservation of strategic sector for the government, and small-scale sector for the small entrepreneur. It also regulated the flow of incremental incomes by progressive income tax rates.

Agricultural growth and redistributive phase: Plan strategy and its basis

The monsoon failures of 1965 and 1966 and the consequent decline in agricultural output called for a new agricultural strategy for the green revolution. Of course, it paid dividends as reflected in estimates of foodgrain output, which increased from 63.3 million tonnes in 1965–6 to 94.9 million tonnes in 1970–71. However, anxieties about sustainability of agricultural growth in the face of a demand constraint led to a revision in development strategy in terms of 'Growth with Redistribution'. This phase of the Indian development planning process, which provided for 'Garibi Hatao' (Abolish Poverty), was quite explicit and ambitious in its goals for poverty reduction through redistribution:

> The Plan formulation was based on an assessment of the progress made till then. It believed that 'growth with redistribution' had actually led to a reduction in poverty and even cited the following numbers: There was growth in real per capita consumption. There was an improvement in distribution too. Between 1960–1 and 1977–8, consumption share of the bottom half of the population increased by 0.28 per cent per annum in rural areas and 0.44 per cent per annum in urban areas while that for upper half of the population declined by 0.12 per cent per annum and 0.17 per cent per annum in rural and urban areas, respectively. Estimates of summary measures like the Lorenz ratios based on grouped consumption data at current prices declined by 0.38 per cent per annum in rural and 0.59 per cent per annum in urban areas (GoI, 1981; p. 82).

The plan formulated the strategy for poverty reduction under the premises of separability and independence. It sought to reduce poverty during the plan period partly by growth and partly by redistribution. It sought to bring down rural poverty from 50.70 per cent to 40.47 per cent and urban poverty from 40.31 per cent to 33.71 per cent by growth. The plan provided for a further reduction in both rural and urban poverty to the targeted level of 30 per cent by redistribution (ibid). Statistically, redistribution is represented as a reduction in inequality. The Sixth Plan exercise on poverty reduction called for a reduction in inequality by 27.42 per cent in the rural and 8.93 per cent in urban areas (Suryanarayana, 1983).

As regards the operational part of the redistributive exercise, the Plan formulation is not explicit and left this entirely to the disconnected sets of fiscal policies and welfare programmes.

The reform phase

This phase focused largely on macro policies for growth with stability and structural adjustment. In pursuit of growth with efficiency and equity, an emphasis was laid on targeting and reduction of subsidies.[4] Market-led growth dynamics permitted enough leeway for income distribution to chart out its own course to illustrate the first stage of the inverted-U phase. Accordingly available studies (for instance, Rao, Shand and Kalirajan, 1999) have found that state domestic products for major states are diverging (based on estimated standard growth regressions for conditional convergence), which would indicate worsening income distribution. This evidence on the regional dimension combined with the macro evidence that there has been a progressive shift in sectoral origin of income from the primary sector to the tertiary, where dualism is higher than even that in the secondary sector (Mazumdar and Sarkar, 2007) would only go to prove that income distribution in India has been worsening.

The Eleventh Five-Year Plan, of course, harps at length on 'inclusive growth', though without really defining or measuring it. In other words, this is an era characterised by much hype on theoretical reasoning, but with little empirical understanding/operational content. For instance, it is not clear how the government proposes to implement its plan strategies and policies in a liberal era dominated by the market as against the previous strategy of implementation by physical regulation of the economy in terms of physical licensing and quantitative controls.

3.3 Assessment and verification

Plan targets for growth and redistribution: Assessment

While the strategies formulated to initiate the development process during the first three five-year plans seem to be based on a reasonable understanding of constraints and opportunities, those for the Second Phase of the planned development process were not. The income distribution parameter as a factor determining the development process either in terms of its impact on savings or investment did not figure explicitly in any plan formulation. The very design of the initial Plan strategies provided for increases in income inequality. For instance, in pursuit of economic development with unlimited supply of labour a la Lewis (1954), planners sought to ensure stability of wages and surplus for reinvestment, which in a sense implied providing for increases in concentration of wealth and income.[5] This is one factor that several studies have lost sight of. At the same time, it must be noted that much had been made of the redistributive dimension of programmes like ceilings on landholdings, taxation and subsidies. The government had explored every option to mop up the surplus at the margin by progressive direct income taxes up to 97.5 per cent. Instead of curbing concentration of white income, it had ended up with the generation of black income, which according to some estimates, had reached levels as much as the white component.

Income/consumption distribution explicitly figured in the plan exercises during the Phase II in working out redistributive targets at the macro level and final household demand vectors via Leontief at the disaggregated sectoral level to set targets for industrial capacity creating, and hence, planning by licensing. However, the redistributive exercises were largely academic and unrealistic for the following reasons.

First, the choice of strategy was based on an unrealistic assessment of past trends in poverty and inequality. Its assessment was technically faulty since it was based on NSS estimates of size distribution of consumption at current prices, which, by ignoring grouping bias and changes in relative prices, leads to incorrect inferences. Estimates of inequality, with corrections for grouping bias and changes in relative prices, do not show any improvement of consumption distribution during the period 1961–2 to 1977–78 (Suryanarayana, 1986).

Second, the choice of strategy was unrealistic even within the framework used for working out plan-related estimates: The Fifth and Sixth Plan exercises were carried out within the two-parameter log-normal framework to characterise size distribution of consumption (GoI, 1973; 1981). But even this framework does not hold out much scope for a redistributive programme at levels of income and poverty observed for India (Surynarayana, 1986). The summary of messages on poverty-growth-inequality relationships emerging from an analysis based on the two-parameter log-normal framework is as follows:

Economic growth reduces poverty under all conditions though the pace of reduction would vary depending upon the levels of income and poverty. This reduction in poverty will take place at an increasing rate if poverty is less than 50 per cent, occur at a decreasing rate if poverty is greater than 50 per cent, and will be maximum when poverty is equal to 50 per cent.

The response of poverty to redistributive efforts depends upon the size of the cake itself. It goes without saying that when the average size of the cake itself is small (say, less than the subsistence norm), a reduction (increase) in inequality might even increase (reduce) poverty.

> Partial derivatives based on log-normal specification show that an increase in inequality will increase poverty when it is less than 50 per cent, decrease it when it is greater than 50 per cent; and be neutral when poverty is 50 per cent.

Thus, the precise impact of a growth or redistribution strategy on poverty reduction would depend upon the mean level of income itself, that is, at what stage of development the country is currently placed. While a growth strategy is uniformly poverty-reducing, though the pace of reduction varies at different stages, a redistribution strategy can reduce poverty only when the size of the cake is large enough so that the poverty level is not acute. This finding makes a clear case for strategies for growth in the interest of the poor. However, the Indian plan exercise for the Sixth Plan did not recognise the limited scope for a redistributive exercise; instead, it laid considerable emphasis on it.

Third, the ambitions for redistribution were unrealistic, given the evidence that, contrary to plan evaluation, there was hardly any improvement in consumption distribution. Calculations within the Sixth Plan two-parameter log-normal framework have shown that realisation of the Sixth Plan redistributive targets would call for a reduction in inequality (Gini ratio) in consumption distribution from 0.305 in the base year (1979–80) to 0.221 in the terminal year (1984–5) in rural all-India, that is by about 27 per cent. Corresponding estimates for urban all-India are 0.334 to 0.305, respectively, which is a reduction of nine per cent (Suryanarayana, 1983).

Fourth, the most important limitation of the plan formulation, for that matter any other formulation, was that it was largely academic and had little in terms of formulation of the operational counterpart corresponding to the hypothetical explorations. The final outcomes during the plan period fell far short of the targets based on well-formulated models. India could realise the Sixth Five-Year Plan (1980–5) target of 30 per cent for poverty not in five years but after pursuing planned pro-poor growth for two-and-a-half decades: the incidence of poverty has finally declined to 28.30 per cent in the rural sector and 25.70 per cent in the urban in 2004–5 (GoI, 2007a) thanks largely to growth and not any significant reduction in inequality. Contrary to the Sixth Plan formulation, inequality (Lorenz ratio) in rural consumption distribution has declined marginally from 30.53 per cent to 29.67 per cent while that in the urban one has even increased from 33.50 per cent to 37.24 per cent between 1979–80 and 2004–05.

Finally, policies pursued during the reform era, in spite of all claims about their human face, did not have any clear vision at least in the initial stages. For instance, much was made about targeting welfare programmes like the PDS by minimising the Type II errors, but without really defining the norms and parameters for errors and targeting. The human face bothered little about minimising Type I errors. Still, despite wide declarations, the food subsidy which was Rs 24,500 million in 1990–91, and increased to 262,000 million in 2005–06. This could be because the reforms suggested have little substance and are based on poor appreciation of empirical facts and realities. The Eleventh Five-Year Plan has aimed at 'faster and more inclusive growth' without defining and measuring parameters of inclusive growth. This is a salient feature of the 'reform-syndrome' in India.

Distributional outcomes: verification: consumption/income distribution

Comparable and reliable time series estimates of income distribution are not available for India. Available limited estimates for rural and urban India are those from the National Council of Applied Economic Research, that too for a couple of discrete points in time. Even these estimates are not comparable for conceptual differences and statistical reliability factors. Therefore, studies in general, and policy debates in particular, are carried out with reference to estimates of consumption distribution generated by the National Sample Survey Organisation (NSSO). It may be noted that this data source has provided the basis for the entire literature on poverty and income distribution in India. As already noted in section 3.2, choice of strategy for growth with redistribution in the Sixth Five-Year Plan (1980–5) was based on the observed trends in extent of inequality in the rural and urban consumption distributions for all-India for the sample period 1960–1 to 1977–8. Ahluwalia (1978) too finds a statistically significant trend decline in inequality in rural consumption distribution at current prices during the period 1956–7 to 1973–4 at the all-India level and in seven major states. He cites this evidence to call into question the wisdom behind the view that growth bound by existing institutional constraints would not lead to any poverty alleviation. Such estimates of inequality in consumption have their own methodological limitations for the following reasons.

First, the NSS concept of consumer expenditure covers all private non-productive consumer expenditures incurred by a household. The survey is designed so as to obtain an unbiased estimate of the mean consumer expenditure and not the distribution parameters. For instance, to minimise reporting errors, information on wage payments in kind like prepared food is collected from the employer's household in terms of its constituent items and credited to its account As a result, the NSS tends to underestimate the consumption of the employee's households, who generally belong to the poor landless labour class in rural India and overestimate the consumption of richer employer households. Wage payments in kind constituted about half of the total wage payment in the 1950s and early 1960s. Their share has declined over time to less than five per cent with gradual monetisation of the labour market; hence, NSS distributions for recent years would provide good approximations to the underlying distributions (Suryanarayana, 2000).

Second, there are periodic changes in NSS schedules. The NSS schedules are generally confined to collection of information on household consumption only. But annual surveys between 1964–65 and 1970–71 canvassed an integrated household schedule, which sought information on consumption as well as income from different sources. Households, richer ones in particular, generally tend to understate their income; hence, households seem to have under-reported their consumption by the same proportion to provide consistent and convincing information during these survey years. Such under-reporting seems to have affected estimates of both averages and inequality in consumption distribution (Suryanarayana, 2000).

Third, there are periodic changes in the survey period: The NSS is carried out in the form of successive rounds, which vary from a few weeks to months. The NSS is generally spread over an agricultural year in the form of sub-rounds to take into account seasonal variations in a monsoon-dependent agricultural economy. However, this is not done always. Sometimes the survey period coincides with the calendar year (the 38th NSS round during January–December 1983); there have been surveys limited to an incomplete part of the agricultural year like the 28th round (October 1973 – June 1974). Since, generally, the poor are more vulnerable to seasonal variations than the rich, one would expect larger sampling errors for estimates of consumption of the poor, and hence, also for estimates of extent of inequality.

Fourth, there are accounting inadequacies. Even the most recent data available for the year 2004–5 is not free from problems (Suryanarayana, 2008). The NSS table shows that majority of the households with Antyodaya (a centrally sponsored scheme aiming to provide food at subsidised prices for the poor) and BPL ration cards are in the non-poor/richer monthly per capita expenditure (MPCE) classes. The NSSO provides the following explanation: "It should be mentioned here that the MPCE of a household is based on its consumption expenditure during the last 30 days. A poor household that bought a durable good during the 30 days prior to the date of survey might conceivably be placed in a higher MPCE class than the class in which its usual MPCE lies." (GoI, 2007b, p. 16; Footnote # 3). If so, it would imply that the NSS estimates of consumption distribution do not represent the 'usual MPCE', and hence, does not represent the true distributional profile. However, there is limited empirical support for this explanation by the NSSO. On careful verification of the unit-record data for 2004–5, we find that of the above poverty line households with BPL cards, 76 per cent in the rural and 70 per cent in the urban sector had not spent anything on durables.

The fifth problem is tabulation. The NSS has started publishing unit record data on household consumption schedules only since the 38th round (1983). Prior to the 38th round, the NSSO used to publish tabulated results in the form of size distribution of consumption at current prices. The distributions were defined over unequal class intervals whose width generally increased with level of expenditure. In addition, the class intervals were kept invariant though the consumption data were reported at current prices, which were rising. Since the data on expenditure are in current prices, the class intervals should have been updated in keeping with changing price situations. However, the NSSO did not carry out any such adjustments till 1977–8. This has generated tables involving (1) gradual upward shifts in the population toward higher and wider expenditure classes and (2) concentration in the open-ended class. This had two implications for estimates of inequality: (1) With unequal class intervals, convexity of the Lorenz curve, and hence, extent of inequality was underestimated at a point of time. This generally was the case however robust the Lorenz ratio estimator; and (2) Underestimation of the convexity of the Lorenz curve, and hence, extent of inequality increased over time with progressive clustering of the population in the upper and wider class intervals. This is one reason why several studies on nominal consumption distribution found even a statistically significant decline in the extent of inequality. This is one factor overlooked by almost all the studies on India though there have been several attempts to examine the bias due to grouping of observations at a point of time and parametric and non-parametric corrections for them.[6]

Sixth, there are problems of measuring nominal consumption: Since the data are reported at current prices, inequality in nominal consumption distribution would not reveal the real changes, particularly when the relative prices change. It was Mahalanobis (1963) who noted the differential movements in cereal prices across different decile groups, which was further corroborated by the Committee on Distribution of Income and Levels of Living (GoI, 1969). Vaidyanathan (1974) was one of the first studies to attempt such price correction using fractile group specific price indices. Majority of the studies on consumption inequality in India are based on estimates of consumer expenditure distribution at current prices and have not attempted such price corrections. Hence, one is not sure how far the estimates of changes in inequality are real and different from differential price movements.

The factors listed above seriously compromise the relevance of NSS data for a study on income distribution. Published tabulations being limited in scope and coverage do not help address any of the issues listed above. It is only for the last two issues of under-estimation of inequality and differential impact of inflation that one could explore some methodological options, though there is no way of authenticating their veracity.

Consumption inequality: inequality: pre-reform phase

This section examines some evidence on trends in inequality in consumption distribution in India as a whole during the development era. Estimates of household consumption distribution are available right from the inception of development planning in 1951. However, data sets are reliable and conceptually consistent largely for the period after 1960. For reasons spelt out in the preceding section, there are serious problems of comparability of the NSS distributions. But the scope for addressing all the issues is limited given the available information. Hence, this section will illustrate issues related to grouping bias and differential impact of inflation for different blocks of years depending upon availability of consistent and comparable information on price indices. Therefore, it may be noted that these blocks do not necessarily correspond to the three different policy regimes discussed in Section 3.3.

To begin with, we present estimates of inequality measures at current prices for the period 1961–2 to 1977–8. This is the period when the NSS kept the class intervals virtually unchanged. This sample period covers only one-third and tail end of the first phase of the development era. Table 3.1 to Table 3.3 provide estimates of consumption shares by linear interpolation and Lorenz ratios by different alternative methods. Some salient features are as follows:

1. In general, relative deprivation (measure in terms of percentage shares in sectoral consumption) was much less in rural India than in the urban areas and metropolitan cities. On an average, the poorest

Table 3.1 Estimates of consumption inequality measures: Rural all-India

(At current prices based on group data)

Year	Per cent share in consumption of			Lorenz ratio (%)				
	Bottom 10%	Bottom 40%	Top 10 %	Trapezoidal rule	Two-parameter log-normal model	Uniform intra-group distribution	General Lorenz curve	Beta Lorenz curve
1961–62	3.79	21.53	25.88	31.30	30.30	31.60	31.61	31.71
1963–64	3.90	22.29	24.61	29.70	28.80	30.00	30.01	30.08
1964–65	3.79	22.39	24.56	29.40	28.30	29.70	29.65	29.71
1965–66	3.72	22.04	24.56	29.70	29.60	30.10	30.05	30.13
1966–67	3.63	21.98	23.59	29.30	28.70	29.80	29.69	29.73
1967–68	3.71	22.40	23.45	29.10	28.20	29.60	29.08	29.11
1968–69	3.63	21.71	25.49	30.50	29.70	31.00	30.90	30.97
1969–70	3.77	22.31	24.31	29.30	28.50	29.80	29.74	29.82
1970–71	3.91	22.63	23.25	28.30	27.50	28.90	28.76	28.89
1972–73	3.78	22.41	25.40	29.90	28.30	30.40	30.63	30.67
1973–74	4.00	22.23	22.56	27.60	27.00	28.20	28.19	28.29
1977–78	3.46	20.84	28.34	33.60	31.40	34.00	34.20	34.33

Notes:
The shares in consumption corresponding to different population fractile groups are obtained by linear interpolation.

The estimates of Lorenz ratio with reference to the General and Beta Lorenz specifications are obtained using the POVCAL software.

The estimates of Lorenz ratio for the log-normal model are derived from its parameters, which in turn, are estimated by solving the ordinate of the Lorenz curve corresponding to the bottom half of the population. This is because relevant information required for better and efficient methods could not be obtained owing to grouped data.

Source: [illegible]

Table 3.2 Estimates of consumption inequality measures: Urban all-India

	(At current prices based on group data)							
Year	**Per cent share in consumption of**			**Lorenz Ratio (%)**				
	Bottom 10%	**Bottom 40%**	**Top 10%**	**Trapezoidal rule**	**Two-parameter log-normal model**	**Uniform intra-group distribution**	**General Lorenz curve**	**Beta Lorenz curve**
1961–62	3.03	19.11	29.04	35.70	34.70	36.20	36.37	36.28
1963–64	3.25	19.14	29.09	36.00	34.80	36.60	36.54	36.49
1964–65	3.34	19.51	28.38	34.90	33.90	35.70	35.57	35.52
1965–66	3.46	20.06	27.43	33.90	33.10	34.70	34.51	34.45
1966–67	3.38	19.98	28.00	33.70	32.90	34.90	34.66	34.69
1967–68	3.40	20.21	26.11	33.20	33.00	34.80	34.49	34.50
1968–69	3.42	20.15	25.09	32.90	32.60	34.60	34.15	34.25
1969–70	3.32	19.51	24.90	34.00	33.50	36.20	35.86	35.86
1970–71	3.39	20.05	22.87	32.70	33.00	35.20	34.65	34.69
1972–73	3.44	19.91	27.62	34.10	32.70	34.80	34.70	34.46
1973–74	3.83	21.40	25.38	30.10	30.10	31.00	30.78	30.90
1977–78	3.29	19.91	28.11	34.60	33.20	35.20	35.53	35.74

Notes:
The shares in consumption corresponding to different population fractile groups are obtained by linear interpolation.

The estimates of Lorenz ratio with reference to the General and Beta Lorenz specifications are obtained using the POVCAL software.

The estimates of Lorenz ratio for the log-normal model are derived from its parameters, which in turn, are estimated by solving the ordinate of the Lorenz curve corresponding to the bottom half of the population. This is because relevant information required for better and efficient methods could not be obtained owing to grouped data.

Source: Suryanarayana (1986).

Table 3.3 Estimates of consumption inequality measures: Metropolitan cities

(At current prices based on group data)

Year	**Per cent share in consumption of**			**Lorenz Ratio (%)**				
	Bottom 10%	**Bottom 40%**	**Top 10%**	**Trapezoidal rule**	**Two-parameter log-normal model**	**Uniform intra-group distribution**	**General Lorenz curve**	**Beta Lorenz curve**
1961–62	3.18	18.90	24.17	34.50	32.60	34.30	35.92	36.11
1963–64	3.00	18.54	22.60	34.10	32.60	34.40	35.86	36.07
1964–65	2.95	18.37	21.95	34.70	30.40	32.30	37.63	–
1965–66	2.99	18.82	20.68	33.10	30.60	32.10	35.43	35.61
1966–67	2.99	19.18	18.63	31.10	30.80	32.80	34.05	34.06
1967–68	3.16	19.77	17.69	29.90	31.20	33.10	33.60	33.72
1968–69	3.32	19.53	17.71	30.10	31.50	32.80	34.04	34.28
1969–70	2.97	18.51	16.80	30.20	31.40	33.30	37.51	–
1970–71	2.97	18.54	16.18	29.00	30.60	32.90	33.59	35.59
1972–73	2.92	18.77	28.14	35.70	30.60	32.70	–	–
1973–74	3.33	19.67	27.39	34.60	29.00	30.00	–	–
1977–78	N.A.	N.A.	N.A.	N.A.	N.A.	N.A.	N.A.	N.A.

Notes:
The shares in consumption corresponding to different population fractile groups are obtained by linear interpolation.

The estimates of Lorenz ratio with reference to the General and Beta Lorenz specifications are obtained using the POVCAL software.

The estimates of Lorenz ratio for the log-normal model are derived from its parameters, which in turn, are estimated by solving the ordinate of the Lorenz curve corresponding to the bottom half of the population. This is because relevant information required for better and efficient methods could not be obtained from the grouped data.

decile group and poorest 40 per cent in rural India enjoyed relatively larger shares in consumption than their counterparts in urban India and the metropolitan cities. This picture slightly reverses when we consider the richest decile groups between rural and urban sectors. The urban rich had a larger share in consumption than the rural rich. The same profile does not extend to the metropolitan sector; this could be due to distortions in interpolated estimates of shares in consumption of the top decile group due to progressive bulging of population in the open-ended class intervals in the metropolitan consumption distributions.

2. In general and keeping with the Kuznets's explanation for the inverted-U, the extent of inequality was lower in rural India than in urban India. However, the estimates are not robust thanks to serious grouping bias in the NSS distribution for the metro sector. This is because the NSS used the same set of class intervals across sectors even though the absolute levels of consumption as well as prices were/are in general higher in the metros than in the urban sector, which in turn, were/are higher than in the rural areas.
3. Estimates of inequality are very sensitive to the method used and sector chosen since grouping bias varies across sectors.
4. For similar methodological reasons, unambiguous comments on trends in inequality cannot be made for all the three sectors.
5. However, with necessary statistical corrections for grouping bias as well as for the differential impact of inflation across expenditure groups, which few studies have attempted, one gets reasonably acceptable estimates of inequality across sectors and over time: (1) The extent of inequality in general was higher in the metros than in the urban segment as a whole, which in turn, was higher than in the rural sector; and (2) there is no evidence of a decline in inequality in any of the three regions (Table 3.4).
6. Given that the poor dis-save and only the rich save, the evidence given would imply that inequality in income distribution has worsened. Possibly this is one major reason why it took the country more than two decades to achieve the targets set for the Sixth Five-Year Plan.

How about trends in inequality during phase II of the development era? As regards the period from the second phase, time series estimates of poverty and inequality are not available because the NSSO started conducting quinquennial comprehensive surveys during its 27th round (1972–3). At the same time, reliable and representative retail price indices are available

Table 3.4 Estimates of consumption inequality measures: Metropolitan cities

(At constant prices with adjustment for grouping bias)			
Year	Lorenz Ratio: Adjusted for changes in relative prices		
	Rural	Urban	Metros
1961–62	31.60	36.20	36.70
1963–64	30.20	36.90	36.90
1964–65	30.90	37.10	39.90
1965–66	31.20	36.20	38.00
1966–67	31.40	37.10	37.90
1967–68	32.00	38.00	38.40
1968–69	32.90	36.60	38.10
1969–70	31.80	38.50	40.70
1970–71	30.40	37.30	40.10
1972–73	32.40	37.80	40.00
1973–74	30.50	34.40	39.70
1977–78	35.20	36.00	N. A.

Notes:
Base year budget weighted wholesale price relatives are used as cost of living indices for deflation.

As regards corrections for grouping bias by alternative estimators, the one that yields results, which are acceptable by economic theoretical as well as statistical criteria was the one that assumed uniform intra-group distribution.

Source: Suryanarayana (1986).

for the period from 1970–1 till 1988–9 (Jain and Minhas (1991) and Tendulkar and Jain (1993)). Therefore, as regards the second phase, we have only periodic NSS estimates till 1987–8, which are presented in Table 3.5 and Table 3.6. Some important findings are as follows:

The profile of deprivation across the rural and urban sector continued to be the same. The relative deprivation of the poorer segments was lower in rural India than in urban areas.

The year wise changes in estimates of inequality at current and constant prices vary depending upon the changes in relative prices. The price-adjusted estimates, without any correction for the grouping bias, show some measure of stability in the extent of inequality in rural India and some upward trend in urban India.

However, a profile of growth in real consumption between 1972–3 and 1987–8 shows that the scenario was generally progressive in the rural sector (Figure 3.1)[7].

Table 3.5 Estimates of consumption inequality measures: Rural all-India

Year	At current prices				At 1970–71 prices			
	Consumption share (%) of			Lorenz ratio	Consumption share (%) of			Lorenz ratio
	Bottom 10%	Bottom 40%	Top 10%		Bottom 10%	Bottom 40%	Top 10%	
1970–71	3.91	22.64	23.29	27.70	3.91	22.64	23.29	27.70
1972–73	3.68	21.90	25.47	29.70	3.68	21.86	25.58	29.80
1973–74	4.02	23.28	22.74	26.70	3.97	22.99	23.22	27.30
1977–78	3.46	20.78	28.46	32.60	3.58	21.32	27.69	31.60
1983	3.79	22.09	24.58	29.10	3.87	22.45	24.11	28.40
1986–87	3.85	22.14	24.53	29.10	4.08	23.16	23.32	27.20
1987–88	4.00	22.52	25.21	29.00	4.26	23.64	23.87	26.90
1988–89	4.08	23.25	23.85	27.50	4.31	24.08	22.85	26.00

Notes:
Consumption shares estimates by linear interpolation and Lorenz ratios by trapezoidal rule.

Estimates at constant prices are obtained using representative rural and urban price indices by commodity groups from Jain and Minhas (1991) and Tendulkar and Jain (1993).

Table 3.6 Estimates of consumption inequality measures: Urban all-India

Year	At current prices				At 1970–71 prices			
	Consumption share (%) of			Lorenz ratio	Consumption share (%) of			Lorenz ratio
	Bottom 10%	Bottom 40%	Top 10%		Bottom 10%	Bottom 40%	Top 10%	
1970–71	3.39	20.05	22.87	32.30	3.39	20.05	22.87	32.30
1972–73	3.46	19.94	27.53	33.10	3.36	19.52	28.03	33.90
1973–74	3.84	21.72	25.30	30.20	3.69	21.13	26.01	31.30
1977–78	3.22	19.53	28.76	34.30	3.21	19.50	28.83	34.40
1983	3.41	20.35	27.31	33.00	3.35	20.14	27.49	33.30
1986–87	3.19	19.08	22.59	33.90	3.22	19.13	22.67	33.90
1987–88	3.40	19.58	28.46	34.30	3.47	19.76	28.55	34.10
1988–89	3.43	19.97	26.50	32.90	3.44	19.88	26.78	33.10

Notes:
Consumption shares estimates by linear interpolation and Lorenz ratios by trapezoidal rule.

Estimates at constant prices are obtained using representative rural and urban price indices by commodity groups available in Jain and Minhas (1991) and Tendulkar and Jain (1993).

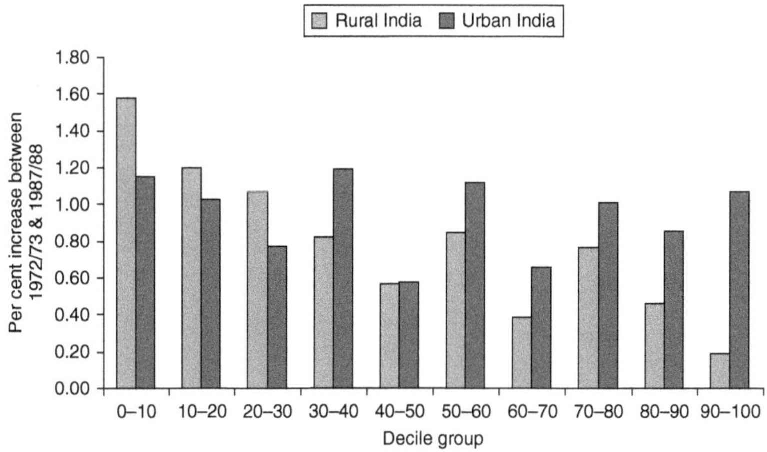

Figure 3.1 Growth in per capita real consumption
Source: Suryanarayana, M. H. (1995b).

Inequality: Reform phase

We proceed now to examine the changes in relative consumption distributions between the initial and terminal years of the reform era. Table 3.7 provides estimates of decile group-wise shares in consumption as well as Lorenz ratio in the all-India rural and urban consumption distribution for the year 1993–4 and 2004–5, respectively.[8] The results, subject to all limitations of prices and grouping bias, show the following:

> The poorer decile groups up to the 90th percentile have experienced a relative decline in their consumption shares, while the richest decile group has enjoyed an increase in both rural and urban all-India. As a result, the Lorenz ratios, even at current prices, have registered an increase.
>
> Thus, the growth phase of India's post-Independence development era has witnessed a decline in absolute deprivation (as reflected in estimates of absolute poverty vide GoI, 2007b: 207), but an increase in relative inequality in consumption distribution. What is disconcerting to note is that the increase in relative inequality has come about due to an increase in concentration of consumption in the top decile group in both rural and urban India.
>
> As is well known, due to positive and increasing savings in the upper income groups, estimates of inequality in consumption would

Table 3.7 Estimates of consumption inequality measures: Rural and urban all-India

(at current prices)

Decile group	**Rural all-India**		**Urban all-India**	
	1993–94	**2004–05**	**1993–94**	**2004–05**
	Consumption share (%)	**Consumption share (%)**	**Consumption share (%)**	**Consumption share (%)**
0–10	4.43	4.08	3.39	3.08
10–20	5.72	5.33	4.55	4.20
20–30	6.59	6.13	5.44	5.07
30–40	7.41	6.91	6.30	5.94
40–50	8.19	7.70	7.26	6.96
50–60	9.14	8.64	8.44	8.15
60–70	10.22	9.72	9.83	9.66
70–80	11.66	11.28	11.84	11.65
80–90	14.14	13.77	15.04	15.20
90–100	22.51	26.44	27.90	30.08
All	100.01	100.00	99.99	99.99
Lorenz ratio (%)	25.64	29.67	33.78	37.24

Note: Consumption share estimates by linear interpolation and Lorenz ratios by trapezoidal rule.

not really reflect the extent of income inequality; it would rather understate it. Available evidence based on income tax records show a sharp increase in inequality even within the richest one per cent of the population. Between 1987–88 and 1999–2000, real income increased by 71 per cent for the top one per cent, 78 per cent for the top 0.05 per cent and 125 per cent for the top 0.01 per cent of the income tax assesses (Banerjee and Piketty, 2005). Other related evidence shows an increase in the extent of wealth inequality and hence, corroborate the findings that income and consumption inequality, increased during the reform era (Jayadev et al., 2007).

3.4 Summing up

On achieving political independence, India embarked upon a strategy of development planning to achieve 'growth with redistribution'. However, plan priorities and strategies have varied across successive five-year plans depending on the emerging constraints and policy imperatives. Economic growth, as measured in terms of 'rate of growth of per capita gross national product', has been quite limited till recently. Given the fact that the extent of increase in per capita income in India has been quite limited during the post-Independence period, the present study does not look for features of Kuznets's 'inverted-U' syndrome – a phenomenon observed in the secular context and over a wide range of income variation.

Redistribution has been conceptualised in terms of a reduction in the extent of inequality in income distribution. To realise this objective, the government has explored and pursued different options, whose variety and intensity have varied over plan periods. Hence, the study found it worthwhile to examine the extent of redistribution, that is, reduction in inequality realised during the development process of the country. For this purpose, the post-independence economic development era of India was classified into three consecutive phases depending upon the policy initiatives and emphasis: Phase I saw the initiation of the development process (1950–65); Phase II provided for a modern agricultural growth strategy (1966–80) along with an explicit programme for poverty alleviation; and Phase III witnessed the neo-liberal reforms for 'structural adjustment with a human face'.

However, evaluation of the effectiveness of redistributive programmes in terms of estimates of income inequality is constrained by the fact that India does not have reliable and comparable estimates of income distribution. The available estimates of income distribution pertain to a few time points in the 1960s and 1970s, but are not comparable in terms of concepts and statistical reliability parameters. Hence, following the conventional approach, the study has utilised estimates of consumption distribution. Estimates of inequality in consumption distribution carried out with limited feasible methodological refinements like price-adjustments for changes in relative prices and inflation, and statistical corrections for grouping bias, of course, do not reveal systematic trends or any evidence of redistribution. This is because of certain features inherent to the data generation process and dynamics of institutional changes associated with the development process: the data sets do not really represent the distribution profile of the given consumption estimate. However, the evidence of no-trend in consumption inequality combined with the fact that savings are a non-linear positive function of income would imply that income inequality in India has increased over time. Other macro evidence like increasing disparities across economic sectors and regions only corroborate this assessment. As regards the reform era, comparable data sets on consumption distribution in the initial and terminal years, unambiguously point to an increase in inequality involving an increase in concentration of consumption in the top decile groups of both rural and urban India.

Notes

1. Per capita income at 1993–4 prices increased from Rs 3687 to Rs 10,071 between 1950–1 and 1999–2000 (GoI), 2007a: S-3).
2. See http://lawmin.nic.in/legislative/Art1-242%20(1–88).doc; p. 17.
3. A detailed list of legislations in 16 major states is provided in Table II of Besley and Burgess (2000).
4. Much of these policy discussions and recommendations, though based on sound theory, were based on a very poor understanding empirical situation (*see* Geetha and Suryanarayana, 1993; Suryanarayana, 1995 a and c, 1996; Suryanarayana and Silva, 2007).
5. It was to ensure stability of wages that programmes like the PDS were initially confined largely to the metros leading what is called the 'urban bias' syndrome (Suryanarayana, 1995c).
6. The most recent one is from Minoiu and Reddy (2007), which examines the performance of POVCAL programme by Datt (1994).
7. These estimates have been obtained with fractile group-specific price adjustment using representative rural and urban consumer retail price indices by commodity groups at the all-India level worked out by Jain and Minhas (1991) and Tendulkar and Jain (1993). For further details, see Suryanarayana 1995b.
8. The NSSO has conducted a major survey during 1999–2000 also. Since there is disagreement about the reliability and comparability of the estimates with those from previous rounds because of differences in the 'reference period', we have not reported those results here. For details regarding this debate, see Deaton and Kozel (2005).

References

Ahluwalia, Montek, S. (1978): 'Rural Poverty and Agricultural Performance in India', *Journal of Development Studies*, Vol. 14: 298–323.

Appu, P. S. (1972): *Ceiling on Agricultural Holdings*, New Delhi: Ministry of Agriculture.

Banerjee, Abhijit and Thomas Piketty (2005): 'Top Indian Incomes, 1922–2000', *The World Bank Economic Review*, Vol. 19, No. 1: 1–20.

Besley, Timothy and Robin Burgess (2000): 'Land Reform, Poverty Reduction and Growth: Evidence from India', *The Quarterly Journal of Economics*, Vol. 115, No. 2: 389–430.

Chakrvarty, Sukhamoy (1987): *Development Planning: The Indian Experience*, Delhi: Oxford University Press.

Datt, Gaurav (1994): 'Computational Tools for Poverty Measurement and Analysis', *Sarvekshana*, 61st Issue, Vol. XVIII, No. 2, New Delhi: National Sample Survey Organisation, Department of Statistics, Government of India: 1–10.

Deaton, Angus and Valerie Kozel (2005): *The Great Indian Poverty Debate*, New Delhi: Macmillan India Ltd.

Geetha S., and M. H. Suryanarayana (1993): 'Revamping PDS: Some Issues and Implications', *Economic and Political Weekly*, Vol. 28, No. 41: 2207–13.

Government of India (1969): *Report of the Committee on Distribution of Income and Levels of Living*, Part II, New Delhi; Planning Commission.

Government of India (1973): *A Technical Note on the Approach to the Fifth Plan of India: 1974–79*, New Delhi: Planning Commission.

Government of India (1981): *A Technical Note on the Sixth Plan of India (1980–85)*, New Delhi: Perspective Planning Division, Planning Commission.

Government of India (2006a): *Household Ownership Holdings in India, 2003. NSS 59th Round (January–December 2003)*, New Delhi: National Sample Survey Organisation.

Government of India (2006b): *Some Aspects of Operational Land Holdings in India, 2002–03. NSS 59th Round (January–December 2003)*, New Delhi: National Sample Survey Organisation.

Government of India (2007a): *Economic Survey 2006–2007*, New Delhi: Ministry of Finance.

Government of India (2007b): *Public Distribution System and Other Sources of Household Consumption 2004–2005, Volume I, NSS 61st Round (July 2004 – June 2005), Report No* 510(61/1.0/3), New Delhi: National Sample Survey Organisation, Ministry of Statistics and Programme Implementation.

Jayadev, Arjun, Sripad Motiram and Vamsi Vakukabharanam (2007): 'Patterns of Wealth Disparities in India during the Liberalization Era', *Economic and Political Weekly*, Vol. 42, No. 38: 3853–63.

Jain, L. R. and B. S. Minhas (1991): 'Rural and Urban Consumer Price Indices by Commodity Groups', *Sarvekshana*, Vol. 15, No. 1: 1–21.

Lewis, W. A. (1954): *Economic Development with Unlimited Supplies of Labour*, The Manchester School of Economic and Social Studies.

Mazumdar, Dipak and Sandip Sarkar (2007): 'Growth of Employment and Earnings in Tertiary Sector, 1983–2000', *Economic and Political Weekly*, Vol. 42, No. 11: 973–81.

Mahalanobis, P. C. (1963): 'A Preliminary Note on the Consumption of Cereals in India', *Sankhyā: The Indian Journal of Statistics*, Series B, Vol. 25, No. 3/4: 217–36.

Minoiu, Camelia and Sanjay Reddy (2007): *The Assessment of Poverty and Inequality through Parametric Estimation of Lorenz Curves: An Evaluation*, ISERP Working Paper 07–02, Columbia University in the City of New York: Institute for Social and Economic Research and Policy.

Perspective Planning Division (1962): 'Perspective of Development: 1961–1976, Implications of Planning for a Minimum Level of Living', reprinted in Srinivasan, T. N. and P. K. Bardhan (eds) *Poverty and Income Distribution in India*, Kolkata: Statistical Publishing Society, 9–38.

Rao, M. Govinda, Ric Shand and K. P. Kalirajan (1999): 'Convergence of Income across Indian States: A Divergent View', *Economic and Political Weekly*, Vol. 34, No. 13: 769–78.

Srinivasan, T. N. and P. K. Bardhan (ed) (1974): *Poverty and Income Distribution in India*, Kolkata: Statistical Publishing Society.

Suryanarayana, M. H. (1983): 'Treatment of Poverty in the Sixth Plan', *Arha Vijnana*, Vol. 25, No. 4: 419–25.

Suryanarayana, M. H. (1986): *The Problem of Distribution in India's Development*, PhD Thesis submitted to the Indian Statistical Institute, Kolkata.

Suryanarayana, M. H. (1995a): 'PDS Reform and Scope for Commodity Based Targeting', *Economic and Political Weekly*, Vol. 30, No. 13: 687–95.

Suryanarayana, M. H. (1995b): 'Growth, Poverty and Levels of Living: Hypotheses, Methods and Policies', *Journal of Indian School of Political Economy*, Vol. 7, No. 2: 203–55.

Suryanarayana, M. H. (1995c): 'PDS: Beyond Implicit Subsidy and Urban Bias', *Food Policy*, Vol. 20, No. 4: 259–78.

Suryanarayana, M. H. (1996): 'Food Security and Calorie Adequacy Across States: Implications for Reform', *Journal of Indian School of Political Economy*, Vol. VIII, No. 2, pp. 203–65.

Suryanarayana, M. H. (2000): 'How Real is the Secular Decline in Rural Poverty?', *Economic and Political Weekly*, Vol. 35, No. 25: 2129–39.

Suryanarayana, M. H. (2008): 'Agflation and the Public Distribution System', *Economic and Political Weekly*, Vol. 43 No. 18: 13–17.

Suryanarayana, M. H. and Dimitri Silva (2007): 'Is Targeting the Poor a Penalty on the Food Insecure? Poverty and Food Insecurity in India', *Journal of Human Development*, Vol. 8, No. 1: 89–106.

Tendulkar, S. D. and L. R. Jain, (1993); 'An Analysis of Inter-State And Inter-Commodity Group Rural-Urban Consumer Price Indices in India; 1983 To 1988–89' *Journal of Indian School of Political Economy*, Vol. 5, No. 2: 267–99.

Vaidyanathan, A. (1974): 'Some Aspects of Inequalities in Living Standards in Rural India' in T. N. Srinivasan, and P. K. Bardhan (ed): *Poverty and Income Distribution in India*, Kolkata: Statistical Publishing Society.

4
Social Protection Policies, Experiences and Challenges

Gita Sen and D. Rajasekhar

4.1 Introduction

Public debates about the relationship between economic strategies, social policies and within them, social protection, date back to at least the nineteenth century.[1] These debates have often been fiercely fought. From the watershed 1834 Poor Law in England and Charles Dickens's workhouses for the indigent poor through the variants of social policy that evolved in continental Europe (Bismarckian versus social democratic approaches to entitlements), and in the US during Roosevelt's New Deal followed by the Kennedy–Johnson expansion of entitlements, to their reversal during the Reagan years in the US, such debates have covered a wide range of issues in the countries of the North. In the South, while debates around social policy are more recent and unevenly developed in different regions, they have often been equally contested. The intensity and scope of such debates within a country usually depends on its economic situation and its historical evolution, the strategy for growth and development and the conjuncture of its political economy.

Social policy is like a pendulum that swings between three points, each representing a distinct rationale for action – a 'welfarist' notion of benevolence, a public goods instrumentality, or a rights/solidarity-based approach. Each rationale embeds a different understanding of the causes of poverty and deprivation, and consequent implications for who should be responsible to address the problem – the individual, household, market or the state.

Welfarist approaches such as those that have resurfaced in recent years under neo-liberal governments in the US often perceive the causes of poverty as attributable to individual characteristics or behaviour, and do not acknowledge the possibility of systemic reasons for deprivation.

As such, neither the state nor anyone else other than the individual concerned is perceived as having a responsibility for protection or promotion. Addressing the problem can, therefore, be passed on to the voluntary benevolence or philanthropy of non-state actors, for profit or non-profit (Foucault, 1991; Lemke, 2000).

At the other pole of the pendulum, the rights/solidarity approach adduces historical and systemic causes that often lie beyond the power of the average poor person or household, and places the onus for action squarely on the state, with non-state actors playing at best a complementary role.[2] Poverty and deprivation are seen as characteristic of specific groups defined and subordinated by economic class, caste, race, ethnicity, gender, or any of a number of other intersecting identities. These identities derive from historical social relations of power and are reproduced by the ongoing political economy. An understanding of this history and political economy is key to recognising that action must be rooted in an affirmation of the empowerment and rights of subordinated people (Sen, 1997).

Somewhere in between these two poles lies the public goods instrumental rationale for collective action. Often arising in historical periods of transition from one to the other pole of the pendulum, this view is less concerned with causes, and more with justification for action, whether in terms of the benefits to future growth (as with universal education, health or gender equality) or governmentality (in terms both of politically managing dissatisfaction, and of ensuring that citizens are motivated, energetic and personally responsible).[3] Enlightened self-interest is the driving force in this view for both public and private action.

Both the rights/solidarity approach and the public goods approach give rise to entitlements. However, while entitlements are programmatic (even if derived from laws), rights are more basic, in that they can be intrinsic, inalienable and reflected in foundational social agreements such as constitutions or the Universal Declaration of Human Rights. Entitlements can be modified or even done away with through programmatic changes, but rights, once acknowledged, are more difficult to change or annul. In this sense, the linking of social protection and social policy, more generally to a rationale of rights, provides them with the strongest foundation for action and demands for accountability.

In development policy debates, the need for social protection to address long-standing vulnerabilities and deprivation and to ameliorate the consequences of growing informalisation of labour (consequent to economic globalisation) came nearer the centre of the agenda in the late 1990s and 2000s. Social protection in its current incarnation (and as a successor to the heavily criticised social safety nets of the previous period) prioritises moving people out of dependency, and has champions of new methods and tools among both instrumentalists and rights advocates (Devereux and Sabates-Wheeler, 2007).

Before discussing the Indian experience with social protection, it is useful to take a comparative look to understand the extent to which Indian dilemmas and challenges are shared by others. Latin American experience with social protection holds many pointers for India, as the region has been at the forefront of policy debate as well as new programmatic approaches involving 'the mainstreaming of poverty, the role and design of transfers, the focus on households and the emerging rights agenda' (Barrientos, Gideon and Molyneux, 2008; p. 772). Social protection in the region evolved through four phases: first, a focus mainly on organised workers during the import substitution industrialisation period up to the 1960s; second, anti-poverty programmes focused on effectiveness and efficiency during the 1970s; third, neo-liberal cost-cutting, targeting and market-based initiatives in the 1980s and early 1990s; and finally, in the late 1990s and 2000s, diverse Latin American countries have seen the emergence of rights-based approaches such as Chile's Chile Solidario, Brazil's Bolsa Familia, and Bolivia's Bolsa Dignidad. As pointed out by Barrientos, Gideon and Molyneux (2008), pro-poor social policies in today's Latin America have had diverse trajectories. They may be intended to complement orthodox economic policies or to ameliorate their negative effects as in Chile. They may also be intended to counter a history of exclusion as in Bolivia. Indeed, recognition of the multidimensionality of poverty and the exclusion of Afro-descendants and indigenous people from the benefits of economic growth and primary product exports despite providing the bulk of unorganised labour is one of the important features of some of the newer rights-based approaches. Bringing this diverse experience together, the United Nations Economic Commission for Latin America and the Caribbean (UNECLAC) called for a 'social covenant structured around the concept of protection ... (that would) be governed by the principles of universality, solidarity and efficiency' (UNECLAC, 2006; p. 16).

Much of the debate tends to be about apparently technical aspects of programmes – whether to target and how? Whether to apply conditions or not? Whether to take account of the implicit gendered assumptions of conditional cash transfer programmes such as Mexico's

Progresa/Opportunidades or to ignore them? and how to ensure financial viability over time? But as Devereux and Sabates-Wheeler (2007, p. 2) say:

> Anyone who believes that design choices in social protection programmes ... are purely pragmatic technical issues ... is missing the point ... Which choices are made, and for what reasons, reflects the kind of society that policymakers and technocrats with power to direct social policy wish to promote...Social protection is self-evidently about a vision of society.

At the same time, the current focus on design issues runs some risk of diverting attention from the basic causes of deprivation and exclusion that have roots both in history and in the contemporary political economy of liberalised markets and flexible labour. Emphasis on programme design issues is undoubtedly necessary, but may well not be sufficient.

4.2 Core challenges for social protection in India

Social protection has evolved in India in a broadly similar manner to the four phases of the Latin American experience, although much of it can only be traced to the period after independence. The 1950s and 1960s witnessed social protection as essentially the preserve of organised workers, including those in the rapidly growing public sector. With growing reaction to the crisis in agriculture and the political turmoil it generated, the 1970s saw anti-poverty programmes emerge as a major thrust via Indira Gandhi's 20-point 'Garibi Hatao' (Abolish Poverty) programme of the 1970s and 1980s. By the mid-1980s, it was clear that these promotional programmes for asset creation and subsidised credit, together with protective programmes for public distribution of food were having an impact on reducing poverty. However, they also had serious problems of scope and reach, as well as of inefficiency and 'leakages'. Nonetheless, the latter part of the 1980s saw the emergence of new approaches focused on popular participation, chief among which was the National Literacy Mission, which focused on illiteracy and educational exclusion among girls and women in a systematic way.

By contrast, the economic reforms of the 1990s brought sharp cuts in budgets for social protection. However, the decline of the Congress Party's dominance led to greater political pressure to win elections, and hence, some reinstatement of these budgets from the mid-1990s on. By the 2000s, driven largely by pressure from below, popular campaigns focused on gaining key rights for the most deprived and excluded – rights to information, work and food. They have challenged the policy terrain, even as economic agendas for market liberalisation have continued apace.

This four-phase trajectory is very similar to the Latin American experience. The major differences are, however, that India's per capita income (and hence, overall financial capacity) is much lower, its poor population much larger, and its levels of absolute deprivation much higher. Importantly, for systems evolving from an initial emphasis on only organised workers, the proportion of unorganised workers is significantly higher in India (over 90 per cent of all workers) as against smaller proportions in Latin American countries, for example, around half of the labour force in Mexico. The biggest challenge for social protection in India is that the scale of need for it is clearly much larger, and cautions against any unidimensional focus on cash transfers as a panacea.

A second important challenge in India is that, as in Latin America, the problem has multiple dimensions in two senses. Income poverty usually goes hand in hand with deprivations in other dimensions – education, health, sanitation, safe housing, clean water, access to family support and child care. Deprivations in these dimensions not only reduce current quality of life, but also affect the possibilities of future generations for a better life. A second sense in which the problem is multidimensional is that economic deprivations tend to cluster along with caste and gender as characteristics that define who is poor and deprived in terms of social protection, functioning and capabilities. Poverty and deprivation are group phenomena, and have to be understood and tackled as such (Sen, 1997).

Gender straddles both types of multidimensionality. The consequences of highly unequal gender relations and preference for a son are experienced in terms of serious differentials in wages and incomes, access to food, education and health services, as well as inter alia, the poor quality and availability of sanitation (including in most schools), fuel, water, the absence of child-care, which significantly increase women's double burdens of housework and employment lengthening and intensifying their working day. This is compounded by the serious problem of violence against women that is widespread and increasingly documented. Even in Latin America, the extent to which the new programmes for cash transfers is built on the unpaid work of women has been raised (Molyneux, 2006; Bradshaw with Viquez, 2008) but still not adequately addressed.

The third challenge is that, because of the overwhelming presence of unorganised workers, deprivation and exclusion are the rules, not the exceptions (Guhan, 1994; Prabhu, 2001). Because of this, as Guhan states:

> Developing countries cannot rely on the formal model alone for social security provision ... social security in poor countries will have to be viewed as part of and fully integrated with anti-poverty policies, with such policies themselves being broadly conceived in view of the complex, multi-dimensional nature of poverty and deprivation. In a context of massive and persistent poverty, the concept of social security has to extend considerably beyond the conventional social insurance model and encompass a large measure of social assistance. The conceptual problem is to situate an operationally useful notion of social security – one that is neither excessively specific (as in the formal model) nor excessively general – within a comprehensive anti-poverty approach. (1994: p. 38)

However rapidly India grows (and the depth of the global economic crisis already challenges the possibility of relying on 'trickle-down' effect), the likelihood of the majority of workers becoming organised in the foreseeable future appears remote. It is also clear, as has been recognised also in Latin America, that workplace-based social security has to be complemented by household and community-based programmes that can address the scope and multi-dimensionality of the problem. A broader, more socially transformative and rights-based approach seems to be the only viable direction.

The fourth challenge is that, notwithstanding some important advances in recent years, such a rights-based approach is still rudimentary in the country, despite its social mobilisation and programmatic innovativeness. High economic growth rates have won over the politically powerful middle classes that have abandoned Gandhian simplicity for ostentatious consumption, and are less concerned with rising economic inequality or the continuing large masses of the underemployed and vulnerable. What this means is that political backing for rights-based social protection for the large mass of unorganised workers is on shaky ground, and programmes could lose support in difficult economic times or with changes of government.

A fifth challenge, and the one that has been most commented on in the Indian literature is a welter of administrative problems, inefficiency and ineffectiveness (Guhan, 1994; Prabhu, 2001). Ad hoc-ism, political one-upmanship, lack of adequate preparation and/or capacity to implement have compounded the absence of clear vision, mission, focus on outcomes and accountability. These problems derive from the political instrumentalism that has marred social protection in India since inception, and not only prevent effective and efficient programme design, management and delivery, but also serve as grist to the mill of fiscal conservatives and political opponents.

4.3 Social security policies and programmes – A review and critique

Social security, defined as measures to assist households and people facing shortages in income and basic survival needs due to work, health- or family-related risks, is an important instrument for the well-being of workers (especially, for those in the unorganised sector) and their family members, as well as those too young, old or unable to earn an income for a variety of reasons. This holds a fortiori in economies with very large unorganised sectors.

The terms organised and formal (unorganised and informal) have often been used interchangeably in the literature, and this has resulted in some confusion because it is often unclear whether the reference is to the enterprise or to its workers. The terms are not synonymous because within large enterprises (usually referred to as 'formal'), not all workers are organised.[4] In large ('formal') firms, there are often a significant number of workers on daily wages, or short-term and insecure contracts, whose rights to both employment and worker benefits are less acknowledged or assured than those of organised workers in the same enterprise or unit. Thus, the formal sector of enterprises often have both organised and unorganised workers (NCEUS, 2006 and 2007). It is much less common, however, to find organised workers in the informal (and often small) enterprises sector. In this chapter, in order to minimise confusion, each time we use the terms 'formal' and 'informal' we will specify whether we are referring to a sector or to workers.

In India, the organised sector has been defined as consisting of all government institutions, and of enterprises using electricity and employing ten or more persons, and those not using electricity but employing 20 or more persons (ILO, 2000: 2). This sector is characterised in part by skilled labour, regular employment and remuneration, use of sophisticated technology and includes registered factories and service establishments. As can be seen, the original definition does not distinguish between an enterprise and its workers. But, while some workers in this sector have a high level of bargaining power, others may well be on short-term contracts or daily wages.

The unorganised sector comprises those workers who do not have a formal work contract. Consequently, they do not have access to social security through the workplace. They are also unable to organise themselves into unions or worker associations for any of a number of reasons including the casual nature of employment, small-size of establishment and low capital-investment per person employed, scattered nature of establishments, and/or superior strength of the employer operating singly or in combination (GoI, 2002).[5]

An important criterion that separates organised from unorganised workers is the availability of and access to different types of social security benefits. The social security measures planned and implemented in India in the post-independence era have been mainly for organised sector workers, despite the fact that the overwhelming majority of the workforce depends on the unorganised labour market for its subsistence.

Guhan (1992, 1994) proposed a categorisation of measures that would constitute a more appropriate framework for social security in poor countries, including promotional measures affecting endowments, exchange entitlements, real incomes and social consumption; preventive measures to avert deprivation; and protective measures intended as part of a safety net to provide relief from deprivation. While this is useful, in practice (as Guhan himself notes) there is considerable overlap between these categories even conceptually, let alone empirically. In particular, many preventive measures such as health insurance are also promotional, since they improve endowments, and the ability to earn incomes.

4.4 Social security policies and programmes for organised sector workers

The Indian Constitution provides strength and spirit to social security legislation for organised workers through the Directive Principles of state policy. These workers are provided with support for contingencies, health insurance, maternity benefits, compensation for work-related accidents and retirement benefits. These mandatory benefits are provided either solely at the cost of employers or on the basis of joint contributions by employers and employees. Social security benefits are entitlements that accrue to employees; however, responsibility for compliance largely rests with employers. The enactments and benefits of major social security benefits for organised sector workers are discussed later. Most of these programmes came into existence at or after the country's independence, as social security for workers in the colonies was not a major concern of the colonial power.

Provident funds

The Employee's Provident Funds and Miscellaneous Provisions Act, 1952, aims to provide social security and timely monetary assistance to industrial employees and their households when they are in distress or unable to meet household and social obligations, and to protect them in old age, disability, early death of the principal income-earning member and such other contingencies. The provident fund is constituted for employees working in factories and other establishments that are engaged in specific industries and with 20 or more employees.[6]

The schemes under the Act are: Employees Provident Fund Scheme, 1952; Employees Deposit Linked Insurance Scheme, 1976; and Employees Pension Scheme, 1995. Mobilising contributions from employees and employers, these schemes provide benefits such as the possibility of withdrawing lump sums after retirement, life insurance cover and pensions.

Health insurance

The Employees State Insurance (ESI) Act was the first social security legislation passed in 1948 in the country after independence, though the question of introducing health insurance engaged the attention of policymakers from the turn of the twentieth century.[7] The ESI scheme is currently applicable to employees drawing wages up to Rs 7500 per month in factories using electricity in the manufacturing process and employing ten or more persons, and non-electricity using factories, shops, hotels and restaurants, cinema and preview theatres, road-motor undertakings and newspaper establishments employing 20 or more persons. The scheme is administered by a corporate body, the Employees' State Insurance Corporation, having members representing employers, employees, central and state governments, the medical profession and the Parliament.

The scheme is financed through contributions from employees (1.75 per cent of wages or nil in the case of those drawing wages less than Rs 50 per day) and employers (4.75 per cent of wages). The respective state government bears 12.5 per cent of the total expenditure on medical care. Under the scheme, cash benefits are provided towards sickness, maternity, temporary disablement, et cetera. Benefits also include medical services provided directly through the ESI network of dispensaries, diagnostic centres and hospitals and indirectly through empanelled private clinics, diagnostic centres and hospitals.

A special programme, the Central Government Health Service (CGHS) was introduced as a contributory plan in 1954 to provide medical coverage to central government employees (both working and retired) and their families. The scheme currently covers 23 cities, while those residing outside these cities are reimbursed for medical expenditure. The contribution from each employee ranges from Rs 15 to Rs 150 per month depending on salary. Pensioners can obtain a lifetime health card by paying a contribution for ten years at the time of retirement.

The scheme offers a range of services through allopathic and homeopathic dispensaries. The facilities of outpatient care, emergency/inpatient care, free drug supply, laboratory and radiological investigations, et cetera, are provided through such dispensaries. Patients are referred to designated hospitals for services that are not available at the dispensary level, and the expenses are reimbursed. About 500 such hospitals are recognised across 17 cities. There are currently one million cardholders and the total number of beneficiaries is 4.3 million.

Over time, the CGHS has run into a number of problems due to rising medical costs and poor administration. As a result, the Sixth Pay Commission has recommended a health insurance scheme for employees and pensioners (excluding those in railways and defence) in place of the CGHS. The scheme will be voluntary subject to payment of the prescribed premium for those who are currently in service or drawing a pension. It will be mandatory for those who join service after introduction of the scheme and for new retirees.

Maternity benefits

The Maternity Benefit Act, 1961, enacted to promote the welfare of working women, provides for maternity leave and payment of monetary benefits during the time when they are unable to work on account of pregnancy. The services of a woman worker cannot be terminated during the period of her absence on account of pregnancy except for gross misconduct. The maximum period for which a woman can get maternity benefit is 12 weeks; six prior to the delivery of the child and six weeks after.

Compensation for work-related accidents

The Workmen's Compensation Act, 1923, was passed to impose an obligation on employers to pay compensation to workers for accidents arising out of and in the course of employment. The Act is applicable to any person who is employed, otherwise than in a clerical capacity in a large number of establishments. The notable exclusions are those covered under the ESI scheme.

Gratuity

The Payment of Gratuity Act, 1972, provides for a scheme of compulsory payment of gratuity to employees engaged in factories, mines, oil fields, plantations, ports, railway companies, motor transport undertakings, shops and other establishments. Every employee is entitled to receive gratuity after he has been in continuous service for five or more years (except in the case of death or permanent disablement), and is paid at the time of termination of service on account of superannuation, retirement, resignation and death. Gratuity benefit is provided at the rate of 15 days' wages for every completed year of service, based on the wages last drawn by the employee. The amount of gratuity payable has a ceiling of Rs 350,000.

The financial viability of social security schemes for organised sector workers has been of concern for some time. This is particularly true for provident funds. An important problem is poor accumulation in a fund as members often withdraw their contributions to pay for higher education, health, housing and other needs. The other and bigger problem is the low rate of return on investment. The contributions of members are invested in select debt instruments with a large and substantial investment being directed towards government securities in order to mitigate risks and provide assured rates of return. The low rates of return on government securities translate into a smaller size of benefits available to the Employee Provident Fund (EPF) member. According to estimates, as much as 20 per cent of the potential earning capacity on investment is lost due to the compulsion to invest in government securities. Thus, the inability to diversify the investment portfolio leads to a substantial reduction in the eventual size of the retirement benefit available to the employee. The fund managers are also restricted by these guidelines, and hence, professional fund managers can do little to obtain higher returns on investment. A related problem is that the financial viability of provident funds remains questionable in the long-run owing to an increase in the life expectancy of the average Indian. Several rules that were formulated keeping in mind the life expectancies prevalent during the 1950s are still being implemented currently.

Despite this, and as can be seen from the previous description, organised workers with regular employment have a reasonable package of benefits that cover major social security needs. Typically, unorganised workers in the same enterprises do not have access to these benefits, and employers even in large enterprises often attempt to replace regular by temporary and contract or daily wage workers in an attempt to reduce costs. Such cost-cutting may work in the short-run, but the employer loses worker motivation, morale and commitment, which may have cost implications in the medium and longer run. In India, the notion of the benevolent employer who is concerned about worker welfare is rare, let alone the recognition by employers of social security as a right, even for workers in large enterprises.

4.5 Unorganised workers – Numbers and composition

The overwhelming majority of the workforce in India is unorganised. The Planning Commission (2006: 18) noted that:

> The social security schemes in India cover only a very small segment of the workers ... Out of an estimated workforce of about 397 million, only 28 million workers are having the benefits of formal social security protection. About 24 million workers were covered under various employees provident funds schemes and 8 million workers were covered under the ESI schemes, in addition to about 4.5 million under the Workmen Compensation Act and about 0.5 million under the Maternity Benefit Act in the year.

Furthermore, the organised sector in India is shrinking in relative terms due to the growth of the contract-work system in several industries, the working of labour laws in a hugely labour surplus economy, and the pressures of globalisation. Rajasekhar and Sreedhar (2002) have shown that workers in the beedi (country cigarette) industry in Karnataka, who were initially covered by statutory provisions such as provident fund, et cetera, have become 'unorganised' by having to withdraw from their accumulated provident funds to meet subsistence and life cycle needs such as child birth, marriages, et cetera (Rajasekhar and Sreedhar, 2002). The agarbatti making and garment manufacturing industries have experienced changes in the mix of workers; the proportion of unorganised workers has increased at the expense of organised workers. Unorganised workers in these industries, the majority of whom were women, obtain wages lower than those prescribed by the government, are outside the formal social security system, and suffer from a range of health problems for which there is no health-care coverage or compensation (Rajasekhar, Suchitra and Manjula, 2007).

The National Commission for Enterprises in the Unorganised Sector (NCEUS) (2007) estimated that the total employment (principal plus subsidiary) in the Indian economy in 2004–5 was 458 million, of which unorganised workers accounted for 395 million (Table 4.1). Of the 395 million unorganised workers, agriculture accounted for 253 million and the remaining 142 million are employed in the non-agricultural sector. The proportion of non-agricultural workers who are unorganised rose from 32 per cent to 36 per cent between 1999–2000 and 2004–5. Agriculture consists almost entirely of unorganised workers who are mainly either self-employed (65 per cent) or 'casual' workers (35 per cent). Even outside agriculture, nearly 72 per cent of the workers were unorganised in 2004–5, an increase of 4 percentage points from 68 per cent in 1999–2000. These workers are mainly self-employed (63 per cent). The rest of the workers in the non-agricultural unorganised sector are more or less equally distributed between the regular (17 per cent) and casual categories (20 per cent).

Between 1999–2000 and 2004–5, total employment in the economy increased from 397 million to 457 million (Table 4.1). But the change in organised employment is actually marginally negative. The increase in employment (for about 61 million workers) has been entirely unorganised, even though employment increased by 8.5 million in formal enterprises. The share of unorganised workers among all workers in formal enterprises increased from 38 per cent to 47 per cent. NCEUS (2007: 4) notes: 'What this means in simple terms is that the entire increase in the employment in the organised sector over this period has been informal in nature that is, without any job and social security. This constitutes what can be termed as informalisation of the formal sector, where any employment increase consists of regular workers without social security benefits and casual or contract workers again without the benefits that should accrue to formal workers'.

4.6 Poverty and vulnerability among unorganised workers

When 92 per cent of the country's workforce is unorganised, it is not surprising that there is a high congruence between this group and the poor and vulnerable sections of the population. NCEUS (2007) attempted, as a first approximation, to measure this congruence by dividing the total population of the country into six groups based on their consumption expenditure. The first group of 'extremely poor' are those who have a monthly per capita consumer expenditure of up to

Table 4.1 Distribution of total Indian workforce by formal and informal sectors in 1999–2000 and 2004–5

	Total Employment (Million)		
Sectors	**Informal/ unorganised workers – number (%)**	**Formal/ organised workers – number (%)**	**Total – number (%)**
		1999–2000	
Informal/ unorganised sector	341.2 (99.6)	1.4 (0.4)	342.6 (100.0)
Formal/ organised sector	20.5 (37.8)	33.7 (62.2)	54.1 (100.0)
Total	361.7 (91.2)	35.0 (8.8)	396.8 (100.0)
		2004–2005	
Informal/ unorganised sector	393.5 (99.6)	1.4 (0.4)	394.9 (100.0)
Formal/ organised sector	29.1 (46.6)	33.4 (53.4)	62.6 (100.0)
Total	422.6 (92.4)	34.9 (7.6)	457.5 (100.0)

Note: Figures in brackets are percentages.
Source: Computed by NCEUS (2007) from National Sample Survey (NSS) 61st Round 2004–2005 and NSS 55th Round, 1999–2000, Employment–Unemployment Survey.

three-fourths of the official poverty line (i.e., an average of Rs 8.90 per capita per day (pcpd) in 2004–5); the second group 'Poor' are those between the extremely poor and up to the official poverty line (average expenditure of Rs. 11.60 pcpd); the third is called 'marginally poor' with per capita consumer expenditure of only 1.25 times the poverty line (i.e., Rs 14.6 pcpd); and the fourth called 'vulnerable' have per capita consumer expenditure of just twice the poverty line (i.e., Rs 20.3 pcpd). If we combine the poor and vulnerable, they would together constitute 77 per cent of the population. This group, totalling 836 million people with an income roughly below US$2 in PPP terms, can be called the poor and vulnerable segment of the Indian population.

It can be seen from Table 4.2 that 79 per cent of the informal or unorganised workers belong to the poor and vulnerable group. 'They have remained poor at a bare subsistence level without any job or social security, working in the most miserable, unhygienic and unliveable

Table 4.2 Percentage distribution of expenditure classes by social identity, informal work status and education, 2004–5

Sl No	Economic status	Social categories (percentage share in own total)				Percentage of unorganised workers	Education* (per cent)	
		SCs/STs	All OBCs except Muslims	All Muslim except SCs/ STs	Others (without SCs/ STs, OBCs & Muslim)		Illiterates	Primary and below primary
1	Extremely poor	10.9	5.1	8.2	2.1	5.8	8.1	5.0
2	Poor	21.5	15.1	19.2	6.4	15	19.0	14.2
3	Marginally poor	22.4	20.4	22.3	11.1	19.6	22.2	19.4
4	Vulnerable	33	39.2	34.8	35.2	38.4	36.9	40.0
5	Middle income	11.1	17.8	13.3	34.2	18.7	12.8	18.9
6	High income	1	2.4	2.2	11	2.7	1.0	2.5
7	Extremely poor and poor (1+2)	32.4	20.3	27.4	8.5	20.8	27.1	19.2
8	Marginal and vulnerable (3+4)	55.4	59.6	57.1	46.3	57.9	59.1	59.4
9	Poor and vulnerable (7+8)	87.8	79.9	84.5	54.8	78.7	86.2	78.6
10	Middle & high income (5+6)	12.2	20.1	15.5	45.2	21.3	13.8	21.4
	All	100.0	100.0	100.0	100.0	100.0	100.0	100.0
	All (million)	302	391	138	258	423	270	164

Note: *Refers to persons aged 15 and above.
Source: Computed by NCEUS (2007) from NSS 61st Round 2004–5, Employment–Unemployment Survey.

Table 4.3 Percentage distribution of unorganised workers across expenditure classes

Status	Total	Self-employed	Regular wage workers	Casual workers
Poor and vulnerable	78.7	74.7	66.7	90.0
Higher income group	21.3	25.3	33.3	10.0
Total	100.0	100.0	100.0	100.0

Source: Computed by NCEUS (2007) from NSS 61st Round 2004–5, Employment–Unemployment Survey.

conditions, throughout this period of high economic growth since the early nineties' (NCEUS 2007).

The relationship between poverty and vulnerability and the type of employment that the unorganised workers engage in, is brought out in Table 4.3. The high congruence between informal work status and poverty/vulnerability becomes almost complete in the case of casual workers, 90 per cent of them belong to the group of poor and vulnerable. As noted earlier, this group includes the overwhelming population of the dalits and adivasis, other backward castes (OBCs) and Muslims. What is also striking is that, even among regular wageworkers, fully two-thirds are poor and vulnerable.

4.7 Coping with risks

As we have seen, an overwhelming majority of unorganised workers are poor and vulnerable, and face a multiplicity of risks. In this section we examine some micro-level evidence of how they cope with risk, in order to understand the contours of their need for social protection from the bottom-up. What risks are faced by the unorganised workers on account of insufficient access to social security? What coping mechanisms do they adopt? An analysis of evidence to answer these two questions is important given the debilitating impact that risks can have on poorer unorganised worker households. Anirudh Krishna found that in parts of India (Rajasthan, Gujarat and Andhra Pradesh) and Africa (Ghana, Uganda and Kenya), between 59 per cent and 88 per cent of a large sample of households attributed their descent into poverty and their inability to escape from it primarily to health and health-related expenses (Krishna, 2003; 2004; Krishna et al., 2004; 2005). Holzmann and Jorgensen (2003) discuss risks caused by four sets of factors – individual, household, community and national.[8]

In this chapter, we have used a broader term – 'emergencies', to include such risks and others. The emergency needs of a household are those that occur suddenly and for which the household may have no (or inadequate) contingency plans or arrangements.[9] They include health emergencies, accidents and deaths, crop failures, drought situations, social functions like wedding and religious/ritualistic ceremonies, social obligations such as village festivals, et cetera. Social functions and obligations are not 'risks' in the sense of being uncertain; but, we treat them as emergencies because poor households tend to perceive even such predictable events as crises.[10] The term 'emergencies' has thus been used to include both predictable and unpredictable events, because, for households that have a deficit in risk-management capacity, even predictable events can have negative effects on the households' asset base or indebtedness.

In order to provide an in-depth understanding of how households experience and address such risks, we draw on evidence from a set of recent studies conducted in three of the Southern states of the country. Rajasekhar et al. (2006), Rajasekhar, Manjula and Suchitra (2006) and Rajasekhar, Suchitra and Manjula (2006) collected primary data on household crises from 505 agricultural labourers, 301 construction workers, 104 domestic workers, 151 agarbatti rollers and 152 garment workers, covering both female and male workers belonging to rural as well as urban areas from five districts in Karnataka state.[11] The effectiveness of micro-finance programmes on vulnerability to debt bondage was investigated by Rajasekhar, Narasimha Reddy and Suchitra (2006) using data on 149 unorganised workers in 32 microfinance groups spread over four districts of Andhra Pradesh. The third study is on 131 agricultural workers belonging to the two most disadvantaged caste groups – dalits and adivasis, who have been members of microfinance groups in six districts of Tamil Nadu (Rajasekehar, Suchitra and Manjula 2008). For the first two studies, the data were collected in 2005 and for the last study in 2007.

In all these studies, the sample households were asked about crises or emergencies faced during the three years prior to the survey date. Unfortunately, the household level data were not collected in a manner that would allow the analysis to examine the working of gender relations within the household or the impact or burdens of crises by gender. However, disaggregated data by SCs/STs and other households have been provided. In Table 4.4, the data on proportion of households facing at least one crisis has been presented. It can be seen that across the states and different groups, well over a third of the households had faced at

Table 4.4 Incidence of emergency needs in unorganised sector households

Category of workers	SC/ST households (%) facing at least one crisis to total SC/ST households	Other households (%) facing at least one crisis to total other households	Households (%) facing at least one crisis
Karnataka (n=1213)			
Agricultural labourers	44.80	38.89	41.39
Construction workers	40.00	43.27	41.86
Domestic workers	29.16	41.07	35.58
Agarbatti workers	60.38	67.68	65.00
Garment workers	42.86	43.06	40.39
Andhra Pradesh (n=149)			
Agricultural labourers	N.A	N.A	64.43
Tamil Nadu (n=131)			
Dalit agricultural labourers	100.00	0.00	90.00
Adivasi agricultural labourers	100.0	0.00	83.10

Sources: Rajasekhar et al. (2006); Rajasekhar, Manjula and Suchitra (2006); Rajasekhar, Suchitra and Manjula (2006); Rajasekhar, Reddy and Suchitra (2006) and Rajasekhar, Suchitra and Manjula (2008).

least one crisis in the reference period, with domestic workers having the lowest incidence at 35.58 per cent. The incidence was over 80 per cent among unorganised agricultural workers belonging to the two most disadvantaged groups of dalits and adivasis.

Table 4.5 shows the distribution of all crises faced by these households. Health emergencies were the single most common crisis faced across the categories of workers, followed by death of household members and marriages and other social obligations. The combination of health, accidents and death accounted for over 75 per cent of the crises faced by each group. Thus, a large proportion of the crises were on account of inability to access social security benefits relating to life cover, accident benefit and health insurance.

Such crises impose a heavy cost burden on unorganised worker households. Table 4.6 presents the total expenditure on all crises faced by the different categories of workers and the distribution of this expenditure across the sources from which they were financed. Significantly, own resources covered at most 31 per cent of spending, while borrowing from moneylenders was the dominant source of finance, with anywhere

Table 4.5 Distribution of all emergencies faced by households by type

(Per cent)

Categories of workers	Death of household member	Health crises	Marriages and social obligations	Accidents	Other	Total (No)
Karnataka						
Agricultural labourers	23.77	47.09	16.59	11.66	0.90	223
Construction workers	14.60	48.91	19.71	16.06	0.73	137
Domestic workers	15.79	52.63	23.68	7.89	0.00	38
Agarbatti workers	14.53	58.91	18.75	7.69	0.12	117
Garment workers	7.25	77.72	13.04	1.45	0.80	69
Andhra Pradesh						
Agricultural labourers	12.50	50.00	20.83	7.29	9.38	96
Tamil Nadu						
Dalits	7.25	59.42	17.39	8.70	7.25	69
Adivasis	11.27	47.89	21.13	11.27	8.45	71

Sources: Rajasekhar et al. (2006); Rajasekhar, Manjula and Suchitra (2006); Rajasekhar, Suchitra and Manjula (2006); Rajasekhar, Reddy and Suchitra (2006) and Rajasekhar, Suchitra and Manjula (2008).

between 37 per cent and 60 per cent of the total expenditure being from this source (Ray 1998). A considerably smaller but still a significant share of the expenditure was through borrowing from relatives, another example of informal mechanisms of risk management, that is, drawing upon family and other social capital. Important to note is the limited role played by the employers of unorganised workers. Also, while sale of assets is not a major source, this may refer only to the immediate source to fund crisis expenditure, and may not refer to loss of assets consequent on having to repay moneylenders over time.

Table 4.7 presents the ratio of the expenditure on crises incurred by agricultural labourers, construction workers and domestic workers in Karnataka to the average monthly per capita income (PCI) of the households.[12]

The agricultural workers were the worst off as nearly 48 per cent of them spent more than two-and-a-half times their monthly PCI on

Table 4.6 Distribution of total expenditure on crises by sources from which financed

Categories of workers	Sources of financing for the household crises faced by unorganised workers (Per cent)							
	Own sources	Moneylenders	Relatives	SHGs	Employer	Sale of assets	Other source	Total expenditure (in Rs)
Karnataka								
Agricultural labourers	18.06	54.92	12.21	0.00	8.49	2.79	3.53	2,684,600 (12,039)
Construction workers	25.32	48.29	12.17	0.00	4.26	3.04	6.92	2,795,100 (20,402)
Domestic worker	18.65	50.79	17.28	0.00	2.61	3.62	7.06	552,650 (14,543)
Agarbatti workers	21.86	37.01	24.27	0.00	2.19	8.90	5.77	2,150,500 (18,380)
Garment workers	30.86	59.26	4.94	0.00	0.00	2.47	2.47	845,000 (12,246)
Andhra Pradesh								
Agricultural labourers	3.03	54.13	22.84	5.10	2.49	11.05	1.36	1,403,100 (14,616)
Tamil Nadu								
Dalits	30.74	32.79	6.53	11.59	0.00	4.02	14.33	544,300 (7,888)
Adivasis	16.56	58.66	4.29	10.20	0.00	3.05	7.24	524,700 (7,390)

Sources: Rajasekhar et al. (2006); Rajasekhar, Manjula and Suchitra (2006); Rajasekhar, Suchitra and Manjula (2006); Rajasekhar, Reddy and Suchitra (2006) and Rajasekhar, Suchitra and Manjula (2008).

Note: Total expenditure in the last column includes the total amount spent by all the households on crises during the reference period. Figures in crises, and almost 30 per cent spent 100–200 per cent of the same. Comparatively, construction workers were better-off but even for them, the ratio was over 100 per cent for nearly 60 per cent of the households. The domestic workers' expenditure to income ratio was not as high as were the ratios for agricultural and construction workers.

A large contributor to the debilitating impact of borrowing from moneylenders during a crisis is high interest rates. On many occasions, these workers paid interest for years at a stretch, without managing to return any of the principal. The following is an analysis of the costs of borrowing incurred by these workers. Table 4.8 shows the proportion of households by interest paid to the amount borrowed. From Table 4.8, it is clear that costs incurred by the workers in the form of interest payments were substantial. Payment of more than 100 per cent of the amount borrowed merely by way of interest indicates a situation of absolute vulnerability.

The above analysis shows that there has been extreme dependence by the unorganised workers on informal forms of risk management, primarily borrowing at high rates of interest from moneylenders. Two phenomena remain concealed in this analysis in that it shows only how the households faced the crises through dependence on particular sources. However, unorganised workers also resorted to reducing household consumption (including for food and education) to meet these

Table 4.7 Distribution of workers (%) by proportion of expenditure to average monthly per capita income

Categories of workers	**<100 per cent**	**100–250 per cent**	**>250 per cent**
Agricultural	22.92	29.17	47.92
Construction	41.82	25.45	32.73
Domestic	72.27	22.73	5.00

Source: Rajasekhar et al. (2006).

Table 4.8 Distribution of households (%) by worker categories and proportion of interest amount paid to principal amount

Categories of workers	**<50 per cent**	**50–100 per cent**	**>100 per cent**
Agricultural	76.43	15.71	7.86
Construction	84.95	10.75	4.30
Domestic	75.00	10.71	14.29

Source: Rajasekhar et al. (2006).

needs (Rajasekhar et al., 2006: 70). There were also some households who had faced risks of varying degrees, but were unable to do anything about them, and therefore, simply carried on with life as though nothing had happened. For example, many health problems would go untreated by these households because they did not have the resources to address them. It is in this context that the dependence on borrowings is significant. While borrowing from moneylenders or others at high rates of interest may seem to be the most disabling form of coping with risks, even worse than this is the situation of households or persons who are unable even to borrow.

Two types of households do not depend heavily on borrowing. One type is well off enough that it depends on sources such as savings, or own resources. But the other type is poor and vulnerable households that cannot borrow from any sources because they are not creditworthy enough even for the moneylender. This applies also to dependence on sale or pledge of assets. Some households do not depend on these sources because they do not need to, but other households cannot depend on them since they are so vulnerable that they do not possess any assets.

In sum, unorganised worker households face crises relating to emergencies due to health, death and accidents, all of which arise on account of insufficient and unreliable access to social security benefits. There is high dependence by the unorganised workers on informal sources to manage their risks, primarily borrowing at high rates of interest from moneylenders. This exposes the unorganised worker households further to vulnerability and leads to greater impoverishment.

Our foray into micro evidence leads to the following conclusions: that insecurity is very common, that borrowing from informal sources at high interest rates is central to risk management, and that social networks are essential to the strategies and survival of poor and vulnerable households. How has the state addressed these problems?

4.8 Social security policies and programmes for unorganised sector workers

Since the 1970s, there have been a growing number of attempts by the government to direct programmes at the different risks faced by unorganised workers. However, unlike social security benefits for organised sector workers that take the form of entitlements and are partly budget-financed, those for unorganised sector workers have traditionally taken the form of ad hoc schemes that have not been animated by a notion of entitlements, let alone rights. It is only recently that a rights-based approach has begun making inroads into thinking about social security for unorganised workers.

Promotional social assistance programmes

In India, social assistance policies and programmes, implemented in bits and pieces since independence, aim to ensure that unorganised worker households have access to basic entitlements such as food and nutrition, housing, health and education. In addition, the government has implemented schemes to ensure creation of employment and income generation opportunities for unorganised workers. Thus, direct and indirect poverty alleviation programmes implemented in India since the late 1970s fall into this category. Beginning with the Integrated Rural Development Programme in 1980, a number of direct poverty alleviation programmes have been implemented for poor households.

These programmes have witnessed a shift in strategy and approach. Initially, subsidised credit was provided to each poor household to support asset development. This was followed by a shift towards employment generation and food-for-work, especially during drought years when landless agricultural labourers are under great stress. More recently, women from poor households have been organised into self-help groups, and subsidised credit is provided to the household through the women members of these groups. Currently, Swarna Jayanti Gram Swarozgar Yojna (SGSY) is the nationwide direct poverty alleviation programme, which covers all aspects of self-employment and assistance through credit-cum-subsidy programmes.

From among the plethora of programmes over the years, we focus on those dealing with employment and food security for closer scrutiny, because they illuminate a number of issues linked to viability, targeting and the shift to a rights-based approach.

Employment guarantees – the Right to Work

Nationwide wage employment programmes, under various names, have been implemented under different political regimes for the last three decades not only to provide wage employment, but also to improve the quality of productive assets in rural areas.[13] A more important recent development has been the enactment of the National Rural Employment Guarantee Act (NREGA), under which it is mandatory for the state to provide 100 days of employment per household to job seekers in rural areas. The enactment of the NREGA marks an important shift from employment as a benefit of an ad hoc scheme or as charity/welfare, to regarding employment as right. The NREGA is a key result of the right to work movement in the country. In view of the employment insecurity faced, especially by agricultural labourers in India, the NREGA, 2005, is both timely and significant. On February 2, 2006, the Act came into force in 200 of India's most backward districts. During 2007–8, the Act was extended to another 130 districts. From April 2008 onwards, the Act covers all of rural India.

The Act attempts to strengthen livelihood security for rural households by providing at least 100 days of guaranteed wage employment in each financial year to every household, whose adult members volunteer to do unskilled manual work. In addition, every applicant is entitled to a daily unemployment allowance when s/he is not provided employment within 15 days of receipt of her/his application seeking employment. This allowance will be at least one-fourth of the wage rate for the first 30 days during the financial year and at least half of the wage rate for the remaining period (GoI, 2005). This Act is a step forward in India's history of employment generation programmes because, for the first time, the state has formally taken on a legal responsibility to provide employment to those seeking it.

Notwithstanding its potential, the NREGA's working has faced challenges. Reviewing two years of experience of NREGA, Ambasta, Vijay Shankar and Shah (2008) have noted the following problems. First, the programme has been implemented by a bureaucracy that is poorly motivated, sometimes corrupt, and has its hands full with a host of other responsibilities. Added to that, there has been a serious shortage of staff at the lower levels where the programme has to be implemented.[14] Second, there have been delays in the execution of works and payment of wages. Third, there has been little effort at social mobilisation, and hence, of people's planning as had been envisaged. This has contributed to the poor quality of work undertaken. Fourth, the bureaucracy is not always willing to implement the strict provisions of NREGA and sometimes actively sabotages them. Fifth, the schedule of payment rates, applied to measure labour productivity and arrive at wages is inappropriate. Finally, there is very little by way of social audit of the programme by the citizens of a village or by a gram panchayat (elected village council).

In addition the report of the Comptroller and Auditor General (CAG) stated that the promise of 100 days of employment per household has not been met. Even the official figures show an all-India average of 33 days of work provided to 25.5 million households. Worse still, the number of people taking up the work has been lower than the job cards issued, raising the issue of corruption and collusion in the working of the muster rolls. Despite explicitly requiring that there should be no contractors allowed under the Act, the presence of contractors appears to be pervasive.

Despite these problems, the NREGA marks a watershed since it is the first major programme built on recognition of the right to work. Ambasta, Vijay Shankar and Shah (2008: 49) write that 'the NREGA ranks among the most powerful initiatives ever undertaken for transformation of rural livelihoods in India. The unprecedented commitment of financial resources is matched only by its imaginative architecture that promises a radically fresh programme of rural development'.

Food security – the Public Distribution System (PDS)

In addition to the attempt to provide incomes through work, the other major social security measure in India has been the PDS. Food security requires both physical access to food and economic access through purchasing power. Because of the pervasive problem of food insecurity in the country, and despite its long history as a programme with universal access, the PDS system has been generally viewed as an instrument to ensure physical access to food at reasonable prices for the poorest sections of the population. The PDS is thus complementary to other instruments such as employment generation and poverty alleviation programmes geared towards ensuring at least a minimum income, and thereby, the wherewithal to purchase food.

The PDS system evolved during the Second World War from the system of fair price shops intended to regulate speculative trading in foodgrains. This system further evolved into the system of statutory rationing in 1942. During the post-independence period, the Government of India used food policy to ensure price stability and food security for the emerging working class in the era of planned industrial development. The policy was regulated to ensure the availability of food in the urban and food-deficit areas of the country, which led to the measures being dubbed as having an 'urban bias' (Suryanarayana, 1995).

After the food and agricultural crisis of the mid-1960s, the green revolution introduced to promote agricultural growth had its own impact on the PDS system and led to considerable integration between food and agricultural policies. Although the production of foodgrains increased, this development was restricted to certain regions of the country and particular crops. This led to the widening of disparities in incomes and food production across different regions. Cereal prices rose exhibiting staircase-type movements owing to the procurement and buffer-stock policy of the government (ibid.). Prices and regional disparities in prices increased due to the need to ensure adequate stocks through procurement and minimum support prices for farmers. As a consequence of higher foodgrain prices, there was greater reliance on the PDS to achieve food security, especially in food-deficit regions.

However, the urban bias of the PDS and its inadequate coverage, especially in some of the poorer states, was a continuing source of concern. As a consequence, the Sixth Five-Year Plan (1980–5) emphasised the need to expand the reach of the programme towards its 'universalisation' across the country.[15] It aimed at achieving this by strengthening the infrastructure and extending the system to backward, remote and inaccessible areas and developing the system in rural areas to a greater extent than was previously envisaged. The Seventh Plan (1985–90) incorporated the PDS as part of the Minimum Needs Programme, to ensure equitable physical access to foodgrains in addition to price stability and control.

The system of financing the procurement of foodgrains has been oriented towards the producers as the government enhanced minimum support prices and procurement prices substantially over a period of years. As this was at least partially passed on through PDS prices, it led to a reduction in the price differentials between the PDS prices and the market prices of foodgrains. Consumers do not rely on the PDS unless the price differentials between the market and the PDS prices of foodgrains are large enough to compensate for considerations of quality and inconvenience; or if they cannot afford foodgrains under the free market system. The incentive to avail of the PDS reduces as a consequence of a convergence of prices. The increase in support and procurement prices also diminishes the incentive for farmers to reduce inefficiencies in agriculture. The impact of PDS on containing inflation has been offset by the monetisation of the budget deficit to meet food subsidies.

The growing challenge of rising food subsidies during times of fiscal stringency led to the transformation of the PDS from a universal to a targeted programme. Reforming the PDS system by targeting only the poor and excluding the non-poor was aimed at reducing the mounting cost of food subsidies and the budgetary deficit of the central government. The targeted PDS was introduced in 1997 as part of the economic reforms agenda of the Government of India. Under this system BPL and APL groups are subject to differential prices with subsidised foodgrains accessible only to the former. The population was bifurcated into these two groups based on the poverty lines estimated by the Planning Commission for the year 1993–4. The estimates of poverty corresponding to these norms were 37 per cent for rural and 32 per cent for urban India. Under the revised scheme, PDS offtake declined from 19.6 million tonnes in 1996–7 to an annual average of 17.5 million tonnes during 1997–2000. Price instability, as measured by the ratio of the wholesale price index for cereals to that of all commodities, increased by 17.4 per cent between 1997–8 and 1999–2000, and declined sharply by 13.3 per cent between 1999–2000 and 2001–2 (Suryanarayana, 2008).

The targeted version of the PDS has resulted in errors of omission of eligible poor households (Type I error in targeting) and excess coverage of ineligible non-poor households (Type II error) (ibid.). Swaminathan (2008) points out, based on evidence from the 61st Round of the National Sample Survey that 'targeting has led to high rates of exclusion of needy households from the ...system, and a clear deterioration of coverage in states like Kerala where the universal PDS was most effective'. The main concerns for the PDS are not only related to coverage, but also to the quality, availability and transaction costs that may act as a deterrent to its optimum utilisation.

The flaws of the targeted PDS have led to sharp and ongoing debate about the best solutions. Against the call to make the PDS a genuinely universal system, Suryanarayana and Silva (2007) argue that a multipronged and regionally varied approach to food security is what is needed. According to them, the revamp of the system should incorporate promotion of broad-based agricultural growth to boost domestic production through non-price instruments, ensuring physical access to food in rural areas of food-deficit regions where physical access is of great importance. In areas where both physical and economic access is needed, the focus should be on integrated poverty alleviation and food distribution programmes. In foodgrain-surplus states and urban areas, employment programmes supplemented by food stamps should be used in order to minimise both the procurement effort and reduce the food subsidy. Whether the political economy of the country will allow such variations in entitlements for something so basic as the right to food is however open to question. These issues have been made especially relevant by the near 20 per cent inflation in food prices during 2009–10, consequent on a combination of poor rainfall, policy-linked reduction in food stocks, and soaring prices of food in international markets as part of the fallout of the global financial crisis of 2008.

Protective social assistance programmes

In addition to promotive schemes for asset building, employment creation and food security, a number of protective social assistance schemes have been implemented for unorganised worker households living below the poverty line. These include old age pensions, maternity benefits, family benefit, disability pensions and widow pensions. While the first three are schemes sponsored by the central government, the last two are present in most of the states and are handled by state governments. The amount of old age pension, which was until recently Rs 75 per month, has gone up to Rs 200 per month since 2006–7. An amount of Rs 10,000 is provided as family benefit to households that lose the principal income-earning member in an accident or natural death. The amount of maternity benefit is Rs 500 per birth up to two live births. The widow pension is Rs 75 per month per beneficiary. The amounts of benefits are, thus, quite small and inadequate to address the problem of acute poverty and vulnerability faced by old people, widows, the disabled and those households that have lost their main income earner. Maternal benefits have been nominally increasing from time to time, but there is a real question about access, as we discuss later.

Figure 4.1 shows that the performance of social assistance schemes in the country, in terms of number of persons assisted varied during the period 1995–6 to 2005–6.[16] Old age pension has been the largest programme. The number of persons assisted, which was 2.93 million persons in 1995–6, increased to 7.32 millions in 1997–8, declined steeply in the late 1990s (due to resource constraints) and picked up from 2001–02.[17] In contrast, the number of persons assisted under family benefit and maternity scheme, 0.01 million and 0.60 million, respectively, in 1995–6, increased in the late 1990s and declined thereafter. While the number of beneficiaries under

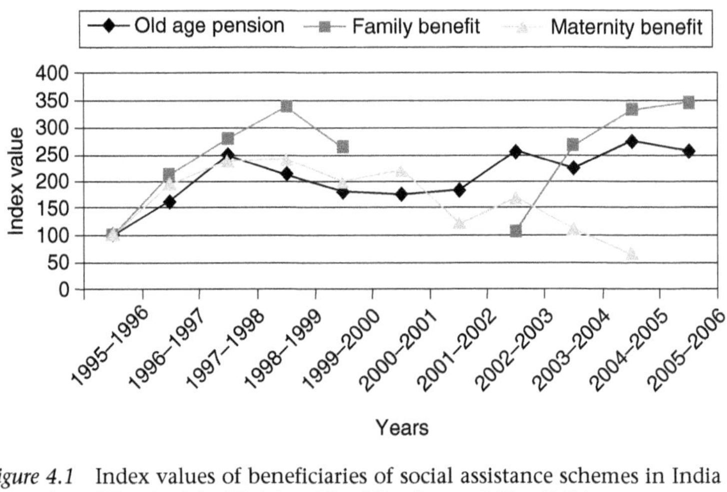

Figure 4.1 Index values of beneficiaries of social assistance schemes in India
Source: *Annual Reports* of the Ministry of Rural Development, New Delhi.
Note: The programme was started in 1995–96.

the family benefit scheme increased from 2002–3 to 2005–06, those under the maternity scheme declined but this is partly because new maternity schemes under different names came into existence.

What factors have influenced access to these social assistance schemes? Financial constraints compelling the State Governments to tighten the eligibility criteria resulted in restricting old age pensions to only the destitute among BPL households, and exclusion of a large number of unorganised workers living in vulnerable conditions. Poor access to old age pensions has been due to low awareness levels among potential beneficiaries about the schemes – eligibility conditions, whom to approach and how to approach – and difficult documentation requirements. These together with poor responsiveness from the concerned officials and high opportunity cost of wage labour income foregone by having to go around visiting various government offices often forces unorganised workers to depend on middlemen and thus spend considerable amounts in transactions costs. Access to maternity benefits has been adversely affected by the mandatory rule of institutional delivery. Institutional delivery to access meagre amounts of maternity benefits is costly for the poor as involves costs on account of travel, and staying away from home. There is also probably a gender dimension in that, given the nature of gender power relations; pregnant women may be unable to get permission or support from husbands or other family members for institutional delivery. The flagship National Rural Health Mission has in the second half of the 2000s begun however to make significant changes in this by giving long-overdue priority to reducing maternal mortality, and providing incentives and other programmatic inputs to promote institutional deliveries. Finally, poor bargaining power on account of limited membership in trade unions and peoples' organisations such as SHGs has adversely affected access to social assistance schemes.

In contrast to these programmes whose coverage has been quite limited, insurance programmes have entered in an important way, and we examine two of these here. Some of these insurance programmes have shown better results through innovative design, tapping into the synergies provided by SHGs and non-governmental involvement, and at least partially addressing the reasons for poor people's lack of interest. Social insurance is one such area.

Social insurance

In the year 2000, a 'group-based social insurance scheme', the Janashree Bhima Yojana (JBY), was introduced for persons in the age group of 18 to 60 years, belonging to BPL households.[18] Half of the annual premium of Rs 200 is subsidised by the Central Government. The insurance cover provided is up to Rs 20,000 in case of natural death, Rs 50,000 in case of accidental death or permanent disability, and Rs 25,000 in case of partial disability. An innovative feature of the scheme has been that two school-going children of insurers are provided with scholarships of Rs 100 each per month, to complete school education.

Two positive features of this programme are: it has led to improved coverage of unorganised workers (Table 4.9), and its popularity is attested to by an over 60 per cent renewal rate. As a group-based scheme, SHGs have been able to access the programme. While the motivation and follow-up work by NGOs contributed to improved coverage, peer pressure within the group has led to improved renewal rates. The associated scholarship scheme for school children has also been an important mover to sustain renewal rates. Claim ratios have been low because the SHGs assess the claims before submitting them to higher authorities.

Two lessons flow from this experience. First, social security schemes implemented through SHGs are likely to result in good outcomes in terms of improved coverage and lower incidence of adverse selection and moral hazard problems. This is because they build on the social networks that we have seen to be important to risk management among poor people. Second, social security products need to be innovative as in the case of JBY that sought to combine life/disability insurance with scholarships for school-going children. People living on the margins of survival often do not perceive the benefits of insurance – something for which they have to pay but from which they may never obtain anything tangible in return. The opportunity costs become too high, and poor people will often gamble with risks. However, the education scholarship provides something tangible that is linked to their children's future, and this makes the insurance seem more worthwhile.

The scheme could have had an even better coverage, if knowledge about it among potential beneficiaries were higher. Rajasekhar and Manjula (2005) found that less than five per cent of a sample of unorganised workers in Karnataka knew about JBY. Furthermore, by limiting the benefits only to BPL households, the scheme (like many other such programmes) ignores the reality that, while all BPL households are likely to be in the unorganised sector, the reverse is not necessarily true. The BPL criterion is a very minimalist and inappropriate approach to extend social security to unorganised workers (Rao, Rajasekhar and Suchitra, 2006). Finally, the poor are sceptical of contributing to a scheme wherein they realise that they will not get any returns unless the eventuality that they have taken the insurance for, occurs. Even

Table 4.9 Progress in the coverage of social insurance scheme in India

Years	Number of lives	Rate of renewal	Number of claims	Claim ratio	Amount (Rs in millions) claimed	Per capita benefit (Rs)
2000–01	215,637	0.00	186	0.09	3.5	18,817
2001–02	819,012	76.71	4,309	0.53	87.8	20,376
2002–03	1,158,239	63.67	9,685	0.84	196.2	20,258
2003–04	2,507,024	66.88	15,248	0.61	311.2	20,409
2004–05	3,539,654	68.60	16,902	0.48	349.7	20,690
2005–06	6,341,054	NA	NA	NA	NA	NA

Source: LIC (2006). Booklet on Social Security Group Insurance Schemes. Mumbai: Life Insurance Corporation of India – Pension and Group Scheme Department.

though the scholarships for children provide a tangible incentive, combining insurance with a savings scheme with a return would be likely to generate more enrolment. This clearly raises an important question about the attitude to risk and risk management among people who perceive their lives as being full of risks in any case, and who have their own approaches to risk management that include reliance on social capital and family networks rather than individualised (at the level of the individual household) risk mitigation.

Health insurance

Unorganised workers have until recently been expected to access health services from the public health-care delivery system. The early years of economic reforms in the country led to a serious increase in inequities in access to health services as evidenced by the National Sample Survey (Sen, Iyer and George, 2002). The cost of health care has emerged as a major barrier to access. Micro evidence cited earlier in this chapter also shows that health emergencies are among the top reasons for household impoverishment. Health financing by the government has been very low, and most health expenditures (rich and poor alike) are out of pocket (NCMH, 2005). After many years of neglect, government attention to health has increased recently with the rolling out of the ambitious National Rural Health Mission (NRHM), and a similar urban health programme is currently on the anvil.

Whether and how to shift from or combine a poorly funded public health system with other ways of improving access such as health insurance is hotly debated at present. A group-based programme, the Universal Health Insurance Scheme (UHIS), was launched by the Central Government in 2004. This was intended to mark a significant paradigm shift towards universal insurance coverage in the health policy of the country.[19] The government provides a subsidy of Rs 100 that remains fixed whether it is an individual who buys the insurance or a family of five or seven. The benefits provided are as follows. In case of hospitalisation, the scheme provides medical expenses up to Rs 30,000 per household. If an earning member falls sick, it compensates for loss of livelihood at the rate of Rs 50 per day up to a maximum of 15 days. In case of death of the earning head of the household due to personal accident, Rs 25,000 is to be given to the nominee. Unfortunately, while the scheme was initially open to all households, its coverage and subsidy later became restricted to only BPL households, thereby doing away with its intended universality. Partly this was a response to the fact that early evidence on coverage suggested that BPL insurers were only a small fraction of the total numbers.

The UHIS was expected to cover ten million individuals in its first year, but performance has been more modest (Bhat and Saha, 2004; Ahuja and De, 2004). Around 417,000 households or 1.16 million individuals were insured in 2004 in all states and union territories (Ahuja, 2004). Nearly 48 per cent of them were from rural areas. Around 50 per cent of the policies sold were accounted for by four states alone: Maharashtra, Andhra Pradesh, Tamil Nadu and Gujarat. Only 11,408 persons belonged to the BPL category, which is roughly one per cent of the total persons covered. This suggests that it was mostly non-BPL people who had been buying the policy, in spite of the subsidy being offered to the BPL households.

In 2004–5, therefore, the government revised the UHIS to provide a higher subsidy to BPL households, and made this subsidy variable depending on the household size of the insured. While the benefits provided under the scheme were not altered, the uniform subsidy of Rs 100 formerly available to all three categories of members – individual, family of five and family of seven – was increased to Rs 200, Rs 300 and Rs 400, respectively. Accordingly, the effective premium (net of subsidy) paid by the BPL household was reduced to Rs 165, Rs 248 and Rs 330, respectively (GoI, 2004). Limiting the programme to BPL insurers was, however, an unnecessary restriction of the insurance pool, reducing potential cross-subsidies, and increasing the potential subsidy burden on the government.

Health care access for the vulnerable provides a plural picture, combining strengthening of public services, experimentation with community health workers and induction of private health providers under the NRHM and targeted health insurance. After years of drought, a hundred flowers appear to be blooming in the health sector; how long this will last remains to be seen.

4.9 The National Commission for Enterprises in the Unorganised Sector (NCEUS)

In 2004, in order to systematise the patchwork of ad hoc schemes, the NCEUS was set up to investigate the conditions of unorganised sector workers. NCEUS has made a number of recommendations and suggested legislations to expand the coverage of social security among unorganised workers and to improve the working conditions of the unorganised workers. Two separate reports have been brought out in this regard. The first one was on 'Social Security for Unorganised Workers' and the second on 'Conditions of Work and Promotion of Livelihoods in the Unorganised Sector'.

The Commission is of the view that social security problems of unorganised workers are of two types. The first one 'arises out of deficiency or capability deprivation in terms of inadequate employment, low earnings, low health and educational status, and so on. The second one arises out of adversity in the sense of absence of adequate fallback mechanisms (safety nets) to meet such contingencies as ill health, accident, death and old age' (NCEUS, 2006: 98). While the former can be called as a promotional social security, the latter can be termed as a protective social security. The commission focuses 'on protective social security for workers in the informal economy though the complementarities of promotional social security that should form a part of an overall and integrated social policy' (ibid.).

According to NCEUS, the social security framework in India operates at three levels. The universal programmes and schemes for basic social/human development such as the mission for literacy, schooling, health care services, drinking water and sanitation, technical training, et cetera that should be viewed as foundational to any sound social and economic development policy. These programmes address the issue of creation and enhancement of human capabilities through creating entitlements to all citizens funded by the public exchequer. The effectiveness and advancement of these functions of the state are often a prerequisite for the effectiveness of specific protective social security policies and schemes such as the one proposed here.

The social/human development schemes are intended to provide a measure of socio-economic security to the poorer citizens, irrespective of their status as working or non-working poor. The underlying idea here is to meet both promotional and protective needs. Over time, a number of programmes have come to stay in the country like Integrated Child Development Services (ICDS), PDS, mid-day meal programme, NREGS, et cetera.

The third level should, according to the commission, constitute a social security system for unorganised/informal workers. This should address both deficiency and adversity. The social security concerns arising out of deficiency relate to access to credit/finance (especially, for the self-employed), loans for upgrading skills, loans for housing, children's education, et cetera. Adversity refers to contingencies such as absence of social security cover for ill health, accidents/death and old age.

NCEUS (2006) restricted its recommendations only to protective social security and proposed to cover hospitalisation, maternity, life insurance and old age security. The commission also proposed defined contributions as premiums for insurance to cover (a) hospitalisation, (b) maternity, life insurance and (c) old age security. The State Social Security Boards are expected to negotiate with the insurance provider regarding nature and extent of benefits, taking into account the state-specific contexts, in order to ensure the best possible cover to the registered worker. The commission also suggested legislation providing minimum social security covering life insurance, health insurance and pensions for all the unorgansied workers in the country.

NCEUS's mandate also included doing the preparatory work for appropriate legislation, and this has now become a subject for fierce debate. The commission prepared the Unorganised Sector Workers' Social Security Bill, 2007, proposing contributory life insurance, old age pensions and health insurance for all unorganised sector workers. The bill faced stiff resistance from state governments because the employers' contributions have to be borne by them in case the employer cannot be identified. Since it is difficult to identify the employer for large numbers of the unorganised workers, there was considerable resistance to the enactment of social security legislation for all unorganised workers. As a result, the revised bill proposed social security schemes only for unorganised workers falling below the poverty line.

A watered down version of the original bill was passed in December 2008.[20] Although the passage of the bill by Parliament means that unorganised workers in the country will obtain entitlements in these areas for the first time, the devil as usual is in the details. The mandated mechanisms for implementation have been criticised already as being too weak and subject to discretion. What actually happens and how long it will take for the envisioned central social security authority to be set up and become functional, and how it will function will determine whether the Act remains a paper promise or not.

4.10 Ways forward

While organised workers have benefited from legally mandated and budget-provided social security during the post-independence period, those in the unorganised sector have been largely excluded. It is often stated that all the social security schemes (those initiated by the government and non-government agencies) do not cover even ten per cent of the total number of unorganised workers. Our review of recent approaches and programmes points to the gaps and weaknesses, as well as the potential and promise of new directions.

It is clear that the main problem is not with social security for organised workers but for those who are unorganised. In an earlier section of the chapter, we had identified five key challenges – the large scale of the problem, and therefore, its financing implications, its multidimensionality in terms of different types of deprivation and intersecting social inequalities, a combination of design flaws and weak implementation, the need to shift from trickle-down to rights-based approaches, and weak and unreliable political support for these rights. Our review of key programmes puts meat on the bones of these challenges.

Scale and financing

Expenditure on social security at the central level and across the states has been grossly inadequate over the years. According to the World Labour Report (2000), public sector expenditure on social security in India was 1.8 per cent of the GDP, whereas it was 4.7 per cent in Sri Lanka and 3.6 per cent in China. For the purpose of this comparison, social security expenditure covers pensions, health care, employment, injury, sickness, family, housing and social assistance funds.[21] This is true across the states as well. For example, the state of Karnataka spends only 1.52 per cent (amounting to Rs 3570 million) of its total expenditure on social security measures for the unorganised sector. Tamil Nadu, which is believed to have better functioning social security programmes, spends 2.64 per cent of its total expenditure on social security (CMIE, 2002). Clearly, a significant injection of funds is essential.

However, K.C. Pant, former deputy chairman of the Planning Commission of India noted as far back as 1999 that 'just extending the formal sector schemes to the informal sector would be too simplistic.

One point is often made that if we do so the amount to be redistributed from the income of formal sector employees to those belonging to the informal sector would be enormous and would have implications for further taxation of a very high order. This highlights the imperative need to find new alternatives to ensure social security in the informal sector rather than simply attempting to expand the scope of formal sector schemes'.[22] There are strong instrumental reasons for spending on programmes meant to improve capabilities and productivity of the present and future workforce, such as for education, health, or raising women's productivity through reducing the drudgery of the double burden. Nor can this be avoided given the 60 overhang of low public spending in these areas, which now can clearly act as a brake on the country's growth and development potential. Protective programmes will have to be increasingly funded through a mix of fiscal subventions and insurance. It is in the latter area that there are many lessons to be learned from the experience of other countries as well as the country's own fledgling experiments with group insurance.

An important point to be emphasised in the context of financing is the extent to which, as pointed out earlier in the chapter, poor and vulnerable people have returned to dependence on moneylenders to meet their needs in a crisis. Government policies in this regard appear to be running counter to the needs of the vulnerable. India's policies towards credit and the role of the moneylender have gone through significant ups and downs since the 1970s. The combination of bank nationalisation and emphasis on 'priority sector lending' during the 1970s and 1980s led to a significant erosion of the role of moneylenders and landlords as evidenced by the decline in their share of rural lending from over 75 per cent on average during 1951–61 to less than 25 per cent in 1991 (Shah et al., 2007).[23] Already by the late 1980s, there were a number of questions being raised about the 'efficiency' of priority sector lending. With the economic reforms of the 1990s, banks were largely freed of this requirement in their loan portfolio. Consequently, usurious rural moneylenders have once again become a major source of credit to the poor, while microfinance, although much touted, barely accounts for 5 per cent of rural credit (ibid.). Furthermore, as argued by Shah (2007a), there is an ongoing ideological shift towards accepting moneylenders as a fact of life by incentivising them to behave better.[24]

Multidimensionality

Evidence, both from macro level surveys, such as the National Sample Survey, and various micro level investigations highlights two types of multidimensionality at work – multiple deprivations, and intersecting social relations of power. The majority of unorganised workers also fall within the poor and/vulnerable categories of the NCEUS. Hence, they also suffer from multiple deprivations, which interact with and compound each other. Policy response to this has been through fragmented programmes that work in silos. The NCEUS attempted to address this challenge through its version of the bill for unorganised workers by proposing a unified approach at least to protective social security. It is not clear as yet to what extent this has been watered down by the Act; however, an integrated approach needs to be restored if it has. Speaking before Parliament during the passage of the Act, the then labour minister acknowledged that speed of passage meant there could be some 'shortcomings', which could be corrected in future (InfochangeIndia, 2008).

The second type of multidimensionality derives from the intersections of different identities of oppression and deprivation – economic class, caste and gender being the critical ones in India. Again, there is considerable data to show how significant this is. Those who are poorest are often also dalits and the women among them suffer the most. Social security in the country has had little to do directly with addressing caste, yet it is clear that the need is greatest at the bottom of the caste pyramid.

Where gender is concerned, there is little beyond the patchwork of maternity benefits, and as good as nothing when it comes to dealing with the drudgery imposed by women's multiple burdens of work. One positive aspect of the shift towards programmes located outside the workplace is that women and their needs and potential have come to be better recognised. Despite the often overly instrumental approach to SHGs, they do have considerable potential not only in areas such as saving, but also for such programmes as group insurance, as we have seen.

Design and implementation

As noted earlier in the chapter, because of the multiplicity of schemes and programmes at central and state government levels, the social security system in India has lacked a consistent policy (Prabhu and Iyer, 2001). Schemes have been framed in an ad hoc manner at various points in time in response to the expedience of the day and not conforming to any overall design. These schemes do not represent an overall policy or plan. Piecemeal implementation of promotional and protective social security measures has meant that synergies between the two sets of measures have not been reaped.[25] Since there is no convergence when different departments implement different schemes, the coverage of unorganised workers under various schemes has been minuscule.

Absence of overall cohesion in design and management has also proved to be counterproductive in economic terms (Prabhu and Iyer, 2001). The administrative costs of implementing them are very high relative to the paltry benefits accruing from them, and the negligible impact they have on the target population (Dreze and Sen, 1991). The state welfare boards, which have been administering the social security schemes, have disproportionately high administrative costs. Given the bureaucratic administrative machinery, there are several demands and compulsions of administrative procedures that have to be met, all of which cause delays and keep raising the cost of administering the schemes.

Design and implementation flaws have bedevilled both promotional and protective social security programmes for unorganised sector workers. Radhakrishna (2001) points out the flaws in the PDS. Rajasekhar and Manjula (2005) note that the employment potential of Sampoorna Grameena Rozgar Yojana (SGRY) was low because of the faulty design allowing expenditure on capital-intensive works. The authors conclude that design changes requiring a certain proportion of expenditure to be spent on labour-intensive project works could simultaneously improve the natural resources in villages and increase the amount of employment created. Rajasekhar and Satapathy (2007) point out design flaws, which contributed to low spending on the self-employment generation programmes of SGSY. In related studies, Gayatri (2001), Alam and Antony (2001), Thorat (2001) and Dayal and Karan (2001) point out the flaws in the design and management of schemes for vulnerable groups of women, older people and SCs and STs, and call for a reworking of the policies.[26]

Recent trends afford some hope for improvement. Most important in reducing fragmentation will be the consolidation of programmes under the new Act. However, at present, not all schemes are covered under the Act, and how effectively the Act will function remains to be seen. At the level of design, the experience with group-based social insurance has already yielded positive results. This shows that improvements can be made if certain realities are borne in mind, namely, the need to address poor people's ambivalence towards formal insurance, and the importance of groups and social networks, and the fact that women are central to such networks, and also carry excessive burdens already.

Rights-based approaches

Both in Latin America and in India, rights-based approaches are now seen as showing the way forward to ensure full citizenship and agency for all, to improving accountability, and to providing monitoring mechanisms to correct design flaws and implementation errors. Furthermore when such approaches build on grass-roots social movements as in India and in some countries of Latin America, their positive potential is multiplied through the mobilisation and energy of those at the bottom of the social and economic pyramid.

The challenge is that in the period since economic reforms in India, inequality in wealth, incomes and consumption between the so-called middle class and those below them has increased sharply. While growth is rapid, and their incomes are growing rapidly, this class is happy to have all of India 'shining'. However, this has largely been on the basis of a sense of benevolence and charity, not a sense of equality or solidarity. Charity is unfortunately a weak basis for the kind of sustained effort the country needs to overturn the weak approaches to social security of the last 60 years. A sense of solidarity is a much stronger basis for acknowledgement of the rights of others. But, with the downturn in the globalised economy, will even a sense of charity remain? The answer to this question will profoundly shape not just the future of unorganised workers and the poor and vulnerable, but also the viability of the growth and development process in the country.

Notes

1. In this chapter we use the terms social protection and social security interchangeably because both terms have been used to mean much the same thing in India.
2. For a more detailed discussion of solidarity, see Sen (2008).
3. For more on Foucault's concept of governmentality, see Foucault (1991) and Lemke (2000).
4. Even within the same sector or occupation or industrial classification, organised and unorganised workers, and formal and informal subsectors can be found. For instance, in the food industry, while many hotels and restaurants fall under the formal sector, a great many also come under the informal sector but have organised workers, and all the roadside vendors and eateries are both informal and have only unorganised workers.
5. In the official records of the National Commission on Labour, the unorganised sector in India is simply defined as the residual of the organised sector (GoI, 2002). However, due to the problems of underestimation and insufficient coverage, it is difficult to arrive at this residual estimate.
6. The Act does not automatically become applicable to government employees and those employed in factories and establishments that employ less than 20 workers; but employers and employees can opt for it if they choose.
7. The Royal Commission discussed the possibility of introducing health insurance on labour way back in 1929. The Act incorporated the health insurance scheme for workers developed by B.P. Adarkar with technical assistance provided by the ILO.

8. Individual-level factors (disease and old age) determine the risk exposure of a person regardless of the household or community to which the person belongs. Household level risk factors (high dependency ratios, low social standing, limited access to means of production and low or uncertain returns to labour) relate to the household structure and composition, and to its socio-economic characteristics. Community risk factors are primarily determined by ecological and infrastructural conditions, such as soil degradation, difficult access to basic social services, et cetera. National risk factors relate to laws, policies, geographical and political conditions. They affect the whole population, but tend to place higher burdens on the poor.
9. Holzmann and Jorgensen categorise such prior preparation into two types of risk management strategies – prevention and mitigation, as against a complete lack of preparation in which case the households are forced to cope (coping strategy) with the risk as best as they can.
10. For instance, a less vulnerable household may not perceive a routine wedding as a crisis really. But, a 'highly vulnerable' household may see the same as a crisis, because such an event is likely to render them even more vulnerable.
11. The methodology of identifying the workers was to arrive at the list of workers in the localities known to have these categories of workers and select them randomly.
12. This is calculated by dividing total monthly income by number of persons in the household.
13. One of the political games is that each time a new political party comes to power, it will close previous programmes and/or change their names so that it can take populist credit for them.
14. CAG report also notes 'the main deficiency was the lack of adequate administrative and technical manpower at the Block and GP [Gram Panchayat] levels, especially the programme officer, technical assistants, and employment guarantee assistants. The lack of manpower adversely affected the preparation of plans, scrutiny, approval, monitoring and measurement of works, and maintenance of the stipulated records at the block and GP level. Besides affecting the implementation of the scheme and the provision of employment, this also impacted adversely on transparency, and made it difficult to verify the provision of the legal guarantee of 100 days of employment on demand' (CAG Report, 2008).
15. The term 'universalisation' has been used in this literature to mean both expanding the reach of the PDS to unserved regions and groups, as well as in the sense of universal versus targeted.
16. These data were obtained from various annual reports of the Ministry of Rural Development, New Delhi. It may be noted that the programme was started in 1995–6, and hence, we have provided information from that year.
17. Chapter 3.2 on 'Poverty Alleviation in Rural India: Strategy and Programmes' in Planning Commission, 10th Five Year Plan, 2002–07, http://planningcommission/plans/planrel/fiveyr/10th/volume2/v2_ch3_2.pdf.
18. This is implemented through the Life Insurance Corporation of India. In the Annual Budget of 2008–9, Rs 500 crores of additional allocation was made for the scheme.

19. The scheme followed a three-tier option of premium payment; Re1 per day per year for an individual, Rs 1.50 per day per year for a family of up to five members, and Rs 2 per day per year for a family of up to seven members.
20. There is considerable dissatisfaction with the end product among those who had been advocating for the Act. The feeling is that the government really did not want to pass the bill, but did so after considerably weakening it because of election year compulsions.
21. Some caution is needed in using these comparisons as it is unclear to us whether the coverage in terms of central versus state or provincial government expenditures have been treated uniformly in all countries. There may also be other comparability issues.
22. Inaugural address by K.C. Pant, former Deputy Chairman, Planning Commission, to an International Conference on 'Social Security Policy: Challenges before India and South Asia', 1 November 1999.
23. To the poor, small producers and others who until then had largely been excluded by formal credit mechanisms.
24. Shah (2007a) critiques a recent report by a technical group of the Reserve Bank of India that recommends this, as 'the crowning of the moneylender'.
25. In terms of making promotional social security benefits available to those obtaining protective social security benefits, and vice versa.
26. There are also problems on the demand side, which have been documented, particularly in areas such as education, health and housing. For instance, see De, Noronha and Samson (2001) for demand-side problems in accessing basic education. Kundu (2001) highlights similar problems in accessing health and housing benefits. These services are addressed in the paper by Shah, Rao and Vijay Shankar (2008).

References

Ahuja, Rajeev and Indranil De (2004): 'Health Insurance for the Poor: Need to Strengthen Healthcare Provision', *Economic and Political Weekly*, Vol. 39, No. 41 (October 9): 4491–3.

Ahuja, Rajeev (2004): 'Health Insurance for the Poor', *Economic and Political Weekly*, Vol. 39, No. 28 (July 10): 3171–8.

Alam, Moneer and Piush Antony (2001): 'Social Security for the Aged', in S. Mahendra Dev, Piush Antony and V. Gayathri (eds) *Social and Economic Security in India*, New Delhi: Institute for Human Development.

Ambasta, Pramathesh, P. S. Vijay Shankar and Mihir Shah (2008): 'Two Years of NREGA: The Road Ahead', *Economic and Political Weekly*, Vol. 43, No. 8: 41–50.

Barrientos, Armando, Jasmine Gideon and Maxine Molyneux (2008): 'New Developments in Latin America's Social Policy', *Development and Change*, Vol. 39, No. 5: (September): 759–74.

Bhat, Ramesh and Somen Saha (2004): 'Health Insurance: Not a Panacea', *Economic and Political Weekly*, Vol. 39, No. 33(August 14): 3667–70.

Bradshaw, Sarah with Ana Quiros Viquez (2008): 'Women Beneficiaries or Women Bearing the Cost? A Gendered Analysis of the *Red de Proteccion Social* in Nicaragua', *Development and Change*, Vol. 39, No. 5 (September): 823–44.

CAG Report (2008): 'Performance Audit of the National Rural Employment Guarantee Act', Report No XXXXII of 2008' (March 2008).
CMIE (2002): Public Finance, Economic Intelligence Service, Mumbai: Centre for Monitoring Indian Economy.
Dayal Harishwar and Anup K. Karan (2001): 'Social and Economic Security for the Scheduled Tribes', in S. Mahendra Dev, Piush Antony and V. Gayathri (eds) *Social and Economic Security in India*, New Delhi: Institute for Human Development.
De, Anuradha, Claire Noronha and Meera Samson (2001): 'Education Security for Children: Some Insights from the PROBE Survey', in Mahendra Dev, Piush Antony and V. Gayathri (eds) *Social and Economic Security in India*, New Delhi: Institute for Human Development.
Devereux, S. and R. Sabates-Wheeler (2007): 'Editorial Introduction: Debating Social Protection', in *IDS Bulletin* (Debating Social Protection), Vol. 38, No. 3, pp. 1–7.
Dreze, J. and A. Sen (1991): 'Public Action for Social Security: Foundations and Strategy', in Ahmad, Ehtisham, Jean Dreze, John Hills and Amartya Sen (ed.) *Social Security in Developing Countries*, Oxford, UK: Oxford University Press.
Foucault, Michel (1991): 'Governmentality', in Graham Burchell, Colin Gordon and Peter Miller (eds) *The Foucault Effect: Studies in Governmentality*, Hemel Hempstead: Harvester Wheatsheaf, pp. 87–104.
Gayatri, V. (2001): 'Security for Women Workers', in S. Mahendra Dev, Piush Antony and V. Gayathri (eds) *Social and Economic Security in India*, New Delhi: Institute for Human Development.
GoI (2002): *Report of the National Commission on Labour*, New Delhi: Government of India.
GoI (2004): Speech of the finance minister, P Chidambaram, delivered on July 8, Ministry of Finance, Government of India, Delhi.
GoI (2005): *National Rural Employment Guarantee Bill*, 2005. New Delhi: Government of India. www.nac.nic.in.
Guhan, S. (1992): 'Social Security in India: Looking One Step Ahead', in Barbara Hariss, S. Guhan and R. H. Cassen (ed.) *Poverty in India: Research and Policy*, Bombay: Oxford University Press.
Guhan, S. (1994): 'Social Security Options for Developing Countries', *International Labour Review*, Vol. 133, No. 1: 35–53.
Holzmann, R. and S. Jorgensen (2003): 'Social Risk Management: A New Conceptual Framework for Social Protection and Beyond', *Social Protection Discussion Paper*.
ILO (2000): *India: Social Protection for the Unorganised Sector*. Geneva: International Labour Office.
Infochange India (2008): 'Unorganised Workers' Social Security Bill Scrapes through Parliament', http://infochangeindia.org/200812197544/Livelihoods/News/Unorganised-Workers%E2%80%99-Social-Security-Bill-scrapes-through-Parliament.html.
Krishna, A. (2003): 'Falling into Poverty: Other Side of Poverty Reduction', *Economic and Political Weekly*, Vol. 38, No. 6 (February 8): 533–42.
Krishna, A. (2004): 'Escaping Poverty and Becoming Poor: Who Gains, Who Loses, and Why?' *World Development*, Vol. 32, No. 1: 121–36.
Krishna, A., M. Kapila, M. Porwal and V. Singh (2005): 'Why Growth is not Enough: Household Poverty Dynamics in Northeast Gujarat, India'. *Journal of Development Studies*, Vol. 41, No. 7: 1163–92.

Krishna, A., P. Kristjanson, M. Radeny and W. Nindo (2004): 'Escaping Poverty and Becoming Poor in 20 Kenyan Villages' *Journal of Human Development*, Vol. 5, No. 2: 211–26.

Kundu, Amitabh (2001): 'Access of Urban Poor to Housing Amenities: Aspects Concerning Social Security', in S. Mahendra Dev, Piush Antony and V. Gayathri (eds) *Social and Economic Security in India*, New Delhi: Institute for Human Development.

Lemke, T. (2000): 'Foucault, Governmentality and Critique'. Paper presented at the *Rethinking Marxism Conference*, University of Amherst, MA. September: pp. 21–24.

LIC (2006). Booklet on Social Security Group Insurance Schemes. Mumbai: Life Insurance Corporation of India – Pension and Group Scheme Department.

Molyneux, M. (2006): 'Mothers at the service of the new poverty agenda: Progresa/ Oportunidades, Mexico's Conditional Transfer Programme', in Shahra Razavi and Shirin Hassim (ed) *Gender and Social Policy in a Global Context*, Basingstoke: Palgrave Macmillan, pp 43–67.

NCMH (2005): *Financing and Delivery of Health Care Services in India*, NCMH Background Papers, New Delhi: Ministry of Health and Family Welfare.

NCEUS (2006): *Report on the Unorganised Sector*, New Delhi: National Commission for Enterprises in the Unorganised Sector.

NCEUS (2007): *Report on Conditions of Work and Promotion of Livelihoods in the Unorganised Sector*. New Delhi: Academic Foundation.

Planning Commission (2006). *Report of the Working Group on Social Security*, New Delhi: Planning Commission, Government of India.

Planning Commission, 10th Five Year Plan, 2002–07, http://planningcommission/plans/planrel/fiveyr/10th/volume2/v2_ch3_2.pdf.

Prabhu, K.S. (2001): 'Socio-economic Security in the Context of Pervasive Poverty: A Case Study of India', *The Indian Journal of Labour Economics*, Vol. 44, No. 4: 518–58.

Prabhu, K.S. and S.V. Iyer (2001): 'Public Provision of Social Security: The Challenge in South Asia', *South Asia Economic Journal*, Vol. 2, No. 1.

Radhakrishna, R. (2001): 'Food Security: Emerging Concerns', in S. Mahendra Dev, Piyush Anthony and V. Gayathri (eds) *Social and Economic Security in India*, New Delhi: Institute for Human Development.

Rajasekhar, D. and G. Sreedhar (2002): 'Changing Face of Beedi Industry in Karnataka', *Economic and Political Weekly*, Vol. 37, No. 39 (September 28): 4023–8.

Rajasekhar, D., N.L. Narasimha Reddy and J.Y. Suchitra (2006): *Effectiveness of Micro-Finance Programmes in Reducing Vulnerability to Debt Bondage*, ISEC Research Report, Bangalore: Institute for Social and Economic Change (www.bondedlabour.org).

Rajasekhar, D. and R. Manjula (2005): *Performance of SGSY in Karnataka*. Bangalore: Institute for Social and Economic Change (mimeo).

Rajasekhar, D., R. Manjula and J. Y. Suchitra (2006). *Social Security Needs and Willingness to Contribute to Social Security: Garment Workers in Karnataka*, GTZ (mimeo).

Rajasekhar, D. and Sachidananda Satapathy (2007): 'An Assessment of a Major Anti-Poverty Programme (SGSY) for Women in India', *Indian Development Review*, Vol. 4, No. 2.

Rajasekhar, D., J.Y. Suchitra and R. Manjula (2007): 'Women Workers in Urban Informal Employment: the Status of Agarbathi and Garment Workers in Karnataka', *Indian Journal of Labour Economics*.

Rajasekhar, D., J.Y. Suchitra and R. Manjula (2008): *Assessing the Micro-Finance Needs of Vulnerable Groups*, Bangalore: Institute for Social and Economic Change (mimeo).

Rajasekhar, D., J.Y. Suchitra, S. Madheswaran and G. K. Karanth (2006): *Design and Management of Social Security Benefits for the Unorganised Sector Workers in Karnataka*. New Delhi: GTZ.

Rajasekhar, D., J.Y. Suchitra and R. Manjula (2006): *Social Security Needs and Willingness to Contribute to Social Security: Agarbathi Workers in Karnataka*. GTZ (mimeo).

Rao, V.M., D. Rajasekhar and J.Y. Suchitra (2006): 'The Unorganised Worker: Deprivations, Social Security and Policy Implications', *Economic and Political Weekly*, Vol. 41, No. 19 (August 12): 1913–19.

Ray, Debraj (1998): *Development Economics*, New Delhi: Oxford University Press.

Sen, G. (1997): 'Empowerment as an Approach to Poverty', *Human Development Papers 1997 – Poverty and Human Development*, New York: UNDP.

Sen, G. (2008): 'The Role of Solidarity in Institutions of Governance' in B. Hettne (ed) *Human Values and Global Governance, Studies in Development, Security and Culture, vol. 2*. New York: Palgrave Macmillan, pp. 177–87.

Sen, G., A. Iyer and A. George (2002): 'Structural Reforms and Health Equity: A Comparison of NSS Surveys of 1986–87 and 1995–96', *Economic and Political Weekly*, Vol. 37, No. 14 (April 6): 1342–52.

Shah, M. (2007a): 'The Crowning of the Moneylender', *The Hindu*, September 1.

Shah, M., R. Rao and P. S. Vijay Shankar (2007): 'Rural Credit in 20th Century India: Overview of History and Perspectives', *Economic and Political Weekly*, Vol. 42, No. 8 (April 14): 1351–64.

Suryanarayana, M. H. (2008): 'Agflation and the Public Distribution System', *Economic and Political Weekly*, Vol. 43, No. 18: 13–17.

Suryanarayana, M. H. and Dimitri Silva (2007): 'Is Targeting the Poor a Penalty on the Food Insecure? Poverty and Food Insecurity in India', *Journal of Human Development*, Vol. 8, No. 1: 89–106.

Suryanarayana, M. H. (1995): 'PDS: Beyond Implicit Subsidy and Urban Bias – the Indian Experience', *Food Policy*, Vol. 20, No. 4: 259–78.

Swaminathan, M. (2008): 'Public Distribution System and Social Exclusion', *The Hindu*, May 7.

Thorat, Sukhadeo (2001): 'Social Security for Scheduled Castes in the Unorganised Sector', in S. Mahendra Dev, Piyush Anthony and V. Gayathri (eds) *Social and Economic Security in India*, New Delhi: Institute for Human Development.

UNECLAC (2006): *Shaping the Future of Social Protection: Access, Financing and Solidarity – Summary*, Report prepared for the 31st session of the Economic Commission for Latin

American and the Caribbean, Montevideo, 20–24, March. Distr.: General. LC/G.2295(SES.31/4).

World Labour Report (2000): Income Security and Social Protection in a Changing World, Geneva: ILO.

5
Rethinking Reforms: A New Vision for the Social Sector in India*

P. S. Vijay Shankar and Mihir Shah

5.1 Introduction – Growth without human development

India today presents a striking contrast of development and deprivation. Nearly two decades after the unleashing of economic reforms, there is no doubt that GDP growth has accelerated. The rate of GDP growth has consistently been above five per cent during the last two decades (Nagaraj, in this volume). India is the 12th largest economy in the world in terms of GDP and is also one of the fastest growing economies in the world today (World Bank, 2008). In terms of indicators of quality of life as well, India has had some successes. Life expectancy at birth has nearly doubled from around 36 years in 1951 to about 65 years in 2001 (NHP, 2002). The infant mortality rate, which stood at 146 in 1951, has come down to 58 according to the recent estimate (SRS, 2006). Under-five child mortality rate has declined to 17.8 from 57.3 at the time of independence. Similar improvements are also found in literacy levels and school enrolment ratios.

Impressive as these achievements are, they pale into insignificance when confronted with the fact that access to basic services like health, education, drinking water and sanitation has been denied to large sections of the population. After six decades of planned development, 80 per cent of Indians still earn less than US$2 a day. The number of officially poor has doubled over this period (World Bank, 2004). Nearly 77 per cent of India's population, 836 million people, have a per capita consumption expenditure of less than or equal to Rs 20 per day (roughly US$2 in PPP terms) (NCEUS, 2007). The latest National Family Health Survey-3 (2005–6) provides data on the shocking levels of nutritional deprivation prevailing in the country. Over the last seven years (since the previous NFHS-2 survey of 1998–9), the proportion of anaemic children under-three has gone up from 74 per cent to 79 per cent. Nearly half of India's children under three years continue to remain underweight and this proportion has declined only marginally from 52 per cent in 1992–3 to 46 per cent in 2005–6. We must remember that these 13 years almost completely overlap with the 'reform phase' in the Indian economy. Full immunisation coverage in rural areas is still alarmingly low, at 40 per cent. India has the highest percentage (87 per cent) of pregnant anaemic women in the world (World Bank, 2007). Even if India manages to attain the Millennium Development Goals (MDGs) for health by 2015, it is estimated that 500 million people will still lack access to sanitation and 334 million to safe drinking water (WaterAid, 2006).

5.2 Inter-regional disparities

There are sharp inter-regional variations within India. While there are some areas where substantial improvements have taken place, backwardness is concentrated in a few pockets. While the indicators of the levels of living in some southern states like Kerala and Tamil Nadu are comparable to many developed countries, those in large, densely populated, northern states like Uttar Pradesh (UP), Rajasthan, Orissa and Madhya Pradesh (MP) are closer to that of the poorest parts of the world, such as sub-Saharan Africa (Figure 5.1).

Disparities in human development: Towards an explanation

India's poor performance in this respect comes out more starkly when compared with that of other countries, with comparable per capita income levels. Analysing the comparative performance of countries in terms of human development, Dreze and Sen (2002) classify them into 'growth-led' and 'support-led' experiences. It would be wrong to understand this distinction to mean that in the former set of countries, the state did not play an important role. For even there, state support played a very active role in creating and directing markets and fostering an incentive structure conducive for growth. The state also fostered human development, which laid a strong basis for long-term growth. The real difference is that 'support-led' countries were able to achieve remarkable successes in human development, even while their macro-rates of growth remained modest. It has been suggested that in societies with a more equitable distribution of control over assets and income, political power will be more equally distributed. Such societies tend to foster institutions that promote participatory and inclusive growth, and ensure access of public

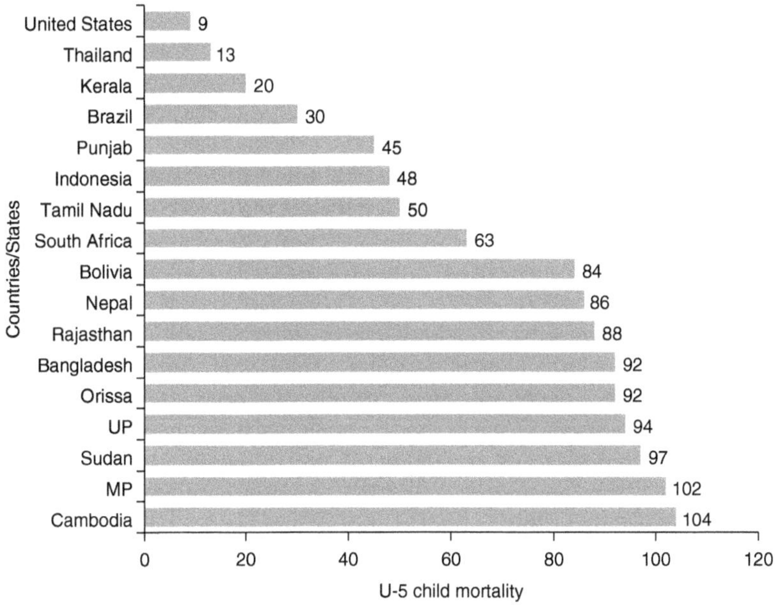

Figure 5.1 Comparison of other countries with Indian states in under-5 mortality, 2000
Source: World Bank, 2007.

goods to larger sections of the people (World Bank, 2006b; Engerman and Sokoloff, 2001). Moving further, we argue that even with a highly unequal initial distribution, if there is a significant movement towards social and economic equality in a society, this can lead to a redistribution of public investment and public goods in favour of the marginalised and the disadvantaged. And, once set in motion, the institutional and social processes assume dynamics of their own and get entrenched in political agendas of the existing coalitions of social forces. In the context of a vibrant, grass-root democracy, electoral competition between rival political formations drives this process forward and the growth process becomes more inclusive. On the other hand, if there is high inequality in societies and there is no significant movement towards equality, 'bad' institutions get promoted and the distribution of public goods becomes even more skewed in favour of the more privileged. Democracy and electoral competition in such situations stagnate and the growth process becomes exclusive. We suggest that this could partly explain the regional variations and spatial configurations in the delivery of basic services in India.

The rest of the chapter is organised as follows. Section 5.3 provides an overview of the broad trends in provisioning of these basic services under successive policy regimes since independence. Section 5.4 analyses sectoral performance in drinking water, sanitation, primary health care and elementary education. Section 5.5 suggests a vision for public sector reform that would move us towards universalisation of these basic services with quality. Section 5.6 brings together the major conclusions of the study.

5.3 Overview of trends under different policy regimes

We now examine how the challenge of universalisation with quality of four basic services – drinking water, sanitation, primary health care and elementary education – in rural India has been addressed in various policy regimes. Access to basic services is fundamental to human development and a better quality of life. Moreover, it governs the individual's development in the social environment and the kind of opportunities that s/he can get in future. The underlying idea is best captured in what James Tobin has called 'specific egalitarianism'.[1] In any society, there are certain specific services/goods that should be distributed less unequally than people's ability to pay for them. These are mostly public goods, access to which determines access to many others. Hence, we must make special arrangements so that their distribution is less unequal than the configuration that would result from an unequal distribution of income (Tobin, 1970). This is an area of strong public action, which fosters robust institutions that ensure universal access to and an egalitarian distribution of key basic services.

At the time of independence, India had a huge backlog of underdevelopment inherited from its colonial past. There was a clear consensus that underdevelopment on this scale could not be addressed through the market mechanism alone. India's five-year plans emphasised raising the level of savings, creation of capital stock through rapid industrialisation and an inter-sectoral shift of labour from agriculture to industry. This approach could be described as a 'growth-first' or 'trickle-down' strategy, inasmuch as it promised improvements in consumption only at the end of the accumulation process (Chakravarty, 1987). While the so-called 'productive' sectors received large investments, allocations for the 'social' sectors were far from substantial, even by the standards of those days. Public spending on education in India was never more than three per cent of the GDP until the middle of 1970s, and that on health nowhere near even one per cent of GDP during the entire 60-year period after independence.

By the end of the Third Five-Year Plan, it had become clear that economic growth could not by itself solve the problem of poverty and inequality. There was widespread dissatisfaction that Indian planning had failed to deliver on its promise. Severe doubts were cast on the 'growth-first' strategy and the concerns of the resulting distribution of income came to the foreground. The Fifth Plan (1974–9), for the first time, placed poverty eradication as the primary objective of planned development.

These developments led to the emergence of a spate of anti-poverty and social welfare programmes in the 1970s, increasing the level of involvement of the state in social sectors. Water, education and health now became part of the package of 'minimum needs' to be provided to all, irrespective of their position in the social and economic hierarchy. We can also see a regionally diverging trend in public action and a wide range of variations in public investments and social sector outcomes since early 1970s (Kohli, 2008). By 1990, these inter-regional differences in the indicators of well-being such as child mortality rates, life expectancy and literacy rates, consolidated into definite patterns. This has given rise to a regionally concentrated pattern of human deprivation in India.

It is now generally agreed that India's GDP growth rate picked up after 1980 and gathered further momentum after 1990. However, this acceleration in growth rate did not improve the performance of social sectors. There was a strong shift in policy in favour of a reduced role of the state and of alternative modes of service delivery. The perceived need for fiscal prudence and for curtailing the profligacy of 'populist' governments reflected the rise of a fundamentalism centred on a management of the fiscal deficit. Another major trend in this period was the strengthening of political decentralisation. With the enactment of the 73rd Constitutional Amendment in 1992, local self-governing bodies (or panchayat raj institutions – PRIs) were expected to play a major role in service delivery. The failure of most government programmes was identified with the absence of 'people's participation' and 'beneficiary control'. In reality, the move towards decentralisation remained incomplete, as the transfer of functions was not matched by a similar transfer of sufficient funds or creation of a cadre of functionaries. Moreover, as there was very little attention devoted to building their capacities or equipping them to deliver development, the PRIs had limited ability to undertake planning, implementation and monitoring of development projects in most parts of the country.

The combined impact of the discourse of government failure and a strong thrust towards political decentralisation can be summed up as universalisation without quality. With the growing pressure for universalisation of basic services on the one hand, and haunted by fiscal fundamentalism on the other, governments in these states took to the easy and low-cost route of entrusting the local communities or the PRIs the responsibility of managing these services. The result has been a severe loss of quality or service provision, especially in basic services like water, sanitation, education and health.

How did public investment move in response to these policy changes? The aggregate social sector expenditure (SSE = expenditure on social and community services plus rural development) in real terms is shown in Figure 5.2.

The chart shows that the SSE grew steadily in real terms during the 1990s. Several studies have reported that SSE initially fell in the early part of 1990s, both as a proportion of GDP and of aggregate public expenditure (Dev and Mooij, 2002; Shariff et al, 2002; and Joshi, 2006). However, the expenditure quickly recovered in the second half of the 1990s, a finding that Nagaraj (2000) also confirms. Our own finding, calculated from the Indian Public Finance Statistics, show that there was no overall reduction in SSE during the 1990s either as a proportion of GDP or in real per capita terms. As a proportion of aggregate public expenditure, it showed a decline during the period 1998–9 and 2003–4, which seems to have been reversed subsequently. While expenditure did rise in real terms, with universalisation as the driving force, the outcome seems to be a thinner spreading of resources across larger areas, resulting in an appalling neglect of the quality of services provided.

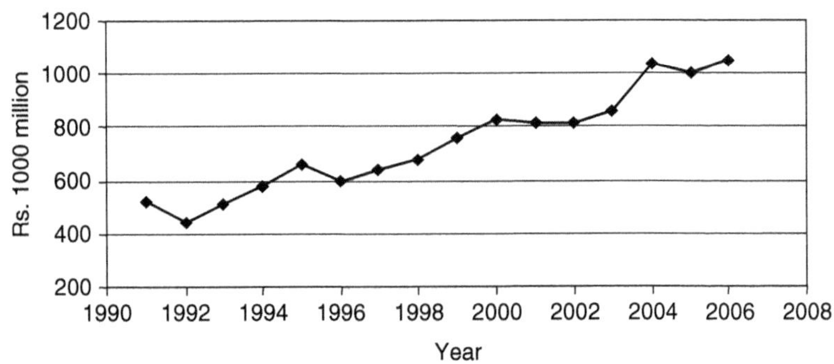

Figure 5.2 Trends in social sector expenditure, 1990–2006 at constant 1993–4 prices (Rs 1000 million)
Source: Calculated from Indian Public Finance Statistics, various issues.

5.4 Sectoral performance

Drinking water supply and sanitation (DWSS)

India has been spending considerable sums on drinking water and sanitation in recent years. Expenditure on DWSS was part of the health budget till 1987–8 after which it was separated. We have excluded the initial plan years (1950–65), as the expenditure in these years was insignificant (Table 5.1). A substantial rise (nine times, at an annual compound rate of seven per cent pa) is visible in expenditure in real terms. What has been the impact of this rise in investment on the long-term performance of the country in DWSS?

Drinking water supply

Historically, drinking water in rural areas in India has been provisioned outside the sphere of the state through the network of private or community-operated wells, ponds and small-scale irrigation reservoirs. The share of self-provisioning was somewhat lower in the urban centres, where the elected local self-government bodies like the municipalities and municipal corporations were in charge of providing drinking water. Even though the provision of safe, drinking water supply (DWS) was included in the national agenda during the initial years of the planning era, it was not considered as one of the priority areas. The Water Supply

Table 5.1 Plan-wise investment in DWSS at current and constant prices, 1969–2007

	(Rs Million)					
	At current prices			**At constant (1999–2000) prices**		
Plan Period	**Rural**	**Urban**	**Total**	**Rural**	**Urban**	**Total**
IV Plan (1969–74)	2,080	2,510	4,590	20,610	24,870	45,480
V Plan (1974–79)	5,520	5,400	10,920	36,750	35,910	72,660
VI Plan (1980–85)	16,630	23,350	39,980	66,860	93,830	160,690
VII Plan (1985–90)	45,350	25,580	70,930	123,490	69,640	193,130
VIII Plan (1992–97)	93,660	73,160	166,820	131,630	102,820	234,450
IX Plan (1997–02)	209,140	186,240	395,380	211,210	188,080	399,290
X Plan (2002–07)	241,040	223,170	464,210	213,940	198,080	412,020

Source: Planning Commission (2007).

and Sanitation programme launched in 1954 was part of the health plan. Subsequent plans made only nominal allocations for DWSS.

Towards the middle of the Fourth Plan, concerns were raised about the deteriorating water supply and sanitation situation in both rural and urban areas. It was widely felt that there is a need for public provisioning of drinking water through specially designed programmes. The central government launched the Accelerated Rural Water Supply Programme (ARWSP) in 1972–3 to help the states to increase the coverage of DWS. This was the first major programme focused wholly on water supply to rural areas. The programme, for the first time, specified the national norms for drinking water. However, even after laying down these standards, the coverage of households with safe, potable drinking water and sanitation facilities did not improve significantly. The Sixth Plan (1980–5) document mentions that in 1980, there were about 0.19 million villages in the country that needed water supply provision on a priority basis (Planning Commission 1980, 23:45). In 1986, the National Drinking Water Mission (NDWM, later renamed as the Rajiv Gandhi NDWM) was set up to strengthen the rural water supply system. It aimed to cover 137,155 residual villages with water-related problems. The National Water Policy (NWP) drafted by the Ministry of Water Resources in 1987 stated that DWS is the first charge of water resources in the country. Still, the numbers of habitations with safe drinking water and population excluded from this basic service remained high.

The underlying reason for the persistence of the drinking water problem in spite of these major policy drives is to be found in the deep structural changes taking place in the agrarian water economy of the country. Since the green revolution of the mid-1960s, demand for water in irrigation had gone up tremendously. The gross irrigated area went up from 28.6 million hectares in 1960–3 (triennium average) to 76.5 million hectares in 1999–2000 at an average annual growth rate of 2.69 per cent. Nearly 84 per cent of the additions to this new irrigated area have been from groundwater sources. The increasing demand for water for irrigation has exerted an immense pressure on the available water resources and progressively contributed to the worsening drinking water problem.

The World Bank-funded, Sector Reform Pilot Project (SRP) of late 1990s marked a policy shift in the DWS sector. This shift was towards a 'demand-driven approach', implying that the investments in the sector should be designed in accordance with the demand of users. The SRP in drinking water was scaled up throughout the country under a new programme, the Swajaldhara, which was launched on 25 December

2002. How has the coverage of households with safe drinking water supply moved over the years in response to the policy changes and changes in investments? Has the shift to demand-driven programmes like Swajaldhara contributed to an increase in coverage of households?

According to the most recent estimates of the Eleventh Plan document, the coverage of rural households with safe drinking water in 2007 stood at 89 per cent in rural areas and 91 per cent in urban areas (Planning Commission, 2008), implying that India is safely placed in terms of attaining the millennium development goal of drinking water security. However, this rosy picture provided by government data is totally at variance with the reality of growing water shortage and conflicts over water. The coverage data is so out-of-touch with reality primarily on account of the very definition of 'coverage' in official sources. The norms defining a 'fully covered' habitation are completely silent on several key aspects that determine access by needy households. It is obvious that the mere fact of the presence of a water source, such as a hand pump, does not guarantee that it is able to supply the required amount of water per household (WaterAid, 2006). Equally important, these norms do not take into account the reliability of the water source and the seasonal variations in water supply. Finally, the norms are silent on the alarming aspect of growing quality problems in the water supplied for drinking. High fluoride concentration in groundwater, beyond the permissible limit of 1.5 ppm, is a major issue affecting a large segment of rural population to the tune of 25 million spread over more than 200 districts in 17 states. The population at risk is estimated at around 66 million. The presence of excess arsenic in groundwater has been reported from West Bengal. Nearly 13.8 million people in 75 blocks are reported at risk. It is also reported that around 0.2 million people in West Bengal have arsenic-related skin manifestations (MoRD, 2004). These water quality issues do not find any mention in the official statistics on coverage.

Partly in recognition of the inadequacy of the definition of 'coverage', the eleventh Plan document as well as some of the recent assessments by the MoRD (MoRD, 2004), talks about cases of 'slippage' of fully covered habitats to partial coverage. Of the reason quoted for this slippage, the most important is the 'drying up of the source', accounting for a major portion of the slippage. This is a reflection of the growing crisis of groundwater in India. Annual extraction of groundwater in India is estimated to be 210 BCuM, by far the highest in the world. With such high levels of extraction, the groundwater levels in the country are reportedly going down at an alarming rate. The recently published Expert Group Report on Groundwater Management and Ownership (Planning Commission, 2007) notes that in 2004, 28 per cent of the blocks in the country were in the category of semi-critical, critical or overexploited, compared to seven per cent in 1995. If this progressive lowering of the water table continues, many more of the 'fully covered' habitations could experience a slip back. The knee-jerk response of the government at all levels to any drinking water crisis has been to install new water sources, mostly based on groundwater. There is clearly the need to develop a new and integrated approach to meeting growing water demand in rural and urban areas. The first step in this direction is to go beyond the spurious statistics such as the coverage data and create a strong database, with properly designed surveys, to bring out the actual situation on the ground with respect to drinking water availability in the country.

Sanitation

Sanitation coverage in India was extremely poorly developed in the pre-independence period. The Environmental Hygiene Committee (1949) notes that underground sewers existed only in 35 towns and even they served only 33 to 75 per cent of the population in each town (Guha, 2004). The First Plan document notes that only three per cent of the total population had some sort of sewerage system. Even as a few initiatives were taken to expand coverage of drinking water supply, sanitation continued to remain an area of complete neglect. The situation even in the early 1980s was appalling, to say the least. The percentage of rural households with latrines was as low as one per cent (Planning Commission, 2002). The Sixth Plan document felt that the UN's call for 100 per cent coverage by 1990 could only be met 'through a large-scale mobilisation of voluntary effort at the village level' (Planning Commission, 1980, 23:49), which was as good as saying that it was impossible. In 1980, of the 3,119 towns, only 198 had sewerage facilities and only 27 per cent of urban households had access to safe latrines.

To raise sanitation coverage and to bring states at par with each other, the central government launched the first major nationwide programme on sanitation called the Central Rural Sanitation Programme (CRSP) in 1986. However, the programme did not make a significant difference to this massive problem. In 1999, the government restructured CRSP to a 'demand-driven' approach, similar to the one adopted for drinking water under Swajaldhara. This Total Sanitation Campaign (TSC) proposed to incentivise changes in attitudes and behaviour rather than fund infrastructure. The emphasis of TSC was on 'Information, Education and Communication (IEC), human resource development, capacity development activities to increase awareness among the rural people and generation of demand for sanitary facilities' (GoI, 2007).

Indeed, according to the official sources, the 'community-led and people centred initiatives' under TSC seems to have raised the sanitation coverage substantially in rural areas. While in 1997–8, only about 1.3 million toilets were built, the figure seems to have jumped to about 10 million in 2007–8 (Saxena, 2008). How authentic is this picture? Examining the subsidy structure of TSC for individual household latrines (the most significant quantitative component of TSC), it becomes clear that this programme is only a case of attempted universalisation at the cost of quality. The TSC Guidelines (GoI, 2007) make it clear that the maximum subsidy per toilet available to a BPL household would be a paltry Rs 1200. No less a person than the Prime Minister of India, in his address to the Third South Asian Conference on Sanitation in November 2008, admitted that '20 per cent of the toilets built in our country are not functional because of a variety of factors, from poor construction to the lack of adequate maintenance'. The TSC appears to constitute a complete abdication by the state of its duty to provide basic sanitary facilities to the people. By assuming that the real bottleneck was 'cultural or attitudinal', it shifts the burden of investing in improved sanitation on to the people. The subsidy provided is completely inadequate in providing proper sanitation. It is also important to note that in village sanitation, the way waste management and disposal is done is equally important. The NSS data on number of villages (per 1000 villages) with drainage system and the type of drainage show that at the national level, only one-third of the villages had any drainage system, mostly of open kutcha variant. Over 85 per cent of villages in Orissa, Chhattisgarh, Gujarat, Rajasthan, Jharkhand, MP and West Bengal did not have any sewerage facilities in 2004.

Health

Early approaches to public health: The Bhore Committee

Health services in nineteenth century India emerged as a response to the specific military and administrative needs of the colonial government. This ensured that the British lived in residentially segregated 'enclaves' with good environmental sanitation (Dasgupta, 2005). Organised medical activities had very little spread outside the cantonment area and civil lines. It was only in times of severe epidemic outbursts like cholera, kala azar or visceral leishmaniasis, plague or small pox that the medical personnel stepped outside these confines. Even though the public health movement was already well-established in Britain by the end of the nineteenth century with its strong support to sanitary services for prevention of diseases, sanitation in India did not get much official support and was confined to the areas around which the white population lived (Qadeer, 2005).

The details of a well-developed national public health-care system were put forward by the Health Survey and Development Committee headed by Joseph Bhore (hence known as the Bhore Committee) in 1946. The Bhore Committee made the first comprehensive health plan for India, along the lines of the National Health Service of England. It was the Bhore Committee that suggested for the first time a three-tier system of implementation in health sector (comprising primary, secondary and tertiary health units). The Bhore Committee's proposal boils down to two major recommendations: (1) creation of a strong state-supported national health system capable of delivering health care to all sections of the people at subsidised cost; and (2) promotion of an integrated approach combining preventive and curative services from a larger public health perspective.

The new era of family planning

At the time of independence itself, therefore, India had good advice on how to design a comprehensive health-care system with a public health perspective. The clarity and detail of the proposal is in marked contrast with the anaemic, muddled and ad hoc manner in which health planning has been undertaken in India in the 60 years that ensued. Until the 1960s, the health initiatives focused mainly on managing epidemics, necessitated by the fact that epidemic diseases contributed significantly to the total mortality in the country (Dasgupta, 2005). Mass campaigns were started to eradicate the various diseases. These separate countrywide campaigns were launched against malaria, smallpox, tuberculosis, leprosy, filaria, trachoma and cholera. As a result of these interventions, mortality rates came down sharply. However, birth rates did not show a similar decline. At the same time, owing to two successive monsoon failures in the mid-1960s, food production declined drastically from 89 million tonnes in 1964–5 to 65 million tonnes in 1965–6, necessitating import of wheat from the US under PL 480. The threat of rapid population growth coupled with food shortages gave rise to the fear of a Malthusian population explosion and re-emergence of famines on an unprecedented scale.

In response, since the mid-1960s India embarked on a massive campaign for population control through family planning. The objective was to bring down the birth rate from 41 per thousand to a target of

20–25 per 1000 by the mid-1970s. The network of public clinics to deliver sterilisation and other contraceptive services expanded rapidly and the number of health personnel engaged in family planning was also increased (Dasgupta, 2005). Family planning was made into a separate department in 1972 within the Ministry of Health. As a proportion of the total public expenditure on health, expenditure on family planning went up from around 3.7 per cent in the early 1960s to nearly 15 per cent in the early 1990s. Preventive care was now given an even lower priority than before when compared to curative medical services on the one hand (for which there seems to have been a steadily rising demand) and family planning on the other.

Following the declaration of Emergency in 1975, the National Population Policy of 1976 called for a 'frontal attack on problems of population' and asked state governments to 'pass suitable legislation to make family planning compulsory for citizens'. This technology-centred and target-oriented approach to population control completely ignored the underlying social and gender-related factors governing reproductive behaviour in any society. It failed to take into account the role of female literacy and child survival in reducing birth rates (as shown in the examples of states like Kerala). Though it was widely criticised, the ideology of technology-and-target-centric family planning continued to dominate health policy in India for many more years to come. It was replaced by a target-free, reproductive health approach in India only in 1996. However, the National Population Policy 2000 again showed signs of the continuing obsession with targeted population control. The strategies proposed remained techno-centric, demographically oriented, focusing on women (Qadeer, 2005).[2]

Return of public health? – The National Health Policies

High rate of population growth and mortality rates of women and children, high incidence of malnourishment, diarrhoeal diseases and communicable diseases – these were the elements of a distressing macro-picture of health in the country in the 1980s. Lack of access to safe drinking water and poor environmental sanitation were among the major contributory causes of the high incidence of disease and mortality. With the setback of the family planning overdrive and with the overall picture of the health sector continuing to be deplorable, it seemed as if the health sector was poised to move towards a multi-sectoral, public health-oriented approach in the beginning of the 1980s. Such a move was strongly favoured by the Alma-Ata declaration of 1978, which recognised health (physical, mental and social well being) as a fundamental human right. The National Health Policy of 1983 recommended 'universal, comprehensive primary health-care services which are relevant to the actual needs and priorities of the community at a cost which people can afford' (NHP, 1983, 3–4). For the first time after the Bhore Committee, the government started talking in terms of universalising the health-care system. The revised National Health Policy of 2002 reiterated the concern of universalisation of health care. The NHP 2002 recommended increasing public expenditure from 0.9 per cent to 2 per cent of GDP by 2010 and allocating 55 per cent of public health investment to the primary health sector. It has also made provision for a mandatory two-year rural posting to all medical students before awarding the graduate medical degree. Simultaneously, in line with the earlier policy, NHP 2002 emphasised the role of private sector in health, while calling for legislation to regulating private clinical establishments.

Trends in public expenditure on health

We now examine how public expenditure on health responded to these policy changes over the years. India has one of the lowest ratios of public expenditure on health to total public expenditure in the world (21 per cent). This ratio is half of the public spending in ideologically 'free market' countries such as the US (45 per cent) or Chile (44 per cent) (World Bank, 2006a). It was lower than the ratios of the East Asian countries and India's neighbouring countries such as Sri Lanka.

The data show that although public expenditure on health in real terms has gone up by more than four times since the 1980s and the per capita real expenditure has risen by more than ten times during the same period, public expenditure as a proportion of the GDP has never been above one per cent in the entire post-independence period in India (Table 5.2).

Tracking the impact of this investment and policy changes on key health indicators, we find that there are some substantial achievements in life expectancy, reduction of birth and death rates, et cetera (Table 5.3). However, the progress achieved is far short of expectations, especially in the case of infant, child and maternal survival rates.

Against this background a poorly performing public sector health system, the NRHM was launched as a focused intervention in 2005. The NRHM proposes to bring about a significant reduction in infant mortality rate (IMR) and maternal mortality rate (MMR), universalise access to public health services by the year 2012. The NRHM reiterates the commitment of the government to raise public expenditure on health

Table 5.2 Trends in public expenditure on health in India, 1950–2004

	Public expenditure on health (Rs Million)		Public expenditure on health as per cent of		Per capita public expenditure on health (Rs)	
	Current prices	Constant (1999–2000) prices	GDP	Public expenditure	Current prices	Constant (1999–2000) prices
1950–51	219	4,954	0.2	2.7	0.61	13.83
1955–56	510	13,237	0.5	4.6	1.27	32.97
1960–61	1,077	21,659	0.6	5.4	2.45	49.28
1965–66	1,686	24,929	0.6	3.8	3.41	50.42
1970–71	3,351	37,472	0.7	3.8	6.11	68.32
1975–76	6,785	48,049	0.8	3.8	9.91	70.18
1980–81	12,857	61,501	0.9	3.5	17.35	82.99
1985–86	29,661	94,260	1.0	4.4	35.52	112.88
1991–92	56,296	117,968	0.9	3.3	60.13	126.00
1995–96	104,128	133,628	0.9	3.6	112.21	144.00
2000–01	188,067	181,670	0.8	3.3	184.50	178.22
2003–04	280,283	243,468	1.0	3.8	214.62	186.43

Source: Calculated from National Accounts Statistics, Various years.
Note: The data is drawn from the National Accounts Statistics of various years. Expenditure at constant 1999–2000 prices is worked out using the GDP deflator.

to 2–3 per cent of the GDP from its current level of 0.9 per cent. It is still too early to discuss the impact of the NRHM. However, reports from the field and ministry's own evaluations show that the most remarkable of NRHM's achievements is in terms of institutionalisation of deliveries and expansion of immunisation coverage. The NRHM has also not been able to substantially step up public investment in health, which still continues languish around one per cent of the GDP.

Current scenario

National averages conceal wide regional variations. As a result, the health indicators in backward states like Bihar, UP, MP, Jharkhand and Orissa are not only far below the national level, but are comparable to those in the poorest parts of the world. The health sector in the

Table 5.3 Performance of key health indicators, 1951–2002

Indicator	1951	1961	1971	1981	1991	2002
Decadal rate of growth of population (per cent)	NA	21.6	24.8	24.7	23.9	21.4
Life expectancy (years)	32.1	41.3	45.6	50.4	58.7	63.0
Crude birth rate (per 1,000)	40	42	37	33.9	29.5	25.4
Crude death rate (per 1,000)	27	23	15	12.5	9.8	8.0
Infant mortality rate (per 1,000 live births)	140	114	129	110	80	66
Under-5 child mortality (per 1,000)	NA	NA	171	152	94	73
Neo-natal mortality rate (per 1,000)	NA	NA	NA	70	51	40
Maternal mortality rate (per 100,000 deliveries)	NA	NA	NA	NA	NA	407
Hospital beds (per 10,000 population)	3.2	5.7	6.4	8.3	9.5	11.3
Registered medical practitioners (per 10,000 population)	1.7	1.9	2.8	3.9	4.7	5.6

Source: MoHFW, 2007.

backward regions of the country still suffers from gross neglect and under-investment. While one primary health centre (PHC – the second level in the three-tier health system) caters to two villages in Kerala and 14 villages in Tamil Nadu, the number of villages it caters to is as much as 99 in Jharkhand, 73 in Orissa and 48 in MP. Even allowing for differences in population densities, this shows that the existing infrastructure in poorer states is inadequate to ensure health security to its target population. It is also remarkable that nearly 70 per cent of the hospitals and 75 per cent of hospital beds are in urban areas, which have only about 30 per cent of the population (Planning Commission, 2002). This shows the huge rural–urban gap in health-care facilities in India.

Of more serious concern is the fact that even when a health unit is physically present, the kind of services it can provide is severely limited by the absence of key health personnel. The extent of shortfall (the difference between personnel required and personnel actually present) is considerable in the case of female health workers and nurses and midwives at both the PHC and community health centre (CHC) levels (DLHS, 2008). Further, the problem of shortfall is compounded by 'absenteeism' of the key health service providers, which has been highlighted by several studies (Banerjee, Deaton and Duflo, 2004; Hammer, Iyer and Shamji, 2007). Since many of the health-care centres normally have a staff strength of one person, absence here means that the facility does not function at all on those days. The health-care centres are also found lacking in basic facilities like electricity, drinking water and sufficient number of rooms and beds (DLHS, 2008).

With their inadequate numbers, low staff strength and poor infrastructure, it is natural that outreach and quality of key health services is low. Table 5.4 summarises the data from the three successive rounds of National Family Health Surveys, spanning the 13-year period from 1992–3 to 2005–6, which overlaps the radically new phase of reform, globalisation and high growth in the Indian economy.

As we can see from the table, the coverage of health services did not experience a comparable acceleration and continued to grow at a slow pace. As a result, in 2004–5, 50 per cent of pregnant women and 60 per cent of children remained excluded from these key health services.

How critical is the influence of these services on infant and child mortality? We have tried to assess this by correlating the district-level estimates of IMR (Irudaya Rajan et al., 2008) with the information from the DLHS database on percentage of population covered by three health-care indicators (percentage of women receiving full ANC, percentage of institutional deliveries and percentage of children 12–23 months fully immunised). The regression coefficients indicate that the districts with better coverage of health-care services had a lower rate of infant mortality. We have also constructed a composite index of health care combining these three indicators. When we correlate the IMR with

Table 5.4 Coverage of key health care services over the years

		NFHS-1 1992–93	NFHS-2 1998–99	NFHS-3 2005–06
1	Per cent of women receiving three ante-natal care (ANC) visits	43.9	44.2	50.7
2	Per cent of institutional deliveries	26.1	33.6	40.7
3	Per cent of safe deliveries (deliveries attended by skilled personnel)	35.1	42.4	48.8
4	Per cent of children (12–23 months) fully immunised	35.5	42.0	43.5

Source: MoHFW, 2007.

this composite index of health care, the association becomes stronger (Table 5.5 and Figure 5.3).

Growth of private provisioning

With systems of public delivery in such disarray, it is natural that the private players get a bigger role. As we have mentioned before, India's health system is one of the most privatised in the world. Sen, Iyer and George (2002), in an insightful study, compare evidence from successive rounds of the NSS (42nd and 52nd) and show that the role of private providers has steadily been on the rise in both institutionalised and non-institutional treatments. Compiling the data from three rounds of NSS (42nd, 52nd and 60th Round), we also find evidence for a steady decline in the share of public providers in institutional treatments in both rural and urban areas (Table 5.6).

Table 5.5 District-level regression coefficients with IMR and key health variables

	RSQ	Level of significance (%)
Per cent of women receiving full ANC	0.2973	95
Per cent of institutional deliveries	0.3370	95
Per cent of safe deliveries	0.3541	95
Per cent of children (12–23 months) fully immunised	0.2110	NS
Composite index (full ANC, safe deliveries, full immunisaton)	0.3642	95

Source: Calculated from NFHS-3 Results.

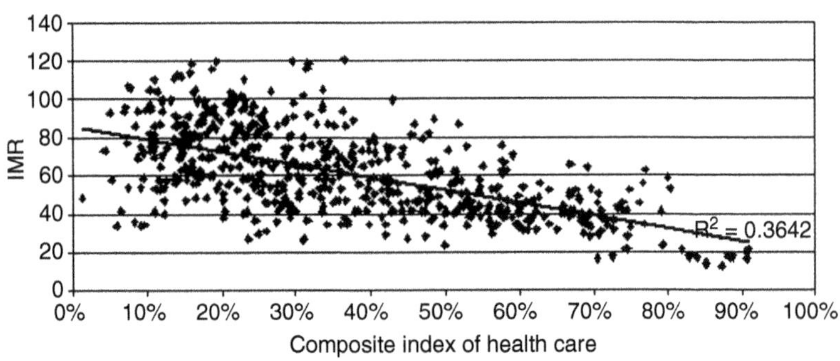

Figure 5.3 IMR and composite index of health care

Table 5.6 Share of public and private sector in health provision, 1986–87 to 2004, NSS Rounds

Type of provider	Share in rural			Share in urban		
	1986–87	1995–96	2004	1986–87	1995–96	2004
Non-institutional treatment						
Public providers	25.5	19.0	22.0	27.1	19.0	19.0
Private providers	74.5	80.0	78.0	72.9	81.0	81.0
Total	100.0	100.0	100.0	100.0	100.0	100.0
Institutional (hospitalised) treatment						
Government hospital	59.7	43.8	41.7	60.3	43.1	38.2
Private hospital	40.3	56.2	58.3	39.7	56.9	61.8
Total	100.0	100.0	100.0	100.0	100.0	100.0

Source: NSSO, various rounds.

The table shows that despite this decline, around 40 per cent of hospitalised treatment still takes place in public facilities, reflecting the heavy dependence of low-income groups and the most vulnerable sections such as SC/ST households on public health providers. The endemic inequalities in our health system seem to have only worsened in recent years, with the poor still holding on to the ineffective public systems, while the demand for private provision is on the rise from those who can afford the steeply rising cost of health services.

We saw that the public health systems, particularly in the poorest parts of the country, are located at a distance from the people whom it is supposed to serve and is fraught with multiple problems of the absence of basic facilities, lack of key personnel, poor maintenance of existing facilities and poor monitoring systems. However, it is the only hope for the poor of getting affordable health care. Given the way the public health-care system is organised, it is unlikely that the health indicators of these areas will improve for many years to come. The system, particularly the primary care system, is unprepared to deliver even the minimal services expected of it. Consequently, when shocks like hunger deaths, epidemic outbursts and natural calamities occur, it reaches a point of perilous collapse. This system needs a total revamp. We argue that it is possible to achieve a significant improvement in health-care delivery if we scale up public investment on health, 'reform' the implementation system and focus on the few regions and districts where the problem is the most acute.

Elementary education

Initial years

Universalisation of elementary education (UEE) has been one of the important goals of India's development planning (Constitution of India, Article 45). The effort in the early planning phase was to increase enrolment in schools and to raise the literacy rate. The number of primary schools, mostly in the public sector, nearly doubled from 0.2 million in 1950–1 to over 0.4 million in 1970–1. Expenditure on education at current prices went up almost five times between 1950–1 and 1964–5. Expenditure per pupil nearly doubled from Rs 35.6 in 1950–1 to Rs 62.6 in 1964–5. This step up in expenditure did bring in some positive results, especially in the form of higher enrolment of girls. However, this rise was woefully inadequate compared to the increase in the number of children requiring schooling. Thus, UEE remained a distant dream. The literacy rates continued to be low, barely crossing the figure of one-third of the population by 1971. Nearly half of the enrolled children dropped out by the time they reached Class IV.

Kothari Commission and the National Education Policy, 1968

Kothari Commission The need to focus attention on elementary education was felt for the first time during the Third Plan. In 1964, the government appointed an Education Commission under the chair D.S. Kothari, to conduct a comprehensive study of the education system. The report of the Kothari Commission was submitted in 1966 and marked a watershed in the history of education in India. The Kothari Commission recommended a continuous expansion of educational opportunities and an intensive effort to raise quality of education at all levels, especially the primary level. It also stressed the need to link education with productivity and employment through vocational education. By far the most important recommendation of the Commission was to raise the proportion of gross national product (GNP) allocated to education to six per cent by 1985–86 (GoI, 1966: 893). This figure has subsequently become a standard point of reference, to be endorsed by all major policy statements and studies. This figure has also found its way to the manifestoes of all political parties. However, as we shall see shortly, the actual expenditure on education has never actually reached this figure, even 40 years after this report was submitted.

The report of the Kothari Commission was followed up with the National Education Policy statement in 1968, which emphasised free and compulsory education for all and accepted the Kothari

Commission's recommendation of allocating six per cent of the GNP to education. However, the overall rise in the literacy rate was moderate and in 1981, India had as many as 380 million illiterates, one of the largest in the world.

The New Education Policy (NEP), 1986 A new Human Resources Development ministry was set up in 1984. A New Education Policy (NEP) was announced in 1986. Since existing schools lacked essential facilities, NEP 1986 recommended for all schools at least two, sufficiently large all-weather classrooms with necessary blackboards, maps, charts and other learning materials. It also recommended that each school should have at least two teachers, one of them a woman and the number should gradually increase to one teacher per class (NEP, 1986). As a follow-up to NEP 1986, a programme called 'Operation Blackboard' was initiated in 1986–7. This programme had three components: (1) enhancement of school infrastructure by constructing additional classrooms; (2) increasing the number of teachers per school to two at least and (3) introducing essential teaching materials in schools. Nearly six years after the commencement of this programme, the Sixth All-India Educational Survey conducted in 1993, found that nearly 17 per cent of the primary schools in India were run on open spaces and another 15 per cent were either in tents or thatched sheds (Tilak, 2006). It is clear, therefore, that the achievements under Operation Blackboard fell far short of expectations.

District Primary Education Programme and Sarva Shiksha Abhiyan

In the early 1990s, the stark nature of educational backwardness in many parts of India was clearly visible. In 1991, India had 404 million illiterates. Nearly two-thirds of the people belonging to SC/ST groups were illiterate. An estimated 33 million children of school-going age were out of school. Seventy per cent of the enrolled children dropped out of the educational system by the time they reached Class VIII. Against this background, the government launched another programme with the District Primary Education Programme (DPEP) in 1994 in seven states and later expanded it to four more states. The DPEP envisaged a decentralised programme addressing local needs for education with the active involvement of the local community. In 2001, the DPEP was scaled up as Sarva Shiksha Abhiyan ('Education for All' movement or SSA). The Constitution was amended in 2002 (93rd Amendment) to decree free and compulsory education to all children between the ages 6 and 14. The goal of SSA is to provide meaningful and quality education to all children between the ages 6 and 14 by 2010. Envisaged in partnership with the state governments, the SSA is a centrally sponsored scheme that seeks greater decentralisation of the school system with community ownership of schools.

Public expenditure on education

Were these changes reflected in a rise in public expenditure on education? Table 5.7 summarises the trends in expenditure at current and constant prices as well as in proportion to the GDP and aggregate public expenditure. It shows that there has been a steady rise over the years in the share of public expenditure in GDP and aggregate public expenditure, even though the rise remains far less than the stated goal of six per cent of the GDP. Public expenditure on education steadily rose from half-a-per cent of GDP in 1950–1 to two per cent by 1970 and 3–4 per cent at present. As a per cent of total public expenditure, it stagnated around 10–11 per cent for 25 years after 1955 and rose to around 13 per cent in the last 25 years.

While analysing public expenditure on education, we must remember that for 40 years after independence until 1990, the share of elementary education in education expenditure never rose above 50 per cent. This contrasts with the consistently higher share of elementary education

Table 5.7 Trends in public expenditure on education, 1950–2006

Year	Public expenditure on education (Rs million)		Public expenditure on education as per cent of		Per capita public expenditure on education (Rs)	
	Current prices	Constant (1999–2000) Prices	GDP	Public expenditure	Current prices	Constant prices
1951–52	640	14,610	0.6	7.90	1.8	40.0
1955–56	1,180	30,740	1.1	10.7	3.0	78.2
1960–61	2,400	48,180	1.4	11.9	5.5	111.0
1965–66	4,330	63,970	1.5	9.80	8.9	131.9
1970–71	8,920	99,780	1.9	10.2	16.5	184.4
1975–76	18,490	130,970	2.2	10.3	30.5	215.8
1980–81	38,840	185,800	2.7	10.7	57.2	273.6
1985–86	87,130	276,890	3.1	12.9	115.4	366.7
1990–91	196,160	411,050	3.4	13.4	233.8	489.9
1995–96	381,780	489,940	3.2	13.3	411.4	528.0
2000–01	824,860	796,810	3.9	14.4	809.5	782.0
2005–06	1,190,290	948,470	3.3	13.1	1,075.2	856.8

Source: Calculated from National Accounts Statistics, Various years.
Note: Expenditure at constant 1999–2000 prices is worked out using the GDP deflator.

in total education expenditure of the other Asian countries like South Korea and Thailand since early 1960s (Haq, 1997).[3] The mass literacy rates of the East Asian countries in 1960 were already at a higher level than what has been achieved by India even today. With hindsight, it can now be argued that the composition and rate of growth of output could have been vastly different, had sufficient attention been paid to elementary education (Balakrishnan, 2007).

Current scenario

Rising enrolments? Since late 1990s, an enormous emphasis has been placed on raising the enrolment rates in schools. The Report of the Eleventh Plan Working Group on Elementary Education states that 87 per cent of the rural habitations had access to a primary school within one km in 2004 (Planning Commission, 2008). Over successive NSS rounds (42nd, 52nd and 61st), school attendance has improved and the proportion of children in age group 6–13 years not attending schools has come down. However, we cannot escape the fact that there were about 22 million out-of-school children in 2004–5, which, by no means, is a small number.[4] Parts of these out-of-school children are those who never enrolled and the other part is those who have dropped out of schools. The NSS data indicate that nearly half of the out-of-school children are concentrated in the two states of UP and Bihar. These two states together with MP and West Bengal account for over-two thirds of the out-of-school children in India (Deolalikar, 2005). The incidence of out-of-school children is higher among the STs (22 per cent) and SCs and Muslims (20 per cent), compared to other caste groups/communities (Deepa Shankar, 2007). Therefore, the probability is high that any randomly chosen out-of-school child will be a tribal girl, SC or Muslim girl born in a rural labour household in UP, Bihar or MP. This clearly brings out the regionally and socially concentrated nature of deprivation in India, which could only be handled by a targeted intervention.

Pitiable condition of government schools A significant fact to remember here is that unlike health, education (especially elementary education) in India is still largely provided by the public. Of the total 1.04 million elementary schools over 85 per cent are managed by government (43 per cent) or local bodies (42 per cent) (MoHRD, 2007).[5] Hence, we need to focus on the condition of government schools in the most backward states of the country. In the euphoria created by official statistics about rising enrolment rates, we forget the miserable conditions under which government schools in many parts of the country operate. At the all-India level, half of the schools in rural areas have two classrooms or less. 34 per cent of elementary schools in Jharkhand and 26 per cent in MP do not have classrooms. They are 'open air' schools! 64 per cent of schools in Assam and 19 per cent in West Bengal have only one classroom (Table 5.8). It is a commonly observed phenomenon in these areas that all children from Class I to V are huddled into a single classroom and taught together. Needless to say, very little fruitful learning is possible under such conditions.

Availability of teachers Paradoxically, even as enrolment rates go up, there are reports from states that the pace of teacher recruitment is going down. States like MP and Rajasthan have tried to 'rationalise' the numbers of teachers by appointing persons on contract or resorting to 'para-teachers' on a large scale. Such 'cost-saving' schemes are now in existence under different names in many states. In 2006–7, there were 0.51 million para- teachers in India (NUEPA, 2008). The minimum qualification prescribed for the para-teacher is higher secondary or secondary in most states and Rajasthan even allows Class VIII for male and Class V for female teachers (Govinda and Josephine, 2005). There is very little provision for pre-service or in-service training. With so little attention given to capacity-building of the teachers, one can imagine the quality of teaching that they are able to provide to children. The appointment of para-teachers as a cost-saving measure provides a route of an easy escape for the state to abdicate its responsibility of providing quality education to the children, and instead, creates a false feeling of universal access to education. The guarantee of education is clearly incomplete if it ignores the quality of teaching provided and the learning outcomes that the system produces. The risk is that schemes like employment guarantee scheme (EGS) could accentuate the gap between public and private schools and limit the equalising impact of

Table 5.8 Distribution of schools (%) by number of classrooms, all-India and states

Classrooms	**India**	**Assam**	**Jharkhand**	**Madhya Pradesh**	**West Bengal**
No room	9	3	34	26	1
1 room	12	64	6	11	19
2 rooms	30	18	33	28	29
3 or more rooms	49	15	27	35	49

Source: DISE, 2006.

educational development on rural society (Leclercq, 2002; Pritchett and Pande, 2006).

A clear result of this move to appoint para-teachers is the proliferation of 'single-teacher schools' in many north Indian states (Table 5.9). At the all-India level, 14 per cent of the schools are single-teacher schools. This percentage is as high as 31 per cent in Rajasthan, 30 per cent in Jharkhand and 27 per cent in MP. More than two-thirds of the schools in MP and Jharkhand have only two teachers and less. As in the case of health provision, a serious issue is that of the absenteeism of the teacher. Studies have shown that on average, 25 per cent of teachers in government primary schools in rural India were absent from school on a given day (Kremer et al., 2005; Banerjee and Duflo, 2005).

Facilities in schools There are now fairly accepted norms about the facilities a school should have (CABE, 2005). Apart from adequate number of classrooms and teachers, these include separate toilets for girls and boys, drinking water facility, kitchen for cooking mid-day meals, minimum amount of teaching learning equipment, play materials, electrification and at least one personal computer. The real world of a government school is far removed from this idyllic world of norms. The district information system for education (DISE) data shows that 85 per cent of schools in India do not have electricity connections and over half do not even have common toilets. Amazingly, 28 per cent of schools in Jharkhand and 15 per cent in Rajasthan and Bihar do not even have a blackboard! Compared to an average pupil/teacher ratio (PTR) of 40 for India as a whole, nearly one-fifth of the schools in UP and Bihar have a PTR of over 100. These schools are clearly overcrowded. Another indicator of the overcrowding in classrooms is the student/classroom ratio (SCR). Against the national average of 42, more than half the primary schools in Bihar and UP have an SCR of over 60. A considerable part of the teachers' time is spent in managing

Table 5.9 Distribution of schools (%) by number of teachers, all-India and states

Teachers	India	Jharkhand	MP	Orissa	Rajasthan
No teacher	2	0	1	0	1
One teacher	14	27	30	13	31
Two teachers	34	37	37	37	25
Three or more teachers	50	36	32	50	43

Source: DISE, 2006.

these overcrowded classrooms rather than doing any meaningful teaching activity.

Poor learning outcomes Operating under such stupendously adverse conditions, it is not difficult to imagine that the schools in these laggard states can in no way provide an environment conducive to enjoyment either in teaching or in learning. The DISE data is remarkably silent on the quality of teaching that goes on here. In fact, no government system seems to be in place to monitor the learning outcomes of the elementary educational system, except the system of examinations. The World Bank (2006a) summarises the results of quality monitoring of primary education by different studies (Table 5.10).

There is, till date, no comprehensive official assessment of the quality of learning in schools. Until the basic problem of improving school facilities, increasing access to schools by the disadvantaged sections and tackling teacher absenteeism is resolved, slogans like 'Education for all' will remain in the realm of wishful thinking.

5.5 A new vision of reforms

Targeted interventions

While the overall performance of the social sectors in India is a matter of concern, what is even more worrying is the concentration of distress

Table 5.10 Examples of low learning achievement in primary schools

Study and reference population	Example of learning achievement
Pratichi Trust 2002 – Three districts in West Bengal	Only one of 14 (7 per cent) children in class III and IV who were not privately tutored could write their own name
Banerjee and others 2004 – Urban schools in Vadadora and Mumbai	Less than half of children in class IV (47 per cent) reached Math Standard I competence
Baseline diagnostic test districts of Andhra Pradesh (AP)	Only 12 per cent of children in class II to V could do single digit subtraction; only 54 per cent could answer a question that required counting to three
Baseline test in Jaunpur district in UP of children aged 7–14 in government schools	72 per cent could do no numerical operations and 51 per cent could not read simple sentences

Source: World Bank, 2006a.

in a few regions, districts and blocks. While this regional configuration of distress is shaped partly by the pre-existing social inequalities, it is also determined by the strength or weakness of public action in correcting these. Given their highly unequal distribution across regions, the best way to universalising access to public goods seems to be to concentrate our interventions on the states/districts/blocks where the problem is the most acute. This also flows from the perspective of social equity that dictates that it is the ethical duty of a nation to protect the most vulnerable sections of its population as a matter of priority. Using a diverse set of criteria, the Planning Commission has prepared a list of 170 most backward and 'extremist-affected' districts in the country (Planning Commission, 2005). Our calculations show that 82 per cent of these districts have a high IMR, 66 per cent have a low female literacy rate and 64 per cent have a high incidence of SCs and STs compared to the national average. Fifty five of these 170 districts are also classified by the Planning Commission as 'extremist-affected', implying that the level of popular discontent in these districts has crossed the threshold of tolerance and has taken violent forms. These districts represent an overlap between high concentration of disadvantaged sections, poor service delivery, extreme deprivation and violent protest.

We also note that the district in India is still too large a unit to capture differences accurately. There are sharp intra-district variations in development indicators, which could only be captured by going below further to the level of blocks. All states have developed their own disaggregated databases on development indicators, which could be used for a mapping of backwardness and concentration of deprivation at the block level. Using such maps, we would be able to identify the 1000 most backward blocks from a total of 6000 blocks in India, in terms of the availability of basic services like drinking water, sanitation, health and education. If energies of intervention and reform are concentrated on these most backward blocks, a significant impact on improving service delivery could be achieved. Within these blocks, groups of villages could be identified as hunger and malnutrition 'hot-spots'", where special attention needs to be provided. The broad framework within which an action programme could be drawn up and implemented is suggested in the next section.

Stepping up public investment

Reforms in the public sector in rural India presuppose a heavy dose of public investment. It is true that such investment would continue to go down the drain in the absence of reforms. But it equally must be admitted that without a big push, reforms would be impossible to implement. We need to arrive at the broad orders of magnitude of the step up required in public investment for universalisation in the social sector in India.

The National Commission on Macroeconomics and Health (NCMH) has made an estimate of the cost of drinking water security in 2005 (NCMH, 2005). The estimated cost is that of covering 30 per cent of the uncovered habitations with piped water supply and the remaining 70 per cent with hand pumps. The unit cost of the piped water supply scheme is taken as Rs 1200 per capita and that of the hand pump scheme as Rs 140 per capita as per government norms. The estimated amount comes to Rs 175,930 million. We feel this figure could be a gross underestimate because, as discussed above, the household coverage data used in this estimates could be defective. Unless proper surveys are conducted and a real picture of availability obtained, estimation of cost is not possible.

In the case of sanitation, we feel the government subsidy per toilet should at least be Rs 6000 per toilet for new construction and Rs 3000 per toilet for upgrading existing low-quality constructions. In 2008, there were 157.4 million rural households in India, of which 57 per cent (89.7 million) had a toilet. This leaves a gap of 67.7 million households in need of new toilet construction. At a cost norm of Rs. 6000 per toilet, the amount required works out to Rs 406,130 million. We also estimate that 50.3 million households supposed to have been provided with a toilet under TSC will need an investment of Rs. 3000 per toilet for upgrading their existing toilet. This figure works out to Rs 151,060 million. Thus, in our estimate, the total amount required to cover all households with quality sanitation is Rs 557,190 million. If we stagger this investment over a period of five years, the annual expenditure comes to Rs 111,440 million, which works out to about 0.3 per cent to 0.4 per cent of the GDP. Considering the importance of household sanitation, we feel this is an investment, which the nation has to make to compensate for the monumental neglect of this crucial component of public health during the last 60 years.

The NCMH has made a comprehensive estimate of additional expenditure required for universalisation of health care in India (NCMH, 2005). They estimate that the additional expenditure required comes to Rs 740,000 million (2.2 per cent of the GDP), of which Rs 340,000 million is the capital investment required to revive the battered infrastructure of health care in India. Along with current level of 0.9 per cent of the GDP committed to health, this raises the public expenditure to three per cent of the GDP.

The most recent estimate of universalisation of elementary education is the one prepared by the Central Advisory Board on Education (CABE) report (CABE, 2005). The estimates of the CABE report are based on the assumptions about pupil/teacher ratios and teacher salaries, on the basis of which it has constructed several scenarios. The additional annual expenditure required on elementary education emerging from these estimates is in the range of Rs 642,390 million to Rs 872,920 million per annum. It may be remembered that at present the expenditure on elementary education is about Rs 560,000 million or nearly two per cent of the GDP. The CABE Committee's proposal implies at least a doubling of expenditure over a five-year period. Though the first scenario (1A) is the most expensive, the CABE report strongly supports it in the interest of quality; it is also equitable and provides adequate remuneration to the teacher who is to be the main instrument for providing the right to education (CABE, 2005).

5.6 Conclusions

Over the last decade, India has emerged as one of the fastest growing economies in the world, an attractive destination for foreign capital. But for millions of its poorest people it has not been a very happy time. The social sectors we have dealt with in this paper have both an 'intrinsic and instrumental' (Dreze and Sen, 2002) value for our citizens. They govern both their present well being and future prospects. But they do so not just for the citizens. These public goods also determine the future trajectory of growth of the Indian economy. Every democratic state in history has invariably delivered basic social services to its citizens. India's record in this regard has been abysmal. With more than 60 years having gone by since independence and the state having failed to deliver on elementary education, primary health care, drinking water and sanitation, there are growing calls for privatisation as the answer to what is indeed a crisis of governance. We believe, however, that such a view is a reflection of great intellectual, policy and political ennui.

Markets fail when there are no profits to be made for capitalists or when the private rate of return on investment is significantly lower than the social rate of return. Reforms in India correctly entail privatisation in sectors like airports, airlines, hotels, cars, et cetera but throughout the world, public goods like health, education and the environment have been provided for or protected by governments. Ever since the Great Depression of the 1930s, capitalist democracies have seen major investments by the state in the fundamental rights of citizens. The difference is that in the

US, Europe, South-East and East Asia, the state has invariably delivered. In India it has failed – both in the magnitude of its effort, as also in its quality. Thus, the suffering of our people is not just a tale of market failure. It is also a failure of governance. The reforms for the poor must address this failure.

A key element in our strategy moving forward is to focus on regions where distress is the maximum. We have shown that there are distinct regions where human development indicators are the weakest. We suggest that for each programme we arrive at a list of the 1000 most backward blocks and begin our interventions from there, bringing them up at least to the national norm within the next five years. We also suggest opening up the state space to greater professionalisation and building partnerships with civil society institutions and centres of professional excellence in each of the social sectors to improve quality of services provided. We need to move urgently beyond what we have characterised as the strategy of 'universalisation without quality' towards providing high-quality elementary education, primary health care, drinking water and sanitation to every citizen of India.

Notes

*Authors wish to thank C. Rammanohar Reddy and R. Nagaraj for comments on an earlier draft. They also wish to thank the participants of the project workshop in Mumbai for useful comments and suggestions on how to improve the chapter.

1. Tobin defines this as 'non-market egalitarian distributions of commodities essential to life and citizenship that are in inelastic supply' (Tobin, 1970).
2. NFHS-3 reports the astonishing fact that for 77 per cent of the women following any 'modern method' of family planning have been sterilised, compared to only two per cent of their husbands (MoHFW, 2007).
3. In 1968, a keen observer of south Asia noted, 'except for Pakistan and India, the South Asian countries seem to spend a larger part – 40 to 65 per cent – of their outlays for instruction on primary education. The proportion seems to be highest in those countries – Malaya, Ceylon, the Philippines and Thailand – which have the highest economic levels and have adopted the longest primary school courses and are nearest to the goal of providing children with elementary education' (Myrdal, 1968: 1665).
4. According to the Eleventh Plan document, this number has now reduced to seven million, out of which 4.8 per cent were never enrolled in school (Planning Commission, 2008).
5. However, in recent years, there has been a robust growth of the private sector in education too, thanks to the poor quality of public provisioning. However, the effects of this are more visible in schools at a higher level and near urban areas.

References

Balakrishnan, Pulapre (2007): 'The Recovery of India: Economic Growth in the Nehru Era', *Economic and Political Weekly*, Vol. 42, No. 45, November 10: 52–66.

Banerjee, Abhijit, Angus Deaton and Esther Duflo (2004): 'Health Care Delivery in Rural Rajasthan', *Economic and Political Weekly*, Vol. 39, No. 9, February 28: 944–49.

Banerjee, Abhijit and Esther Duflo (2005): 'Addressing Absence', Department of Economics, MIT.

CABE (2005): *Report of the Central Advisory Board of Education (CABE) Committee on Free and Compulsory Education Bill and Other Issues Related to Elementary Education*, New Delhi.

Central statistical organisation, *National Accounts Statistics*, Ministry of Statistics and Programme Implementation, Government of India, various issues.

Chakravarty, S. (1987): *Development Planning: The Indian Experience*, New Delhi: Oxford University Press.

Dasgupta, M. (2005): 'Public Health in India – An Overview', *World Bank Policy Research Working Paper 3787*, Washington DC: World Bank.

Deolalikar, A.B (2005): *Attaining the Millennium Development Goals in India: Reducing Infant Mortality, Child Malnutrition, Gender Disparities, and Hunger-Poverty and Increasing School Enrollment*, New Delhi: Oxford University Press.

Dev, Mahendra and J. Mooij (2002): 'Social Sector Expenditures in the 1990s: Analysis of Central and State Budgets', *Economic and Political Weekly*, Vol. 37, No. 9, March 2: 853–66.

DISE (2006): *Elementary Education in India: Analytical Report 2005*, District Information System for Education, New Delhi: NIEPA.

DLHS (2008): *Reproductive and Child Health: Report of the District Level Household and Facility Survey – III*, Ministry of Health and Family Welfare, Government of India.

Dreze, Jean and Amartya Sen (2002): *India: Development and Participation*, New Delhi: Oxford University Press.

Engerman, Stanley and Kenneth Sokoloff (2001): 'Colonialism, Inequality and Long Run Paths of Development', in Abhijt Banerjee, Ronald Benabou and Dilip Mookherjee (eds) *Understanding Poverty*, Oxford University Press.

GoI (1966): *Report of the Education Commission* (Kothari Commission), New Delhi: Government of India.

GoI (2007): *Sustaining the Sanitation Revolution: India Country Paper*, SACOSAN III, New Delhi.

Govinda, R. and Y. Josephine (2005): 'Para Teachers in India: A Review', *Contemporary Education Dialogue*, Vol. 2: 2, Spring.

Guha, Sumit (2004): *Health and Population in South Asia from Earliest Times to Present Day*, Cambridge: Cambridge University Press.

Hammer, Jeffrey, Yamini Aiyar and Saminah Samji (2006): 'Bottom's Up: To the Role of Panchayati Raj Institutions in Health and Health Services', Social Development Papers, South Asia Series, Paper No. 98, Washington DC: The World Bank.

Haq, M. (1997): *Human Development in South Asia*, New Delhi: Oxford University Press.

Joshi, Seema (2006): 'Impact of Economic Reforms on Social Sector Expenditure in India', *Economic and Political Weekly*, Vol. 41, No. 4, January 28: 358–65.

Kohli, Atul (2008): 'State and Redistributive Development in India', *paper for the UNRISD Project*, 'Poverty Reduction and Policy Regimes' (This volume).
Kremer, M., N. Chaudhury, F.H. Rogers, K. Muralidharan and J. Hammer, (2005): 'Teacher Absence in India: A Snapshot', *Journal of the European Economic Association*, Vol. 3, No. 2–3, 658–67.
Leclercq, François (2002): 'The Impact of Education Policy Reforms on the Education System: A Field Study of EGS and Other Primary Schools in Madhya Pradesh', Université de Paris I (Sorbonne), Paris, and Centre de Sciences Humaines, New Delhi.
MoHRD (2007): *Selected Education Statistics, 2004–05*, Ministry of Human Resource Development, New Delhi: Government of India.
MoHFW (2007): *National Family Health Survey–3, National Report*, Ministry of Health and Family Welfare, New Delhi: Government of India.
MoRD (2004): *Rural Water and Sanitation Sector Status and Issues*, Presentation before the Minister of Rural Development, Government of India, New Delhi.
Myrdal, G. (1968): *Asian Drama: An Inquiry into the Poverty of Nations*, 3 vols, London: Allen Lane.
Nagaraj, R., (2000): 'Indian Economy since 1980: Virtuous Growth or Polarisation?', *Economic and Political Weekly*, Vol. 35, No. 32, August 5–11, 2831–38.
Nagaraj, R., (2012): 'Development Strategies and Poverty Reduction – Indian Experience', Chapter 2 of this book.
NCEUS (2007): Report of the National Commission on Enterprises in Unorganised Sector, New Delhi: Government of India.
NCMH (2005): *Report of the National Commission on Macroeconomics and Health*, New Delhi: Ministry of Health and Family Welfare, World Health Organisation and Government of India.
NEP (1986): *New Education Policy, 1986*, New Delhi: Government of India.
NHP (1983): *National Health Policy*, Ministry of Health and Family Welfare, New Delhi: Government of India.
NHP (2002): *National Health Policy, 2002*, New Delhi: Government of India.
NSSO (2005): *Morbidity, Health Care and the Condition of the Aged, National Sample Survey, 60th Round*, Ministry of Statistics and Programme Implementation, New Delhi: Government of India.
NSSO (2006): *Status of Education and Vocational Training in India 2004–05, National Sample Survey, 61st Round*, Ministry of Statistics and Programme Implementation, New Delhi: Government of India.
NUEPA (2008): *Elementary Education in India: Progress Towards UEE*, Analytical Report and Tables 2006–07, New Delhi: National University of Educational Planning and Administration (NUEPA).
Planning Commission (1980): *Eighth Five-Year Plan*, Planning Commission, New Delhi: Government of India.
Planning Commission (2002): *Tenth Five-Year Plan*, Vol. I, Planning Commission, New Delhi: Government of India.
Planning Commission (2005): *Report of the Inter-Ministry Task Group on Addressing Regional Imbalances*, Planning Commission, New Delhi: Government of India.
Planning Commission (2007): *Groundwater Management and Ownership: Report of the Expert Group*, Planning Commission, New Delhi: Government of India.
Planning Commission, (2008): *Eleventh Five-Year Plan, 3 vols*, Planning Commission, New Delhi: Government of India.

Pritchett, Lant and Varda Pande (2006): 'Making Primary Education Work for India's Rural Poor: A Proposal for Effective Decentralisation', *Social Development Paper No. 95*, Social Development Department – South Asia, Washington DC: World Bank.

Qadeer, Imrana (2005): 'Continuities and Discontinuities in Public Health: The Indian Experience', in Amiya Bagchi and Krishna Soman (eds) *Maladies, Preventives and Curatives: Debates in Public Health in India*, New Delhi: Tulika Books.

Rajan, S. Irudaya, P. Mohanachandran Nair, K.L. Sheela, Lalitendu Jagatdeb and Nihar Ranjan Mishra (2008): 'Infant and Child Mortality in India: District Level Estimates', New Delhi: Population Foundation of India.

Saxena, N.C. (2008): 'Flush with Success: Rural India is Awash with Sanitation Revolution', http://ddws.gov.in/popups/MediaCorner/Flush,withSuccess.pdf.

Sen, Gita, Aditi Iyer and Asha George (2002): 'Structural Reforms and Health Equity: A Comparison of NSS Surveys, 1986–87 and 1995–96', *Economic and Political Weekly*, Vol. 37, No. 14, April 6: 1342–52.

Shankar, Deepa (2007): 'What is the Progress in Elementary Education Participation in India during the Last Two Decades? An Analysis using NSS Education Rounds', *World Bank Policy Working Paper 42112*, Washington DC: World Bank.

Shariff, Abusaleh, Prabir Ghosh and S.K. Mondal (2002): 'State-Adjusted Public Expenditure on Social Sector and Poverty Alleviation Programmes', *Economic and Political Weekly*, Vol. 37, No. 8, February 23: 767–87.

SRS (2006): *Census of India: Sample Registration System Bulletin*, Vol. 41, No. 1, October, New Delhi.

Tilak, J.B.G. (2006): 'Trends in Public Expenditure on Education: A Contrast between Two Educationally Backward States', *Indian Journal of Political Economy*, Vol. 18, No. 1–2, January–June: 1–34.

Tobin, J. (1970): 'On Limiting the Domain of Inequality', *Journal of Law and Economics*, Vol. 13, No. 2: 263–77.

WaterAid (2006): *Drinking Water and Sanitation – A National Status Paper*, New Delhi: WaterAid India.

World Bank (2004): *Making Services Work for the Poor: World Development Report 2004*, Washington DC: World Bank.

World Bank (2006a): *India – Inclusive Growth and Service Delivery: Building on India's Success*, Development Policy Review, Washington DC: World Bank.

World Bank (2006b): *Equity and Development: World Development Report 2006*, Washington DC: World Bank.

World Bank (2007): *World Development Indicators 2007*, New York: Oxford University Press.

World Bank (2008): *World Development Indicators 2008*, New York: Oxford University Press.

6
Organised Interests, Development Strategies and Social Policies

Vivek Chibber

6.1 Introduction

The relation between organised interests and the state has been a major theme for research for some time now. It has naturally coalesced around the two major forms of state witnessed in the capitalist world during the twentieth century – the welfare state in advanced industrial countries and developmental state in the global South. The former has largely been an accompaniment to the onset of social democracy during the inter-war period, though earlier steps toward its institutionalisation were taken during the late nineteenth century, most notably in Bismarckian Germany. Starting with the wave of labour radicalism that took off after the Great Depression, and continuing into the immediate post-war period, social democratic parties gained influence in large parts of the Western world. At the heart of their agenda was an extremely ambitious programme of social welfare legislation, which was implemented as a direct response to their main social base, the industrial working class. Developmental states, unlike their welfarist counterparts, did not arise as a direct response to working-class pressure, though labour did sometimes figure as part of the political coalition supporting them. The most important constituency behind developmentalism was the domestic capitalist class. This difference in political base reflects the quite distinct dilemmas faced by social interests in advanced and developing countries of the world economy – the former being mainly concerned with accelerating the pace of capitalist development, and the latter with managing its social effects. But the difference in constituencies also directly affected the range of issues taken up by the political elites, and how these tasks have been prioritised.

This paper takes up the relation between organised interests and social policy in a developmental setting. By social policy I shall refer to the distributive dimension of state action – policies aimed at influencing the distribution of wealth and income. The most direct examples of such actions are what are known as social welfare policies, but it also includes state-sponsored employment programmes, and any other programmes that de-link the acquisition of goods from the consumer's participation in the labour market. Social policies, thus, cover the same range of activities normally associated with welfarism. But I shall also take up how the state's developmental commitments affected the distribution of wealth and income. This is because, in developing countries, state planning for growth was explicitly intended to accommodate concerns around distribution – planning was supposed to cover growth and social welfare, even though welfare policies did not figure as a distinct, stand-alone part of policy. So I shall examine the relation between social interests and state policy in the domain of development planning and social welfare.

Even though scholarship on states has coalesced around the two distinct themes of welfarism and developmentalism, it has drawn from a narrow range of theoretical perspectives in both domains. Over the past 25 years or so, as the influence of Parsonian functionalism has declined, state theory has become dominated by three basic approaches: pluralism, state-centrism and class analysis (Alford and Friedland, 1985). But of the three, it is the latter two in particular that have gained prominence, especially in the literature on the two state-forms under consideration here.[1] During the 1970s and into the early 1980s, it was the political economy and class-based approach that exercised a tremendous influence in analyses of the state; in the more recent past, the pendulum has shifted away from class analysis and toward a more state-centred approach.

India scholarship has been characterised by the coexistence of both approaches, though in recent years there has been a noticeable shift away from a serious consideration of the role of organised interests. But the most conspicuous element in the analyses of the Indian state has not been the theoretical approaches that govern it, but rather the subjects that have been taken up. There is a noticeable dearth of research on the evolution of social policies on the subcontinent. There is, no doubt, a rich body of work tracing the effects of various social programmes – their incidence, implementation, success rates and political geography. There is, in other words, considerable descriptive research on state policies. What is lacking is a careful analysis of the politics of policy formation – the role of interest groups, the autonomy of the state, the formation of policy, and so on. While there have been some noteworthy attempts to analyse the policy process, and I will draw upon some of them in this paper, they have been rather sporadic. This is not unusual among developing countries, where attention to the developmental component of state policy has been much more pronounced than to its welfarist side. But India scholarship has, it seems, been harder hit by this phenomenon than many other large developing countries.

The basic proposition of this paper stems from a class-based approach to state policy, and can be stated succinctly: in a capitalist setting, the basic orientation of state policy will be biased toward the interests of the business community, both with respect to social policy and economic policy. This is fundamentally brought about by the fact that states in modern economies depend on tax revenues for their reproduction, and taxes are derived from income coming out of the accumulation process – either as profits or as wages. In order to simply stay afloat, states, therefore, have to place the highest priority to keeping economic growth humming along. Economic growth in capitalism rides on the rate of investment, and investment is not in the hands of the state. By definition, investment in capitalism is in private hands. State policy, therefore, has to be geared fundamentally to maintaining a climate that investors consider appropriate to their profit calculations. Simply on a commitment to its own reproduction, then, the state in capitalism has to give the first preference to the preferences of the investor class, that is, capitalists. This structural power of capital is reinforced by the fact that capitalists also are the most well-financed and connected lobbying group in the political process. The political muscle of this group amplifies their economic power.

This does not mean that other groups are powerless in the policy process. To the extent that they are able to organise themselves and force their presence into the policy process, other social classes can insert their own interests into policy outcomes. In particular, labour can push its agenda if it participates in an organised and mobilised capacity. This is especially important in the analysis of the state's welfare functions, which have expanded in the twentieth century largely in response to demands by organised labour. The birth of the welfare state in the West was either directly or indirectly brought about by a mobilised labour movement, and its expansion appears to have been in tandem with the growth of labour's power (Hicks, 1999; Stephens and Stephens, 2001; Korpi, 1978). But it is important to note that the working class only counteracts capitalists' power in the lobbying process, and that too, rarely as an equal. Labour has no counterpart to capital's structural power, which is based on the latter's control over economic investment. While other groups can confront business as organised actors, they have no parallel power at the structural level.

This means that in all capitalist settings, the baseline direction of policy will be biased toward capitalist interests. In developing countries, this bias can be weakened by two other factors. First, capitalists can be a small and nascent actor in the overall economy, since agriculture typically accounts for a substantial chunk of the GDP. They will, therefore, have less structural power then their counterparts in advanced economies, and might have to share it with landed classes. Second, in addition to their small size, capitalists can be rather more dependent on the state than they are in rich countries – for finance, protection, technology acquisition, et cetera. This gives the state more leverage against local business than it has in industrial economies, a leverage that can be used to cater to other interests. Still, we should not exaggerate the effects of these factors. Though they certainly do modulate the influence of capital, they leave its basic primacy intact. First, even though landed classes might have considerable influence in the global South, they are, by now, typically capitalist landed classes. They represent another sector of capital, not a force arrayed against it. Second, the simple fact that states operate in a global capitalist economy means that they have to give special attention to local entrepreneurs, even if they are small in size. Indeed, one can say that, relative to its share in the economy, capital can be especially privileged in developing countries, since states are committed to creating a hothouse environment for their growth.

The upshot is that in any developing country where the local industry has progressed beyond a certain threshold, the policy orientation of the state will be biased toward the interests of domestic capital – agrarian and industrial. Between the two, there will be a tendency to increase the preference given to industry over agriculture, insofar as the state is committed to development. Within the policy domain, developmental functions will take preference over welfare functions. This is another reflection of a bias toward capital, in that, as I will show later, developmentalism has tended to commit to enhancing profits over wage growth. To the extent that the welfare orientation of the state depend, it will advance more or less in tandem with the growth in the power or the leverage of subordinate groups – the poor and labouring groups in urban and rural sectors, and political parties representing their interests. Here too, we can hazard a prediction: although social policy will be more advanced if subordinate groups have some presence in policy circles, it will be more effective and more munificent in cases where these groups are mobilised, as against simply being represented by intermediaries.

Thus, for the distributive dimension of development policy to be effective, it requires considerable inclusion of the poor and disenfranchised in the policy process; however, the manner in which they are included is of considerable importance. The most common form of inclusion in the developing world has been through various kinds of corporatist structures, which have the effect of relegating these subordinate groups to a passive role. Incorporation of this kind has been far less successful in fostering successful distributive policies. Where such policies have been more successful, working class and peasant organisations have been given, or have wrested for themselves, an active and participatory role in the policy process. This has required, in turn, that subordinate groups either be allowed to organise themselves independently of state control or that the state itself funnel resources toward such organisations of the working population. I will show this through an examination of the Indian case, with some comparative data from other developing countries. It is to be noted that this approach goes against the current thrust in Indian policy circles, where poverty reduction is increasingly relegated to market forces.

6.2 The evolution of policy in Indian development

The evolution of policy in post-independence India has gone through three broad phases, in which the balance between the state's developmental functions and its welfare functions has shifted over time. Table 6.1 summarises the shifts.

The Nehru years

The first period was under the leadership of Jawaharlal Nehru, whose tenure at the helm of the state stretched from 1947 to his death in 1964.

Table 6.1 Phases of state policy

Era	State's role in development	State's role in social policy
Nehru years	High (planned development)	Low (by-product of plans)
Indira Gandhi years	High (state-led development)	Increasing (welfare schemes)
Liberalisation	Low (reliance on market)	Low (reliance on market)

These years were marked by a near-absence of any real welfare policy, except in basic health and education. State policy was geared single-mindedly toward economic development, though under a dirigiste regime. Distributive matters were therefore folded into the domain of economic planning. Planning, for its part, was supposed to have been overseen by a state standing above sectional interests, and hence, able to cater to all social groups. But as we shall see, this was soon revealed to be a serious miscalculation, as dominant groups were able to turn policy outcomes toward their own interests. This not only precluded any real welfarist orientation, it also undermined the distributive goals of economic planning.

The Indira Gandhi era

The second period was largely coterminous with Indira Gandhi's rule, which extended from 1967 to 1980, with a brief hiatus in between. In the Gandhi years, the balance between developmentalism and welfare policy shifted somewhat toward the latter. This was in some measure because of Indira Gandhi's tilt toward the organised left, most of all the Communist Party, which gave a much greater opening to subaltern interests than had been possible under Nehru. But it was probably more powerfully driven by a wave of popular mobilisations starting in the late 1960s, extending into the mid-1970s, which pushed the Indian polity in a more populist direction. This was the period in which distributive measures were set up for the first time and poverty reduction was taken up explicitly as a goal of policy. Some real gains were made on this score, though they remained quite limited.

Liberalisation

The turn toward more market reliance is usually taken to have started in 1991, though in reality it began under Rajiv Gandhi in 1985, when V.P. Singh was the finance minister. Starting then, and more so since the mid-1990s, the state has turned toward a greater reliance on the market both for economic development and for distributional outcomes. This has had two implications for social policy: first, a diminution in the incidence of such policies; second, a shift away from universalism toward more targeted policies, apparently inspired by the American model of means-tested welfare programmes. In some respects this harkens to the Nehru years when social policy was almost absent from the state agenda. But now, it is accompanied by an unbridled and quite open celebration of market forces, as against the state paternalism of Nehru.

6.3 The Nehru years

State policy under the helm of Nehru's leadership was geared single-mindedly toward accelerating the rate of growth. The conventional understanding of the policy agenda that grew out of this commitment is that it led to a kind of dogmatic socialism, an obsessive valorisation of the public sector, to the point of squelching private initiative. A small, weak class of industrialists had little recourse but to go along, and worked to the best of its ability within the parameters established by the state (Bal Dev Nayar, 1989; 1999). In fact, the conventional picture is vastly overdrawn. Nehru was very careful to keep public sector expansion within the bounds that were acceptable to Indian business houses.[2] Almost every major body set up to design policy and new state institutions in the aftermath of independence was dominated by business leaders. It was taken for granted that Indian development would be a capitalist development, based primarily on the private sector. Nehru issued statements espousing socialism to be sure; but he did so while changing the meaning of the term. Socialism for Nehru basically meant a kind of state capitalism, with some influence from highly paternalistic Fabian leanings.[3] And this too, did not touch the dominance of Indian business houses in the industrial sector, nor did it make much of a dent in the power of landed classes. This had grave consequences for both development policy, as well as social policy. For while it was assumed, or hoped, that growth would take care of distribution, the influence of elite groups only further undermined an already weak impulse.

Industrial policy

The first three five-year plans were guided by the basic assumptions of Keynesian growth theory a la Harrod and Lewis, which focused powerfully on securing a jump in the rate of investment. This, in turn, required an increase in the savings rate, which was assumed to depend on funnelling income toward wealth holders. So a firm commitment to boosting investment seemed to depend on clamping down on consumption and increasing savings among asset-holders. If achieved, this would generate an increase in growth and employment, and hence, greater economic security for the poor. Note that, when the political ramifications of this apparently technical schema are considered, it cannot but privilege the interests of the wealthy. I will return to this later. But as regards labour, economic security for labour was taken to be a by-product of the growth process. The role of the state was to ensure that the required investment took place, at the appropriate level and in the warranted direction – this was the meaning of planning.

What would be the place of distribution in this framework? The primary instrument through which labour has pursued its distributive interests in the twentieth century is through collective bargaining. The Indian labour movement had powerful currents pressing for a reliance on this mechanism for setting wages in manufacturing. But while the new government did give lip service to encouraging direct negotiation between employers and employees, it set up various measures that in fact discouraged it. The prospect of disruption through strikes or job actions could not be countenanced in the crisis setting of the post-war years. So the new legislation developed an elaborate apparatus for arbitration of industrial disputes. The Industrial Disputes Act of 1947 forced unions to issue a 14-day notice in the event of a planned strike action, but also empowered the state to send the contending parties to compulsory arbitration if it deemed necessary. The involvement of the state into industrial relations was magnified by the passing of the minimum wage legislation in 1948, which called for the establishment of regional and sectoral wage boards, which would ensure a fair schedule of wages in key lines.

What is noteworthy is that, in the industrial sector, Nehru did not establish instruments specifically geared toward poverty reduction or income redistribution. These were folded into the planning framework, and subordinated to the growth imperative. Nonetheless, the government also did not settle for a complete reliance on the market for fair distributional outcomes. Guided by its basic paternalism, the state introduced itself as a participant and an adjudicator in industrial relations. The aim was to stop short of actually reversing market outcomes, but to still have some influence in their basic direction. If the profit motive was to be harnessed to developmental goals, the state would still smooth out some of its sharper edges.

On paper, the wage legislation and adjudication system seemed promising – since it presumed a basic neutrality vis-a-vis the key actors. But to the extent that investment was assumed to come from the private sector, policy decisions could not but privilege employer interests over those of labour. Nehru and the Indian National Congress fully internalised the imperative to build an appropriately friendly investment climate, to build business confidence. During the first two plans in particular, the worry about keeping business placated quickly overshadowed all other commitments. It would have been a mighty force in its own right under any circumstances. What made it especially pressing was the material situation after 1947. The Partition created a significant economic dislocation, magnifying the marginal effect of even a small downturn in investment. But even more importantly, Indian capitalists went on a political offensive after independence, exacerbating the economic disruption of the years with an investment slow-down. For more than two years, the Congress and the Indian capital were in a stand-off on the basic direction of policy for India's future development (Chibber, 2003, Chapter 6; Kidron, 1965). At the heart of this conflict was the issue of the state's power over the private sector – what would be the scope of industrial planning, what instruments would be put into place to implement it, and what would be the range of powers that planners would arrogate to themselves? The initial designs drawn up by the Congress leaders gave planners great authority to not only draw up economic plans, but also ensure business compliance with their dictates. But this initial vision broke against the shoals of business opposition.

In order to encourage the resumption of investment, planners found themselves scrambling to placate the business community. The first victim was labour policy. Legislation that had been passed would be implemented only if it did not interfere with the plans, and since the plans depended centrally on the participation of private capital, the implementation of labour legislation came to be influenced heavily by the demands of Indian business. The immediate expression of this new dynamic was the successful delay by the Planning Commission in the implementation of the Minimum Wages Act of 1948. Industry was extremely suspicious of any wage boards or statutory wage legislation, and this resulted in the state adopting a very cautious stance on the matter. Hence, there was a ten-year delay in the setting up of the wage boards that were to administer minimum wage legislation. Despite the fact that the law was passed in 1948, it was not until the late 1950s that the boards were in fact set up.[4] This left matters of distribution to individual or to collective bargaining. But here too, the intrusion of the arbitration system favoured employer interests. While the law provided for compulsory arbitration, it did nothing to ensure rapid delivery of a verdict. Management was left with the ability to drag out the proceedings for months, even years (Ramaswamy, 1984: 44–8)). This meant that under the new dispensation, collective bargaining held little value to employers, as their recalcitrance was only likely to deliver the parties to a conciliator or arbitrator, and in such a case, the whole matter would turn on which of the parties would give in first. And with immeasurably greater resources at its command, the odds, of course, always favoured management.

Agriculture

Matters were arguably worse in the agrarian sector. In industrial policy, the state did beat a retreat on many of its more ambitious designs at building a developmental state. Nevertheless, it remained programmatically committed to imposing some discipline of the pattern and direction of private investment – without which planning would be an entirely academic exercise. This, in turn, presumed some degree of discipline on local firms, and an apparatus designed to impose such discipline. Industrial policy required some degree of encroachment on the property rights of local capitalists. With regard to the agrarian sector, however, the retreat of the state was even more dramatic. Congress programmes had for quite some time been announcing a commitment to land reform, one of the cornerstones of its political agenda. But upon its ascension to power, the Nehru government backed off from its agrarian programme. The basic story is very well known, and does not require reiteration.[5] The retreat on land reform occurred in two steps: first, the matter was declared the responsibility and the prerogative of individual states, not the central government; and second, once at the state level, it was allowed to slowly die on the vine – hardly a surprise, as state legislatures were largely dominated by representatives of landed interests. While there was some success in the acquisition of surplus land, the progress of land-to-the-tiller reform never got very far.

The result with regard to organised interests and redistribution was two-fold: first, landed power remained largely intact in many parts of the country, though the limited redistribution that did take place created a new stratum of large peasants. What is relevant here is that the creation of rich peasants did not mitigate the unequal distribution of power, but simply created a new stratum within the rural elite. Economic policy would not, therefore, take on less of an elitist bias – it simply would be turned toward the newly emerging dominant group. Second, the failure of reform left intact a vast ocean of agrarian labourers clutching on to marginal holdings, or surviving as an underemployed rural proletariat. For this class of rural dwellers, there was a pressing need to deliver some kind of economic entitlements, since their own participation in rural markets fetched such meagre returns. Agrarian policy from the First Plan onward had to address this issue, however, cursorily.

The dilemma in the agrarian sector with regard to distributive outcomes was of the same kind as in industrial policy. The basic constraint lay in the development strategy itself, which viewed distribution as a by-product of the growth process. This being the case, welfare concerns were put on the back-burner as all attention came to be focused on boosting agrarian production. In the first three plans, which were drawn up around a heavy industrialisation strategy, this meant viewing the agrarian sector mostly through its supply dimension, not as a source of demand for consumption goods. Indeed, the Mahalanobis strategy was geared toward discouraging consumer goods, as resources were funnelled to heavy industry. This naturally meant that agrarian incomes were not a primary concern, and nor, by extension, was the matter of distribution. Even more, since a mobilisation of the agricultural surplus was of primary importance, any disruption of the reigning institutional structure was viewed with great trepidation. Hence, even while changes in property relations were pushed off the agenda, even a change in operational holdings – as through cooperativisation – failed to gain momentum. As Francine Frankel has chronicled, the commitment to agricultural cooperatives, as declared in Congress's Nagpur Resolution of 1959, remained, like so many other Congress resolutions, largely ornamental (Frankel, 1978, Chapter 5).

The second constraint was that the failure of reform left untouched the power of dominant groups in the countryside. This had the effect of enabling landlords to circumvent or block what little was tried in the way of redistribution or entitlement schemes during Nehru's time. Starting in the Second Plan, especially its latter years, and extending into the Third, Nehru instituted some measures to provide greater security of consumption and incomes to the rural poor. The main such measures were attempts at cooperatives, state trading in foodgrains and the community development programme (CDP). All of these were either responses to the glaring shortcomings in food policy, or, in the case of the CDP, an attempt to reorganise rural resource mobilisation in lieu of asset redistribution. But each one of these programmes came apart through resistance from the landed elites, typically in alliance with local merchants and traders. The fundamental problem of class constraints on state action was never tackled directly, and hence, proved to be the critical weakness of the strategy. The very institutions that were supposed to implement government policy – the Congress Party machine and the local state organisations – were thoroughly penetrated by groups hostile to agrarian policy. Even the halting attempts at reform tried by Nehru foundered against their resistance.

The Nehru years were thus marked by a conspicuous failure with regard to social policy. The basic framework for economic policy was such that it could not directly attend to the interests of the poor. Plans were geared primarily toward increasing the rate of growth, and since investment remained largely in private hands, a commitment to increasing the pace of investment could not, but translate into a special concern with the interests of dominant classes. There was a hope of sorts that the development process itself would deliver greater security to the poor and destitute; and in fairness, the Congress did initiate some attempts at protecting the economic interests of urban and rural workers, though wage and price legislation. But this was based on a fantasy – that the state could remain a neutral actor in the political arena. The ex ante bias toward the wealthy, embedded in any capitalist state, was further reinforced by the growth models that Indian planners adopted; and this favouring of the interests of dominant classes was aggravated by the latter groups' own political muscle, which resisted and undermined the few attempts at redistribution.

6.4 Indira Gandhi and the turn to social policy

The development experience under Nehru's tenure as prime minister was not without its achievements. India posted a respectable growth rate for the three plan periods, and even though land reforms were largely unsuccessful, there were real gains made in the distribution of foodgrains. But the one in which the Nehru era was a clear failure was in poverty reduction. The realisation of this fact among planners gained ground in the mid-1960s. Efforts to address the issue directly were boosted by economic and political developments at Nehru's death, when Indira Gandhi came to power. Gandhi initiated a move to the left in a kind of populist phase, which put the issue of poverty at centre stage. Finally, there was also an upturn in social unrest, which might very well have added to the urgency of the situation in the mind of political elites.

By the middle years of the Third Plan, there was a growing suspicion among planners that whatever the success of the first two plans might have been, there did not seem to have been many gains against poverty. One of the earliest studies of the extent of poverty, and the policy space to tackle it, was taken up by Pitambar Pant in the perspective planning division of the Planning Commission. Pant and his colleagues found that poverty levels remained at alarmingly high levels, and proposed a series of measures that might be taken to marry the growth strategy adopted by the Planning Commission with a minimum standard of living for the poor.[6] It is hard to say how far this concern with poverty reduction would have progressed had circumstances continued along the same groove as had been set by Nehru. After his death, however, an opening emerged that pushed the matter closer to the centre of policymaking.

The critical component of the new dispensation was probably the peculiar situation in which Gandhi found herself as she took power in 1967. While she was nominally the party leader and the prime minister, her base within the organisation was still exceedingly narrow. She found herself with the formal reins of power, but under the authority of the older generation of party bosses, known, ominously enough, as 'the syndicate'. The story of her tussle with this layer of regional bosses is very well known, and need not be reiterated here (see Frankel, 1978). But in 1969, Gandhi engineered a split within the Indian National Congress (INC), launching a new formation under her leadership, the Congress (I), which now became the ruling party. What is relevant for our purposes is the fact that, in launching this new party, Gandhi leaned heavily on the Congress left, which was disaffected with the experience of the past two decades, and reached out to the Communist Party of India for support in Parliament. The launching of the Congress (I) was thus coeval with a leftward turn in the Congress political orientation.

The shift to the left did not come out of the blue. It built on a general upswing of social movements and a commensurate improvement in the non-Congress Left's political fortunes. The parliamentary elections of 1967 were something of a turning point in Indian electoral history. The INC experienced a massive decline in its parliamentary seats. Though it still pulled in a majority of the seats, its share declined from almost three-fourths of the seats in 1962, to just over half in 1967. Meanwhile, the two communist parties and the major socialist parties increased their share of seats by almost 60 per cent, going from 47 seats in 1962 to 78 seats in 1967. To be sure, the right made equally impressive gains, with the Swatantra Party and the Jan Sangh balancing the left parties almost perfectly.[7] But the election showed two things: first, a shocking decline in the Congress Party's hegemony in Indian electoral politics, and second, an apparent polarisation in the political culture along the left–right divide. This electoral shift was accompanied by the outbreak of radical mobilisations in several parts of the country. Rural conflict led by the Maoist break-away groups was especially strong in West Bengal and in Andhra Pradesh, but a wave of radicalisation was sweeping across large parts of the country (Banerjee, 1984). One ought not to exaggerate the threat that these posed: India was not by any means on the verge of a revolutionary upsurge. Nevertheless, the intensification of class conflict was the most significant since 1947.

What, then, was the impact of the rising social conflict, if the threat that it actually posed is questionable? It is likely that its main contribution was to lend credibility and legitimacy to Gandhi's authoritarian populism. That is to say, because there was a real and visible mobilisation from below, which was acknowledged by political elites and magnified by the print media, Gandhi could use it as a lever to prise political capital for herself in her swing to the left. The party split in 1969 marked a turning point in her resort to radical legislation and populist strategies. Most spectacular was the bank nationalisation of 1969, but this was contemporaneous with her adopting the Garibi Hatao slogan, the public railing against large business houses, the passage of the Monopolies and Restrictive Trade Practices Act, and other measures apparently tilted against economic elites. Gandhi was able, in the course of this shift, to lean on the perception that she was responding to a real radicalisation of the population, a mobilisation from below. And in so doing, she could claim to be restoring the waning prestige of the Indian National Congress.

The political context is relevant to our purposes in two respects. First, it opened a greater space for redistributive policies than had been operative before. The combined effect of popular unrest and Gandhi's populist turn put the issue of poverty, and the failure of the plans in alleviating it, at centre stage. On the technical front, it could no longer be claimed, or even hoped, that the growth process itself would make any significant impact on poverty. It was clear that the particular regime of accumulation that India had adopted was generating a stable distributive outcome, one that was tilted markedly toward asset holders. On the political front, the ruling party could not any longer take for granted its hold on power, whether at the centre or in the states. Even had Gandhi not swung to the left after 1969, it is hard to imagine that the ruling party – Congress or not – could have ignored poverty alleviation as a real imperative. The weaknesses in India's economic model were now showing up in the political arena.

The political conjuncture, thus, propelled a move toward welfare measures. Starting in the 1970s, some well known policies were passed that were directed toward the poor – the PDS, the IRDP, the scheme for rural employment and credit programmes for rural producers. Of these, the PDS and the IRDP seem to have emerged as the most ambitious over the next couple of decades, though rural employment schemes have also figured prominently in some states. These new schemes were now added on to the existing expenditures for health and education, to form the backbone of the Indian states' social policy package.

While there was a move to expand the welfare functions of the Indian state, its specific modalities were mediated by the second aspect of the political conjuncture that is relevant for our purposes – the fact that the reforms were mainly the result of inter-elite competition, not a real mobilisation from below. As already noted, Gandhi's turn to populism was justified on grounds of a response to radical threats; these threats, however, were more flash than substance. They certainly pointed to a growing credibility gap for the Congress, but they did not amount to a broad-based mass mobilisation. What was more effective as a proximate cause of the left-ward turn was Gandhi's desire to outflank the party bosses, most of all the syndicate, and to establish her authority as a political leader. This very fact explains the most puzzling aspect of the reforms that she launched, which is their largely ornamental status.

Commentators have noted that while, Gandhi launched the Garibi Hatao campaign with great fanfare, it made little dent in actual policies. The Fourth Plan, launched in 1970, had almost no space for actual poverty alleviation programmes (Patnaik and Patnaik, 2001). Gandhi, for her part, embarked on a media campaign soon after her rout of the syndicate in 1969, to quell rising expectations of a serious radical turn, warning the party base to be realistic about what was actually possible. Of the measures described above, it is probably the IRDP that was a new venture; the PDS built on a system of food distribution put into place by the British (Swaminathan, 2000; Mooij, 1999), which had largely been abandoned in the 1950s and was now revived – and this did not require a great deal of administrative heavy-lifting. And most importantly, any real gains in poverty reduction did not begin registering until the late 1970s, a full decade after the left turn (Patnaik and Patnaik, 2001).

On the basis of the propositions outlined at the outset of this paper, the gap between rhetoric and reality ought not to be a surprise. To the extent that redistributive programmes actually transfer income or assets away from the rich and to the poor, they have required, historically, some genuine pressure on ruling classes and political elites. In its absence, the predicted outcome is what we witness under Gandhi's rule: some measures that score high on visibility but low on actual ambition, meant more to create public opinion than to address the real demands. These measures were meant more to widen her mass base than to actually tackle poverty. Hence, their efficacy remained limited.

In sum, the political context in which social policy has been conducted has established the basic parameters for its scope and scale. The basic thrust of Indian development policy has been to favour the propertied classes over the poor. This has made for little internal momentum for an ambitious social policy agenda. The developmental orientation has itself been a product of the underlying imbalance between labour and capital, but it has also, reciprocally, reinforced this imbalance. In the absence of a real mobilised threat, welfare policy initiatives have been the result of inter-elite competition for votes and mass constituencies. Gandhi's populist turn – more accurately, her turn to authoritarian populism – was the first and one of the most significant of such incidents. The kind of welfare state that this has produced is one in which the efficacy of social policy has been limited, and more geared toward patronage.

Given this basic set of parameters, it should not be surprising that poverty reduction became more prominent as a state initiative in the late 1970s. The Congress rout in 1977 was no accident; it heralded the end of one-party dominance as an accomplished fact in Indian politics. Starting with the Janata experiment, political competition became much more intense than it had been in the preceding three decades of independence. But underlying this was a deeper fissure in Indian politics, brought about by the transformation in rural relations by the green revolution, and by the aggregative effects of land reforms in some parts of the country. By the mid-1970s, traditional sources of political stability in the countryside were starting to break down, as rural class relations underwent a deep transformation (see Kohli, 1990; Corbridge and Harriss, 2000). A new stratum of the rural rich was asserting itself, turning away from the INC, and starting to throw up political formations of its own. The Congress found itself having to scramble to establish new linkages with rural elites, and emerging political leaders – as did other parties. The same incentives that impelled Gandhi toward a faux populism now emerged again, only more powerfully. Social policy, therefore, had a more powerful thrust behind it – while nevertheless remaining limited in its basic scope.

The basic argument about the relation between organised interests and social policy is strengthened if we examine the phenomenon at a subnational level. In recent studies of poverty reduction, the states that have fared most favourably have been those in which unions and popular organisations have been active forces in the political process. Timothy Besley and his colleagues have summarised the relevant findings, and report that West Bengal and Kerala have had the most success in rolling back poverty (Besley et al., 2007). It is worth examining this finding. Kerala is probably the more well known case of the two. It was one of the first states to acquire a ramified PDS system, largely because of mass pressure, as early as 1942–3 (Ramachandran, 1996). Over the course of five decades, a political culture has persisted in which unions and mass organisations have been highly mobilised for political ends. It is significant that, while Kerala's achievements are sometimes identified with the successful history of the CPI(M) there, the latter has not ever held office for an extended period of time. Since it first took office in 1957, the CPI(M) has alternated its rule with the Congress Party, unlike its experience in West Bengal where it has held uninterrupted office for 30 years. In this period, Kerala has consistently scored the highest of any Indian state in per capita welfare measures – despite long periods of sub-par economic growth. This cannot be directly attributed to having a communist party in power, since the Congress has shared office with it. The direct reason is that, in the presence of a highly mobilised and articulate populace, the state faces a real threat to its stability if it ignores mass demands.

West Bengal is in some measures like Kerala, in that it also boasts a highly politicized electorate. But since the CPI(M)'s ascension to power in 1978, it cannot claim to have the same degree of mobilisation as Kerala. Indeed, in some respects, the communists have very adroitly de-mobilised parts of their base.[8] But the CPI(M) is programmatically committed to redistributive policies, and has positioned itself at the left of the political spectrum in West Bengal. It came to power with a very radical programme for redistribution, effected a land reform that, on most every account, was highly successful. This reform has been supplemented with a very ambitious expansion of the PDS, which made the state one of the biggest beneficiaries of the programme by the 1980s (Swaminathan, 2000). Thus, asset redistribution has been supplemented by an extension of entitlements. The findings of Burgess et al. confirm what Atul Kohli found in his research of poverty reduction programmes in the 1980s, that they are most successful in states where a mobilised electorate can be found, and where this base has organised links to a political party (Kohli, 1987).

This is not the only route to successful social policy. Other states have had some success in poverty reduction, though it is significant that, of all the states that score highly in Burgess et al.'s study, it is only Orissa that can claim to base this on state programmes. Other states where poverty has been receding – Andhra Pradesh, Punjab and Haryana – have also experienced high growth rates, so it is possible that it is the latter and not social policy that is behind this phenomenon. But if Orissa's success is real, then it is worth examining the conditions that might explain it.

The general pattern of subnational fortunes with social policy tends to confirm the proposition that welfare measures are directly linked to an organised pressure by the poor. In India since independence, such pressure has not been very high, nor very organised. To the extent that national legislation has tackled the issue, it has been a top-down effort at controlled mobilisation and patronage. This elite competition expanded in the decades after 1970. This explains why poverty reduction in India has been largely a failure, while still exhibiting a definite favourable trend in the decades before the liberal turn.

By the 1990s the Indian state had stabilised its pattern of intervention. Perhaps the most noteworthy point in this regard is that even though the per capita poverty reduction expenditures in India rose between 1970 ands 1990, they remained very low, both on an absolute level and relative to other state expenditures (Mundle and Rao, 1997, Table 7). Second, on an international scale, Indian expenditures remained at average or below average levels.

6.5 India under liberalisation

In the years of India's dirigiste development strategy, welfare policy never occupied an important policy space. I have argued that this was not a simple product of the technical aspects of the economic models that were followed – though these did reinforce the class bias of the policies. The weakness of India's social policies was a direct outcome of the balance of power between social groups – domestic business and landed classes on one side, and workers and the rural poor on the other. In other words, India was never not pro-rich. What shifted in the pre-reform period was the nature of political rule, from a stable polyarchy to a kind of competitive polyarchy. This had two effects: it allowed for the emergence of real measures to attract the poor into new political alliances, but it also kept the range of social policy within strict limits.

Despite the inadequacy of the social policy framework during these years, it cannot be ignored that the 1980s did witness some real progress with regard to poverty reduction. Over the past 15 years, however, in spite of the gains made in the recent past, the state has drawn back from many of its social policy commitments. This has occurred in a context in which the basic framework of dirigisme has also been overturned – bringing in train a shift in the balance of power between dominant and subordinate groups.

In agriculture, income growth has been limited by a general stagnation in the entire sector. Remarkably, however, in spite of the generally unspectacular rates of growth, state support to dominant groups in the rural sector continued on an upward ascent in the 1980s and 1990s (Gulati and Narayanan, 2003). The steady character of this support reflected one of the most important developments in Indian politics during the decades after Nehru's death, which was the emergence of a newly consolidated and assertive lobby of rich farmers (Brass, 1995). In the wake of the spread of new agricultural technologies of the 1970s, subsidies for power and fertilisers became an especially central component of economic policy, since these technologies were, famously, scale-neutral, but input-intensive, – that is, they required heavy investments in power, water, fertilisers, et cetera. So while farmers in some states – particularly in the north and north-west – were certainly able to commit to the use of new techniques, they also pressed their demands that the state defray as much of the costs of this venture as was possible. The first inkling of these new groups' power was the rise of Charan Singh in the Janata Party, culminating in his short premiership (Byres, 1981). But it continued and even accelerated through the 1980s and 1990s, and formed the political basis of the steady rise of agricultural subsidies (*see* Corbridge and Harriss, 2000). The significant point here is that the continued subsidisation during the 1990s represented a quite conspicuous sop to dominant rural classes, even as the rhetoric of scaling back state expenses continued – and more importantly, even as the wage growth in the rural sector showed little improvement (Himanshu, 2005).

The developments in agriculture did not reflect a shift in political power – dominant classes always had an upper hand in the sector – so much as its assertion in a new form. It was in industry that a more palpable shift in power occurred. Research on the politics of liberalisation in industry is still very thin, but some of the broad contours can now be gleaned. Liberalisation began in some significant ways during Rajiv Gandhi's tenure in the mid-1980s, and was adopted as a full-blown policy after 1991. This represented a turn away from the dirigisme of the Nehru–Gandhi years, and was driven by two forces. First, new business groups, which had appeared and matured under the statist regime, found themselves blocked in their further growth because of the cosy nexus that had been established between state planners and established business houses. While Dhirubhai Ambani's Reliance Group has often been pointed to as a driving force in this dynamic, it is probably not representative of the forces behind liberalisation. Reliance was, if anything, a paradigmatic example of adroit manipulation of the licence regime, not of direct opposition to it. More significant, probably, were smaller units that grew as subcontractors and suppliers to dominant houses, and which sought to break into new lines, but found themselves shut out because of state regulation on new investment. These smaller groups established themselves in regional as well as national parties as vocal opponents of the 'licence-quota raj' (*see* also Kohli, 2006a and 2006b).

The other force behind the shift was undoubtedly the political elite with some higher echelons of the economic bureaucracy (Shastri, 1995). Some caution is needed here. Much of the scholarly literature on liberalisation points to the decisions taken by Rajiv Gandhi and by his finance minister, V.P. Singh, to initiate liberalisation in the mid-1980s – making it seem like an autonomous move by the state. But it is also true that Rajiv Gandhi took measures to ensure that there would be a solid base among the Indian business community for this shift – indicating that he expected opposition, and that he was aware that states cannot ignore the sentiments of the most powerful economic actors. Perhaps the most important political measure he took was the promotion of the Confederation of Indian Industries (CII), which had hitherto been a minor business association, mainly of engineering firms, but was now adopted as a major partner of the Indian state. In so doing, he actively sought to create a counterweight to the established business associations like FICCI, which were under the leadership of the biggest business houses (ibid., Chapter 6). Within a few years, the CII became a rival to FICCI and other chambers, and was also the most active supporter of liberalisation.

By the early 1990s, when the wholesale turn away from dirigisme was adopted, the India state had developed a considerable base in the business community in favour of the turn. In addition to the smaller and middling groups that had been chafing under the old regime, there was also now a phalanx of bigger, more dynamic firms in the CII that were allied with the economic bureaucracy. This opened the door to a noticeable shift in social policy as well.

The most direct effect on welfare has been through trends in wages in the organised sector. There is evidence of a more aggressive stance by employers toward industrial disputes, as evidenced in secular rise in lockouts (Datt, 2003; Shyam Sundar, 2004). This increase in lockouts has been concurrent with a drastic decline in strike activity (Anant et al., 2006: 252–3). Employers have, thus, become more aggressive, and labour more cautious, in an environment in which the state has made clear its impatience with labour regulations and protections. Unsurprisingly, this trend in industrial conflict has resulted in a noticeable shift in the distributive sphere – an appreciable decline in the share of wages in the manufacturing sector, and as its concomitant, a jump in the share of profits. A detailed study of industrial relations since the 1980s by Debdas Banerjee reveals a drop in the wage share, from 33 per cent of net value added to 17 per cent between 1985 and 2000; conversely, the profit share rose from around 16 per cent in the mid-1980s to 30 per cent in 2000 (Banerjee, 2005, Figure 2.1). Together, this data points firmly in the direction of a shift in the balance of power away from labour and in capital's favour.

The shift in income shares has occurred in a context where employment generation has been much slower than hoped for. A recent study by R. Nagaraj found a drop of 15 per cent in the number of workers employed in the manufacturing sector between 1995–6 and 2001–2 (Nagaraj, 2004) – in spite of the protections against lay-offs supposedly provided by Indian labour law. Nagaraj refers to this process as 'reforms by stealth', as governments have either decided to not enforce the laws, or have found it harder to do so. Indeed, a spate of recent studies has questioned the proposition that labour law has been a drag on flexibility at all (Shyam Sundar, 2004; Deshpande, 2004). These laws have certainly looked fearsome on paper, but employers appear to have found a great many avenues to avoid their force, especially in recent years. In sum, recent research suggests that not only have the working poor experienced a loss in job opportunities, but that the quality of employment has declined – with less power to negotiate their terms, less leverage against employers, and a declining share of income. The liberalisation era has, it appears, worked to the favour of capital in quite striking ways.

This data makes it especially worrisome that the state has also decided to roll back its social policy commitments at the same time as labour finds its economic fortunes waning. It means, quite directly, that labour is being squeezed from both sides – with less success in the labour market, and with decreasing support from the state. A recent survey by Dev and Mooij shows that social expenditure in the reform decade was noticeably lower than in the 1980s, falling from close to eight per cent of GDP to less than seven per cent by the end of the 1990s (Dev and Mooij, 2002, Table 3).[9]

One indication of the way in which debate reflects the underlying balance of power is with regard to the future of social policy. It is now a growing opinion within the political elite that, if subsidies and entitlements are to continue as a part of state policy, they will have to be packaged as targeted transfers, not universalistic. The United States is viewed as a model in this regard. This has led to a lively debate on whether means-tested programmes are in fact more cost-efficient, and whether they can effectively achieve their purpose, given the difficulty of accurately measuring for income and insecurity (Swaminathan, 2000). Such debates focus carefully on the economic merits of universal versus means-tested programmes. However, there is a political logic to this as well, which is often overlooked. This is the fact that targeted programmes bring with them a severe political liability, for in limiting their scope to one section of the population, they also narrow the support base for such policies. Furthermore, this support base, being the poorest and the most destitute, will also tend to be the weakest politically, since it has the fewest resources for collective action. Finally, in excluding large sections of the population from its ambit, it automatically creates a constituency that gains nothing from the programmes, while nonetheless having to contribute to it through taxation. It thus creates a lobby that sees such programmes as largely a cost, with no direct benefits. And, since this lobby belongs to the wealthier sections, it also has greater resources.

If the future of Indian social policy is in the direction of means-tested programmes, then they are likely to be embattled and on the defensive – much as they are and have been in the US since the passage of the New Deal. It is striking that the programmes that have had the greatest resilience in the US against the neo-liberal assault are those that are universalistic in scope – social security and medicare. The political logic of targeted programmes is a very distinct one, because of the manner in which it interacts with organised interests.

6.6 Conclusions

For most of the twentieth century, state-building and state policy in the developing world was geared toward accelerating the growth process. Almost without exception, the emphasis of policy was thus focused away from distribution and toward asset accumulation. The main exception to this was in the realm of agrarian policy, where land reforms acted as a major source of redistribution, and hence, of poverty reduction. But it needs to be stressed that even though land reforms served the ends of redistribution, they were typically motivated by the growth imperative and not by a social democratic impulse. In any case, the motivation to push growth rates to entirely new trajectories generated, across the developing world, a state form that has come to be known as the developmental state. This form of state was quite distinct in the range of tasks that it took up, when we compare it to the welfare states of the advanced capitalist world. In the latter, growth and accumulation were left more to market forces, and governmental institutions were pushed to intervene more concertedly in the sphere of income distribution. Hence, whereas growth policy was the core of state objectives in the global south, social policy was at the heart of states in the capitalist core.

Institutions for social policy have therefore been less developed in the South – and so has the scholarly study of social policy. Despite the relative paucity of literature on the phenomenon, I have suggested that the basic dynamics of policy in post-independence India conform to the predictions coming from the scholarship on the core states. Insofar as welfare policy is conducted in a capitalist context, it is fair to expect that its success will be positively related to the degree of power and representation achieved by labouring groups. While this is true in advanced economies, it is even more so in the South, where the focus on growth enhancement lends a built-in bias toward asset-holders. Any shift of income away from them requires direct political pressure from its putative recipients.

The Indian case confirms this in a striking fashion. While it is accepted that the failure of land reform was a symptom of the INC's capture by landed classes, it is not widely appreciated that industrial policy also bore the imprint of organised pressure by dominant classes, in this case the giant business houses. For the labouring poor in rural and the industrial sector, therefore, the state did not turn out to be a significant source of poverty alleviation in the early years of independence. What was established in these years under Nehru was a basic framework in which policy was basically geared toward the interests of the dominant classes, but with a great deal of legislation ostensibly aimed at protecting the economic welfare of subordinate groups. But at the same time, these groups were rapidly demobilised and folded into the state apparatus through various institutional means, hence, depriving them of any real mechanism for exerting real political pressure. Legislation, therefore, remained ineffectual, largely ornamental, despite its progressive gloss.

This pattern was modified somewhat during the years of Indira Gandhi's and Rajiv Gandhi's rule, as policy shifted somewhat toward more redistribution. But it still hewed to the basic pattern. Since it was fundamentally driven by deepening inter-elite competition, it was geared toward acquiring patronage and vote banks, not toward actually addressing the root causes of poverty. And since the basic growth model remained the same, the state's orientation was kept steadfastly hitched to elite interests. The places where it was most effective was states where working class mobilisation did achieve lasting success, and where land reform were successfully implemented – much as our theory would predict.

The two decades under liberalisation have not yielded much hope for this pattern to be reversed. With regard to the state's relation to organised interests, the hold of dominant groups over policy has, if anything, tightened. And the space for labouring classes has narrowed, as their political muscle has waned, and their presence in the policy apparatus has become more precarious. Whereas in the years of dirigisme, the state at least gave lip service to poverty reduction, the very idea is now being rejected out of hand. Market forces are now presented as a panacea for achieving what state policy did not over five decades. But this is to take the wrong lesson from the years of economic planning. If international experience is any guide, the way to tackle distribution is by better social policy – not its abandonment.

Notes

1. In sociology, pluralism has very little influence these days. In political science, it is very powerful in the study of electoral politics, which automatically gives it great prominence – but less so in the scholarship on welfare states and the political economy of development. In economics it is probably the dominant approach.
2. This changed in later years, especially the 1970s, and it is very likely that the image of the Leviathan state in Nehru's time is a backward projection of this phenomenon to his years.
3. The identification of Nehru's state capitalism, or statism, with socialism is incredibly common in the literature. For an early – and rare – exception, *see* Michael Kidron, *Foreign Investments in India* (Oxford, 1965).
4. *See* the ILO (1960), p. 33.
5. One informative source for the history of land reform is Appu (1996).
6. *See* the 1962 *Report of the Committee on the Minimum Standard of Living,* in Bardhan and Srinivasan (1974).
7. AICC, *The Fourth General Election: A Statistical Analysis* (1967) Delhi.
8. For a controversial presentation of this argument, *see* Mallick (1992). In my view, Mallick's work – though problematic in several respects – has been too glibly dismissed in the literature.
9. Expenditure rose to close to 7.5 per cent in 2000, but this was likely a result of the implementation of the Fifth Pay Commission's recommendations. *See* also the data in Radhakrishna and Ray, 2005, Chapter Four.

References

Alford, Robert, R. and Roger Friedland (1985): *Powers of Theory: Capitalism, the State, and Democracy*, New York: Cambridge University Press.

AICC (1967): *The Fourth General Election: A Statistical Analysis*, Delhi: All India Congress Committee.

Anant, T.C.A., R. Hasan, P. Mohapatra, R. Nagaraj and S.K. Sasikumar (2006): 'Labour Markets in India: Issues and Perspectives', in J. Felipe and R. Hasan (eds) *Labour Markets in Asia: Issues and Perspectives*, Basingstoke: Palgrave Macmillan, 205–300.

Appu, P.S. (1996): *Land Reforms in India: A Survey of Policy, Legislation and Implementation*, New Delhi: Vikas Publishing House.

Banerjee, Debdas (2005): *Globalisation, Industrial Restructuring, and Labour Standards: Where India Meets the Global*, New Delhi: Sage.

Banerjee, Sumanta (1984): *India's Simmering Revolution: The Naxalite Uprising*, London: Zed Press.

Bardhan, Pranab and T.N. Srinivasan (1974) (eds): *Poverty and Income Distribution in India*, Calcutta: Statistical Publishing House.

Besley, Timothy, Robin Burgess and Berta Estve-Volart (2007): *Delivering on the Promise of Pro-poor Growth: Insights and Lessons from Country Experiences*, New York: Palgrave Macmillan; Washington DC: World Bank.

Brass, Tom (1995) (ed.): *New Farmers' Movements in India*, Essex: Frank Cass.

Byres, Terry (1981): 'The New Technology, Class Formation and Class Action in the Indian Countryside', *Journal of Peasant Studies*, Vol. 8: 405–54.

Chibber, Vivek (2003): *Locked in Place: State-Building and Late Industrialization in India*, Princeton: Princeton University Press.

Corbridge, Stuart and John Harriss (2000): *Reinventing India: Liberalisation, Hindu Nationalism and Popular Democracy*, Delhi: Oxford University Press.

Datt, Ruddar (2003): *Lockouts in India*, Delhi: Manohar Publishers and Distributors.

Deshpande, L.K. et al. (2004): *Liberalisation and Labour: Labour Flexibility in Indian Manufacturing*, Institute for Human Development, New Delhi: Distributed by Manohar Publishers and Distributors.

Dev, S.M. and Jos Mooij (2002): 'Social Sector Expenditures in the 1990s: Analysis of Central and State Budgets', *Economic and Political Weekly*, Vol. 31, No. 9 (March 2): 853–66.

Dreze and Amartya Sen (ed): *Indian Development: Selected Regional Perspectives*, Delhi: Oxford.

Frankel, Francine (1978): *India's Political Economy, 1947–1977: The Gradual Revolution*, Princeton: Princeton University Press.

Gulati, Ashok and Sudha Narayanan (2003): *The Subsidy Syndrome in Indian Agriculture*, Delhi: Oxford University Press.

Hicks, Alexander (1999): *Social Democracy & Welfare Capitalism: A Century of Income Security Politics*, Ithaca: Cornell University Press.

Himanshu (2005): 'Wages in Rural India: Sources, Trends and Comparability', *Indian Journal of Labour Economics*, Vol. 48, No. 2, April–June.

ILO (1960): 'Report to the Government of India on Labour–Management Relations and Some Aspects of Wage Policy', Geneva: International Labour Organization.

Kidron, Michael (1965): *Foreign Investments in India*, Oxford: Oxford University Press.

Kohli, Atul (1987): *The State and Poverty in India: The Politics of Reform*, Cambridge: Cambridge University Press.

Kohli, Atul (1990): *Democracy and Discontent: India's Growing Crisis of Governability*, Cambridge: Cambridge University Press.

Kohli, Atul (2006a): 'Politics of Economic Growth in India, 1980–2005, Part I: The 1980s,' *Economic and Political Weekly*, Vol. 41, No. 13 (April 1): 1251–650.

Kohli, Atul (2006b): 'Politics of Economic Growth in India, 1980–2005, Part II: The 1990s and Beyond,' *Economic and Political Weekly*, Vol. 41, No. 14 (April 8): 1361–70.

Korpi, Walter (1978): *The Working Class in Welfare Capitalism: Work, Unions, and Politics in Sweden*, Boston: Routledge & Kegan Paul.

Mallick, Ross (1992): *Development Policy of a Communist Government: West Bengal since 1977*, Cambridge: Cambridge University Press.
Mooij, Jos (1999): *Food Policy and the Indian State: The Public Distribution System in South India*, Delhi: Oxford University Press.
Mundle, Sudipto and M. Govind Rao (1997): 'Public Expenditure in India: Trends and Issues', in Sudipto Mundle (ed) *Public Finance – Policy Issues for India*, New Delhi: Oxford University Press.
Nagaraj, R. (2004): 'Fall in Organised Manufacturing Employment: A Brief Note', *Economic and Political Weekly*, Vol. 39, No. 30, July 24: 3387–90.
Nayar, Baldev Raj (1999): 'Policy and Performance under Democratic Coalitions: India's United Front Government and Economic Reforms, 1996–98', *Commonwealth & Comparative Politics*, Vol. 37, Issue 2 July 1999, pp. 22–56.
Nayar, Baldev Raj (1989): *India's Mixed Economy: The Role Of Ideology and Interest in its Development*, Mumbai: Popular Prakashan.
Patnaik, Prabhat and Utsa Patnaik (2001): 'The State, Poverty, and Development in India', in Niraja Gopal Jayal and Sudha Pai (ed) *Democratic Governance in India: Challenges of Poverty, Development, and Identity*, New Delhi: Sage.
Radhakrishna, R. and Shovan Ray (2005) (eds): *The Handbook of Poverty in India*, New Delhi: Oxford University Press.
Ramachandran, V.K. (1996): 'Kerala's Development Achievements: A Review', in Jean Dreze and A.K. Sen (ed) *Indian Development: Selected Regional Perspectives*, New York: Oxford University Press.
Ramaswamy, E.A. (1984): Power and Justice: The State in Industrial Relations, Delhi: Oxford University Press.
Shastri, Vanita (1995): *The Political Economy of Policy Formation in India: The Case of Industrial Policy, 1948–1994*, unpublished PhD dissertation, Princeton University.
Shyam Sundar (2004): 'Lockouts in India, 1961–2001', *Economic and Political Weekly* Vol. 39, No. 39, (September 25): 4377–85.
Stephens, John, D. and Evelyn Huber Stephens (2001): *Development and Crisis of the Welfare State: Parties and Policies in Global Markets*, Chicago: The University of Chicago Press.
Swaminathan, Madhura (2000): *Weakening Welfare: The Public Distribution of Food in India*, Delhi: Leftword Press.

7
State and Redistributive Development in India*

Atul Kohli

7.1 Introduction

States in the developing world play an essential role in moulding patterns of development. The Indian state is no exception. Over time, the state in India has shifted from a reluctant pro-capitalist state with a socialist ideology to an enthusiastic pro-capitalist state with some commitment to inclusive growth. This shift has significant implications for the possibility of development with redistribution in India. On the one hand, state's warm embrace of capital has been accompanied by higher rates of economic growth. Since the levels of inequality in India are not enormously skewed, say, in comparison to Latin America, the recent growth acceleration is bound to be poverty reducing. Moreover, growth boosts public revenues that, in principle, could be channelled to the poor. On the other hand, however, the state–capital alliance for growth is leading to widening inequalities along a variety of dimensions: city vs the countryside; across regions; and along class lines, especially within cities. Not only does rapid economic growth then not benefit as many of the poor as it could if inequalities were stable, but the balance of class power within India is shifting decisively towards business and other property-owning classes. This creates the possibility of an even more unequal development in the future. An important question then arises: can democracy and activism of the poor modify this dominant pattern of development?

This paper analyses the changing nature of India's democratic developmental state. While the struggles for more inclusive development are occurring at various levels of the body politic, I argue that the eventual prospects for making India's growth process more inclusive are not encouraging. If rapid growth continues, some of this will necessarily trickle down and help the poor. The Indian state is also likely to devote some of the newly acquired public resources to education, health and other programmes that might help the poor, but more important, provide electoral dividends. Beyond that, however, the scope for hastening this trickle via deliberate redistribution is limited. This is in part because deliberate redistribution is very difficult any where, in part because the Indian state's capacity to implement pro-poor, redistributive policies have always been quite limited, but mainly because of the emerging ruling alliance in India, which at core is an alliance of state and capital for growth. What might add some redistributive thrust to this growth-focused, elitist alliance is the fact that India is a vibrant democracy, with the poor and the near-poor constituting a majority. The excluded majorities are likely to continue to press their own case. A highly elitist apex and a mobilised fringe then define the political context in which India's current development drama is unfolding.

After situating very briefly the Indian state in a comparative context, I analyse below the Indian state's redistributive role at the national, state and local levels. Given the complexity of the subject, the focus is selective. While situating India in a cross-national context, I correct some popular misconceptions, and argue that the developmental capacity of the Indian state is middling, somewhere between the more efficacious states of East Asia and the poorly performing states of sub-Saharan Africa.

When discussing the Indian state at the national level, I suggest that, for the most part, there has been a considerable gap in India between redistributive ambitions and capacity. In the recent decades, however, this gap has narrowed, not because of any significant improvement in state capacity, but because of narrowing ambitions, focusing more on economic growth and less on redistribution. There is significant variation across Indian states in their redistributive capacities. The fact that states such as Kerala and West Bengal have reduced poverty faster than most other Indian states suggests a positive relationship between distribution of power and distribution of economic resources. And finally, the effectiveness of local governments is likely to be critical in the implementation of a variety of (minimal) poverty alleviation programmes that are now on the policy agenda.

7.2 Indian state in a comparative perspective

When assessing any state's capacity to accomplish specific tasks, scholars generally have some standards of comparison in mind. These standards may reflect either a normative ideal or some real world comparison with other similar cases. Let us set aside the issue of the ideals to which one should hold the Indian state. For the present purposes, let us focus on real world comparisons. How well do the capacities of the Indian state, especially redistributive capacities, measure up against those of other developing country states?

Some definitional and analytical clarity is essential at the outset. When discussing the state, I refer to both the political and the bureaucratic institutions of a society. While societal interests, especially dominant interests, always mould state institutions, it is also in the nature of institutions that they take on a life of their own; states thus enjoy some varying measure of autonomy from social forces. When discussing a state's developmental capacity, I refer broadly to a state's capacity to promote growth, as well as to reduce inequalities and poverty. When discussing a state's redistributive capacities, I have in mind, mainly the state's capacity to reduce inequalities and poverty. Poverty and inequalities are, of course, distinguishable; as in contemporary India, inequalities may be widening, but poverty conditions are improving. However, one should not push this distinction too far. Setting aside the case of economic growth enveloping more and more people – often a fairly slow process – most deliberate efforts at poverty alleviation involve some deliberate redistribution, and more important from a political standpoint, are perceived as such. For example, strategies of poverty alleviation may focus on one or more of the following: asset redistribution; welfare provision; creation of human capital; or altering the pattern of economic growth. Since some of these strategies result in clear winners and losers, and others starkly pose the issue of who will pay, strategies of poverty alleviation readily come to be viewed as redistributive policies.

To return to the main issue at hand, let us situate the Indian state in a comparative context, at least briefly. As far as economic growth is concerned, the developmental capacities of the Indian state are middling, somewhere between the more efficacious East Asian states on the one hand, and the poorly performing sub-Saharan African states on the other hand (Kohli, 2004). Indian state presided over an economy that grew at a relatively sluggish rate for some three decades following independence. Since 1980, however, the rate of economic growth in India accelerated. While numerous non-political variables help explain both the overall growth performance, as well as changes overtime, it is the case that the state's role in both promoting and hindering economic growth in India has been significant. The sluggish growth rate in India between 1950 and 1980 was a product of a state-dominated economy in which the state pursued a variety of goals simultaneously, and none too effectively. The roots of this 'soft state' lay in a multi-class social base, a not-too-well-organised ruling party and a bureaucracy that was relatively professional at the apex, but not on the periphery; I have traced the economic consequences of these political traits systematically elsewhere (ibid., Chapter 7). By contrast, the improved economic performance since 1980 can be associated with a narrowing of the state and capital ruling alliance, the state's near-exclusive focus on growth promotion as a priority goal, and institutional insulation of key economic decisions from popular pressures (Kohli, 2012).[1]

As far as deliberate redistribution and poverty alleviation are concerned, the Indian state's capacity must be judged as fairly dismal. The attempts to redistribute land to the landless, to provide education and health to the poor and to create employment via public works type of programmes have all been largely ineffective. The underlying causes include the absence of a real commitment among state elites, poor quality peripheral bureaucracy, but most of all, powerful vested interests who have often opposed or subverted such efforts. When viewed comparatively, however, most developing country states, especially those in Latin America and sub-Saharan Africa, have been even more ineffective than India in checking growing inequalities or in providing for their poor (for some exceptions, (see Sandbrook et al., 2007). While some such East Asian cases as South Korea, or possibly China, indeed provide examples of 'growth with distribution,' it is important that their pathways are understood correctly.

Land redistribution has been an integral component of the relatively egalitarian pathway followed by countries such as China or South Korea. Early land reforms in these cases not only flattened the class profile in the countryside, but also raised peasant incomes, thus, contributing to higher wages for the urban working class by reducing the size of the 'surplus poor'. Revolutionary communists and occupying US forces helped implement land redistribution in China and South Korea, respectively; these political preconditions are not likely to be replicated in India. Much is also made in the development literature of the role of labour-intensive, export-oriented industrialisation in helping reconcile growth with redistribution in these cases. This is fine as it goes, but the fact is that countries such as South Korea pursued both labour-intensive and capital-intensive industrialisation; even in South Korea, the latter was accompanied with growing income disparities. And, of course, growing inequalities in China's recent growth upsurge is quite well known.

The quality of human capital in countries such as China and South Korea is clearly superior to that in India. Here there is much room for improvement in India. Once again, however, how China and South Korea got to where they are needs to be kept in mind. The efforts to improve education and health conditions in China were very much part of the revolutionary transformation of China, a process not likely to be repeated in countries such as India. Even in a non-revolutionary South Korea, certain unique factors contributed to the benign outcome. First, the colonial legacy in the field of primary education was relatively favourable. Second, following land redistribution, landlords often invested their compensations into a system of private education, hoping that their progeny would thus find alternative routes of upward mobility. And finally, of course, public investment into education has been consistently significant, though even here one should not underestimate the role that a growth-oriented authoritarian state expected primary education to play in creating a productive but propagandised working class.

What one might legitimately expect from the Indian state in terms of deliberate redistribution, thus, needs to be tempered by a correct understanding of what others in the developing world have or have not achieved. Relatively egalitarian initial conditions and a more labour-intensive product mix have been important components of reconciling growth with distribution; both of these factors are largely missing in India, especially the first. Investments in education and health have been the other components of creating a more level social field in select East Asian cases. These too were facilitated in part by unique social and political conditions. With a highly stratified society and a narrow ruling coalition, India is, thus, not likely to replicate East Asia. And yet, this is not the whole story! What India has that many other East Asian or Latin American cases have not had, is a sustained democracy. The issue that needs to be raised is, does this make any difference, and if so, how?

7.3 The Indian state, over time

How has the Indian state changed over time, and what are the implications of these changes for development with distribution in India? In what follows, I paint in sweeping (really sweeping, often building on my earlier work) brush strokes the main changes in both India's political and bureaucratic landscapes, and then trace the implications of these changes for such redistributive policy areas as land redistribution, taxation and public investment, building human capital and public works programmes. I argue that political changes, especially since about 1980, have been fairly dramatic: a reluctant pro-capitalist state that flirted with socialism has essentially been supplanted by an enthusiastic pro-capitalist state with a neo-liberal ideology. This narrowing of the political apex, however, has not gone unchallenged, as excluded masses are pursuing both democratic and not-so-democratic means to express their dissatisfaction, especially in a number of states. By contrast, the changes in the bureaucracy have been a lot less dramatic; the basic characteristics of a professional apex and a vast network of not-so-professional lower-level bureaucrats remain intact. The overall result is that the national state has become less redistributive in its intent than in the past on the one hand, but the capacity to implement even these more limited polices has not improved on the other hand.

The nature of India's post-independence developmental state has been studied extensively.[2] I too have developed my views on the subject in a number of publications (Kohli, 1987; Kohli, 1991; Kohli, 2004; and Kohli 2012); only the briefest recapitulation is necessary here. Political power in post-independence India rested mainly in the Congress Party. Led by the likes of Nehru, the early Congress Party was nationalist and socialist in its ideology. While seeking to represent the interests of the 'nation' as a whole, the Congress came to be influenced disproportionately by 'proprietary classes' (Bardhan, 1984). For example, business groups played a significant role in early economic policy-making (Chibber, 2003), and Congress built its political support in the countryside via upper caste, landowning groups, thus incorporating landed interests into the heart of the body politic (Frankel, 2005). Professional urban classes, as well as the well-heeled bureaucrats, exerted considerable influence on the state. And yet, the Congress was never a party of the Indian elite alone. Gandhi mobilised segments of the Indian peasantry into the nationalist movement. Nehru's socialist commitments further broadened Congress' social base, at least promising – though seldom delivering – progress to India's downtrodden.

The Congress Party, with a left-leaning nationalist ideology and a multiclass social base, was never very well organised; the transition from an anti-colonial nationalist movement to a ruling party was never fully accomplished. Of course, the early Congress had some organisational structure: there were paid members; party officers were selected by intra-party elections; those at the lower levels elected those at the higher levels; party offices operated throughout the country, providing some minimal services to supporters; there was some sense of what Congress

Party stood for; and the khadi-clad Congress Party workers were even identifiable by an informal dress code (Weiner, 1967; Kohli 1991). Most of these institutional attributes, however, either did not take deep roots, or were not maintained, leading to a significant organisational erosion during the 1960s and the 1970s. For example, power came to be relatively concentrated at the apex, especially in the person of Indira Gandhi. Moreover, nationalism declined – though slowly – and the commitment to socialism proved superficial fairly quickly. The results included a decline in Congress' public-spiritedness. India's dominant political party then increasingly became an arena in which a variety of private interests competed for personal or sectional benefits. The main organisational characteristic of the Congress Party became long chains of patronage that spread from the centre to a vast periphery.

Following independence, the Congress rulers inherited a relatively well-organised colonial bureaucracy; after some back and forth, India's new rulers also chose to maintain the colonial state structures, building on the well-established core. This turned out to be a Faustian bargain, enhancing the capacity of the new rulers to maintain political stability, but only at the expense of creating a real developmental state. As the Indian Civil Service (ICS) became the Indian Administrative Service (IAS), it grew in numbers but maintained its core characteristics: an exam-based, meritocratic civil service of generalists with its own esprit de corps (Potter, 1996). During the 1950s and the 1960s, the IAS attracted India's 'best and brightest'. The service was also relatively insulated from political interference in these early years, boosting its professionalism. This high quality, professional civil service proved, and has remained since then, vital to India's governance. As a law and order bureaucracy, however, the contribution of this civil service to a more activist state agenda of creating and running factories, promoting exports, or implementing land redistribution, was less successful. Moreover, the quality and professionalism of bureaucracy below the level of the IAS was relatively poor, further diluting the capacity of the new rulers to translate their edicts into real outcomes in the periphery.

As is well known, India's new rulers, especially Nehru, pushed India into adopting an ambitious state-led model of development. Much too much has already been written on this subject; this is also no place to review related debates. Suffice it to note that Nehru's heavy industry-oriented, import-substitution model of growth had mixed results. In spite of neo-liberal criticisms, Nehru's policies successfully laid the foundations of an industrial economy; the roots of the more recent growth upsurge can often be traced back to these early beginnings

(Rodrik and Subramanian, 2004). This is not to suggest that Nehru's model lacked heroic mistakes, such as the neglect of agricultural growth (Myrdal, 1968), or that the system did not develop numerous inefficiencies (Bhagwati and Desai, 1970). Some of these were rooted in ideologically driven policy choices, but for the rest, they resulted from a significant gap between the state's economic ambitions and its political and bureaucratic capacities (Kohli, 2004). On the whole, however, as far as economic growth is concerned, Nehru's economic policies at least led to an impressive growth in India's industry, if not overall (for a balanced overview, *see* Jalan, 1991).

More pertinent for our purposes is how we analyse the impact of the Nehruvian state and its policies for redistribution and poverty alleviation. Here the judgments have to be fairly negative. The simple but powerful fact is that the overall growth rate of the economy was relatively sluggish in these years, population grew at a significant rate and the number of poor in India grew steadily. Below this nearly banal sounding – but tragic – reality of India's slow suffering lay numerous policy choices and poorly implemented policies.

Nehru's emphasis on heavy industry meant the neglect of agriculture, a set of policy decisions with serious negative consequences for India's poor, majority of whom lived in the countryside. It is no exaggeration to suggest in retrospect that there was no systematic policy to promote agricultural growth in Nehru's India. Much reliance was put instead on re-educating the peasantry (via CDPs), and on altering the incentives of the land tiller via land reforms. The former was probably mistaken even in conception, and given the poor quality of peripheral bureaucracy, was certainly implemented very poorly (Myrdal, 1968). The issue of land reforms, however, requires further comment.

There was some success in India in eliminating the largest zamindars (landowners) but much less in ensuring that land was redistributed to the rural landless. Zamindari abolition was thus mainly a political phenomenon (as distinct from a class phenomena), in the sense that many zamindars were allies of the British, lost power as the nationalists gained, and posed an obstacle to the Congress rulers to build political support in the periphery. Congress rulers thus pushed hard and succeeded in reducing the size of zamindari holdings. Those who gained were generally the 'lower gentry', rather than the land tillers. By contrast to zamindari abolition, the several subsequent rounds of land reforms (redistributing land above a certain 'ceiling', or ensuring the rights of tenants) were mostly a failure (Herring, 1983; Appu, 1996). There was some variation on this score across Indian states; I will return to that issue in the next section. On the whole, however, land reforms failed mainly because state authorities in India proved either unwilling or incapable of confronting powerful class interests in the countryside (Myrdal, 1968). Significant factors that contributed to the state's limited capacities on this score included Congress Party's incorporation of landed interests as pillars of party support in the countryside, a federal structure where land redistribution was the responsibility of state governments in which the power of landed classes was especially significant, a less-than-professional lower level bureaucracy that was readily co-opted by the rural powerful, a legal system that was biased in favour of property owners, and a relatively low level of mobilisation and organisation among the potential beneficiaries.

Beyond the neglect of agriculture and failure of land reforms, other notable Nehruvian policies with adverse consequences for the poor included a capital-intensive pattern of industrialisation and the neglect of primary education. The focus on heavy industry reflected both Nehru's vision of how to build a strong and sovereign India (Nayar, 1989), and the prevailing economic logic of the time that since you cannot eat steel, such a focus would enhance savings and facilitate rapid industrialisation (Charkravarty, 1988). Whatever the underlying motives, the consequences were clear: India's industrial growth did not create enough new jobs to make a dent into the growing number of poor. Similarly, a focus on primary education might have not only served important economic goals by raising the quality of human capital, but would have also been an important development end in itself (Sen, 1999). Nehru's focus instead on creating 'pockets of excellence', for example, by creating the Indian Institutes of Technology, remains to this day a much-debated set of policies. Why India's primary education has continued to lag dramatically also remains somewhat of an enigma. Myron Weiner's provocative argument (1991) that the neglect reflected the exclusionary mindset of India's upper caste elites probably has some merit. However, even with a shift in national priorities on primary education, that is currently underway, the fact is that numerous problems of implementation at the level of state governments and below remain; I will return to some of these issues in the next section.

By the 1970s, a new political generation had come into being, the legacy of nationalism was declining, and along with it grew a sense in India that politics was less about the pursuit of ideals, but more about mundane realities of who gets what, when and how. Congress Party was thus in danger of losing its hegemonic hold under the strain of a variety of distributive conflicts. By accentuating populism, Indira Gandhi recreated a new type of Congress hegemony in which power became even more personal. Congress party was further deinstitutionalised, leaders below the apex came to be appointed from the top, often rewarded for little more than loyalty to Indira Gandhi, and even the well-established civil service and the armed forces felt the strain of growing politicisation (Rudolph and Rudolph, 1987; Kohli 1991). While politics has always been in command of economic policymaking in India, the Indira Gandhi years were especially notable for the politicisation of the economy, first in a distributive direction in the 1970s, and then in a more pro-business direction during and following the Emergency in the 1980s.

The Nehruvian model of economic development was accentuated in a populist direction by Indira Gandhi: banks were nationalised, maharajas were stripped of their remaining privileges, anti-monopoly laws were strengthened, new taxes were imposed on the rich, access to credit was broadened, stricter land reform legislation was passed, and public works programmes that may supplement the income of the poor were brought into being. The early 1970s was thus a moment in India with real social democratic possibilities. Unfortunately, the experiment was mostly a failure, not because social democracy in a poor setting is a non-starter (Sandbrook, 2007), but because Indira Gandhi's personal power led more to centralisation and powerlessness (Kohli, 1994) and less to the creation of a well-organised social democratic power bloc that might be capable of confronting dominant class interests.

On the growth front, under pressure from the US, Indira Gandhi adopted the green revolution policies. While overall agricultural growth did not go up significantly, productivity-based growth kicked in, leading to a slow but steady growth in food production that by now has made the perennial threat of famines a distant dream; on balance, this must be judged a positive contribution. As interesting, however, was the fact that the green revolution marked the first major instance of the Indian state actively collaborating with producer classes to facilitate economic growth; while an aberration in those years – especially, in a milieu dominated by the heady rhetoric of socialism – by now this pattern has become the norm of how India produces economic growth. The results included – then as now – some gains in production, but also growing inequalities, certainly across regions, but also possibly along class lines. By contrast, the rate of industrial growth declined during these years: public investments were channelled into a variety of 'consumption' activities aimed at building political support (Bardhan, 1984), and the socialist rhetoric and a variety of new anti-monopoly laws discouraged private investments (Ahluwalia, 1985; Kohli, 2004, Ch. 7).

The failures on the redistribution front were especially glaring because of the gap between promises and outcomes. The main achievement probably was to limit the growth of inequalities, though, as critics will rightly add, this was more a matter of sharing poverty than wealth. Some of the monies invested into poverty alleviation schemes such as employment generation programmes probably also did reach the poor, especially in states with committed leaders and better bureaucracies. By contrast, public education and primary health were ignored. The failure to acquire and to redistribute above-ceiling land, and to improve the lot of tenants, was the most notable failure (Appu, 1996). All the rhetoric and some real legislation aside, the pursuit of land redistribution was left mainly in the hands of state governments. A few state governments made good use of the new, permissive political space, but these were seldom states with Congress governments. In the modal Congress-run state, the political structures consisted of two main hierarchies: a top-down, loyalty- and patronage-based chain that was the Congress party, without a well-organised social base; and a bureaucratic hierarchy, in which the quality of bureaucracy declined as you went down the hierarchy. Where these political hierarchies stopped in the countryside began real social power, that is, the power of landowning elites. Neither the local level party nor the bureaucratic elite were in a position to confront the landed elite; on the contrary, at times, the party and the landed elite were the same people, and nearly always the local bureaucrats were deeply entrenched in local power structures (Kohli, 1987). When, on occasion, some redistributive success seemed close at hand, tenants were either evicted by force or landownership cases that ended up in courts, where they probably still languish.

Starting around 1980, Indian political system began moving in a new direction, especially in terms of developmental priorities, and related to that, in terms of the underlying state–class alliances. After returning to power in 1980, Indira Gandhi increasingly prioritised economic growth, and put the rhetoric of socialism on the back burner. This complex political shift reflected several underlying political realities that I have analysed in detail elsewhere (Kohli, 2012): a growing realisation that redistributive possibilities were increasingly limited; the negative impact that radical rhetoric had on the state's relations with the corporate sector, as well as on the corporate sector's willingness to invest; and of course, relatively low economic growth, especially industrial growth, during the 1970s. Report after report had also underlined the inefficiencies of the public sector, limiting governmental options. Looking for higher rates of economic growth, Indira Gandhi in the early 1980s sought to reorder the state's class underpinnings, tilting it towards capital and against labour. Thus, began a steady process, which, over the next quarter of a century, propelled the power of capital in the Indian polity to near hegemonic proportions.

Indira Gandhi and her son Rajiv Gandhi moved the Indian state away from its socialist ambitions to a growth-promoting state that worked with the corporate sector. The policy shifts were not only of the liberalising types that limited the state's role in markets, but went beyond, actively supporting the profitability of the corporate sector. Liberalising changes included removing a variety of restrictions on the activities of big indigenous business. More activist changes included tax breaks and subsidies to the corporate sector, continuing public investments, expansionist monetary and fiscal policies, a variety of supply-side supports to some such favoured industries as computer and software, and limiting labour's capacity to strike. The impact on growth was significant. As both public and private investments grew, industrial growth picked up. Since the composition of industrial investment shifted towards consumer goods, and since technology imports became possible, productivity of the economy also improved. The 1980s, thus, marked a break in India from the 'Hindu rate of growth' (Nagaraj, 2000; Rodrik and Subramanium, 2004).

The distributional impact of the state's shifting role was mixed, though the negatives were not as negative as what was to follow in the 1990s. State elites increasingly downplayed the rhetoric of socialism. A major fatality of this ideological shift was that land redistribution and tenancy reforms lost lustre as policy options. While these policies had never succeeded much in India, now even their desirability became questionable. The 'computer boys' of Rajiv Gandhi looked instead to integrate India into a global economy. Also, very few new efforts emerged to improve primary education or public health. The pattern of economic growth favoured big business houses.[3] Mercifully, however, both Indira Gandhi and Rajiv Gandhi kept up public investments. In this important sense India, during the 1980s, did not embrace the neo-liberalism that followed in the 1990s, but even then only partially. There was also no real 'state reform' in India in the 1980s in the sense of privatisation of public sector firms or in the sense of shedding or reorganising the bureaucracy. While political interference in the IAS grew, on balance, the IAS remained a privileged, professional and competent civil service. And finally, external opening of the economy remained fairly limited up until the early 1990s. The limited shift in the state's role in India in the 1980s, thus, put a check on the worst forms of growing inequalities that followed in the 1990s. Most important, public investments in agriculture put a brake on the growing rural–urban divide, and by the same token, continuing public investments helped the BIMARU states from following further behind in their relative rates of economic growth.[4]

The state–business alliance for growth has pretty well continued to characterise India's model of development since about 1980, with another important 'liberalising' shift in 1991, when integration with the global economy also picked up speed. Once again, I have analysed the political causes and the growth consequences of this shift in more detail elsewhere (Kohli, 2012). To summarise very briefly, the fiscal and balance-of-payment 'crisis' of the early 1990s provided more the occasion and less the deeper cause of the policy shifts in 1991. Even before 1991, India's ruling elite had sought to liberalise India's economy on numerous occasions, but had run up against a variety of obstacles (Kohli, 1989). By 1991, a number of new forces emerged that facilitated 'liberalisation'; two of these, one external and the other domestic, are especially notable. India's external relations changed dramatically with the decline of the Soviet Union. Needing to shore up its relations with the United States, India increasingly opened its economy to American goods and investors. Within India the most important shift over the 1980s involved shifting policy preferences of big business in India. Whereas the Indian business opposed external liberalisation in the 1980s, by the 1990s, this unified opposition dissolved. Some Indian businesses, especially in the services sector, supported opening of the economy. Import substitution-protected business houses either became more competitive over the 1980s or lost their political capacity to sway policy. As the newer, more globally oriented business houses converged around a refurbished, government-supported chamber of commerce – the Confederation of Indian Industry – the alliance of state elites and of select members of the corporate sector were able to push through an external opening of the economy.

The economic consequences of 'liberalisation' have been widely debated. Our concern here is mainly with distributive issues. On the growth front, suffice it to note that industrial growth did not accelerate in the post-1991 period (though there seems to be some such tendency since 2004–5) and that annual agricultural growth averaged nearly a whole percentage point below that achieved in the 1980s. The higher rates of growth in the services sector compensated for the lower rates of growth in agriculture; the overall rate of economic growth in India in the post-1991 period has, thus, been only marginally higher than in the 1980s. The distributional consequences of the post-1991 pattern of growth, however, have been distinctly less benign.

There is no doubt that a poor country like India desperately needs economic growth. In spite of growing inequalities, it is the case that the relatively high rates of economic growth over the past quarter of a century has helped alleviate some of India's poverty.[5] This needs to be acknowledged fair and square. However, those who stop there also ignore numerous disturbing trends that are making India a starkly more unequal society, with potentially serious political consequences in the future. Declining public investments, for example, have hurt agricultural growth, a sector on which most of India's poor still depend for their livelihood. The same decline has also hurt the growth prospects of India's poorest states, leaving the Bihars and the Uttar Pradeshs of India way behind its Gujarats. The evidence that class inequalities within cities are widening is also fairly clear. And finally, business concentration has increased over the 1990s.[6] Are such growing inequalities an inevitable product of higher rates of economic growth?

The premise of this essay is that such growing inequalities are not totally inevitable, that the state can intervene to modify these patterns, and thus, help India move along a somewhat more an egalitarian pattern of development, as well as hasten the process of poverty alleviation. With land redistribution and tenancy reform pretty well off the policy agenda (whether these should and can be brought back on the policy agenda is a whole separate discussion), most redistributive interventions at the national level will depend on patterns of public investment. Since public investments remain a function of availability of public revenues, improving revenue intake by reforming patterns of taxation ought to be a first order priority of any reform-minded Indian government; some of this is underway in India. With more resources – or by reallocating the use of existing resources – there is a desperate need in India to increase public investment into agriculture and into the poorer states. Not only will this be growth enhancing, but also as Datt and Ravillion (2002) have demonstrated,

> Sectoral and geographical imbalances of growth in India, in the 1990s, may have cut the poverty reducing capacity of economic growth by as much as one half ... Enhanced public investments into such basic areas of human capital formation as primary education and health will also be desirable; the contribution of such investments to both growth and well-being are widely recognized.

Such redistributive reforms face serious political obstacles, however. At issue are both the state's goals and capacities. Given the ideological proclivities of the state elite and the underlying class basis of state power, it seems increasingly unlikely that redistributive reforms will be prioritised. One set of pressures that may push the policy in a more redistributive direction is the simple fact that both rural groups and the poor states within India can be powerful swing factors in electoral politics. However, power of numbers in most democracies is no match for class power. Notice that, even in India, as democracy 'matures', all major political parties, including the communists, prioritise economic growth and pretty well embrace 'liberalisation'. Also notice that, following the 2004 national election, when it became clear that the Congress would need to depend on the CPM to form a government, foreign capital voted with its feet, withdrew funds in hordes, leading to a near crash of the stock market. Sonia Gandhi's concession to the stock market by announcing India's 'pro-liberalising' economic team essentially meant that the democratic verdict was diluted, at least partially.[7] By contrast, the Congress Party won the 2009 elections on a promise of 'inclusive growth'. It is too early to know how this electoral rhetoric will or will not translate into policy outcomes. What is clear nevertheless is that it is very difficult within India's democracy, even for a leadership committed to growth and a neo-liberal ideology, to ignore India's numerous poor.

Beyond issues of ideology and class power that influence the state's priorities, there are also more mundane, but serious obstacles of bureaucratic capacity. Lower level bureaucracy in India remains relatively inefficient, and no serious reforms are under consideration. These inefficiencies hurt numerous redistributive policies, anywhere from tax collection to managing public primary education in the countryside. We will visit these issues again as we travel down the state hierarchy in the following sections.

7.4 Variations across Indian states

While retelling the Indian 'story' in brief, I have argued so far that the redistributive accomplishments of the Indian state have been relatively limited, and that this limitation is best understood in terms of the ideology and organisation of the ruling elites on the one hand, and the class nature of the state on the other. I have also argued that, as the class base of the state has narrowed over time, even the earlier redistributive intent has been diluted. Pursuing similar themes across Indian states may help sharpen the argument further now, for it is the case that the redistributive capacity of provincial states within India varies quite a bit. Since state governments in India are responsible for a host of such policies as land reforms, education and health, it is important to understand how and why their capacities to pursue these policies vary.

In Figures 7.1 and 7.2, Indian states are ranked according to their 'poverty elasticity' (the capacity to reduce poverty) and how much poverty has come down within them over the last couple of decades, respectively. The states that have reduced most poverty include West Bengal, Kerala and Tamil Nadu (Figure 7.2). These are not the states that have grown most rapidly; that credit goes to states like Gujarat and Maharashtra. While economic growth is an important predictor of decline in poverty,[8] as interesting is the fact that states vary enormously in the 'efficiency' with which they reduce poverty for a given level of growth (Figure 7.1). For example, the growth elasticity of poverty in Kerala and West Bengal (–1.23 per cent and –1.7 per cent respectively) are some four times than, say, in Bihar or Madhya Pradesh (MP)

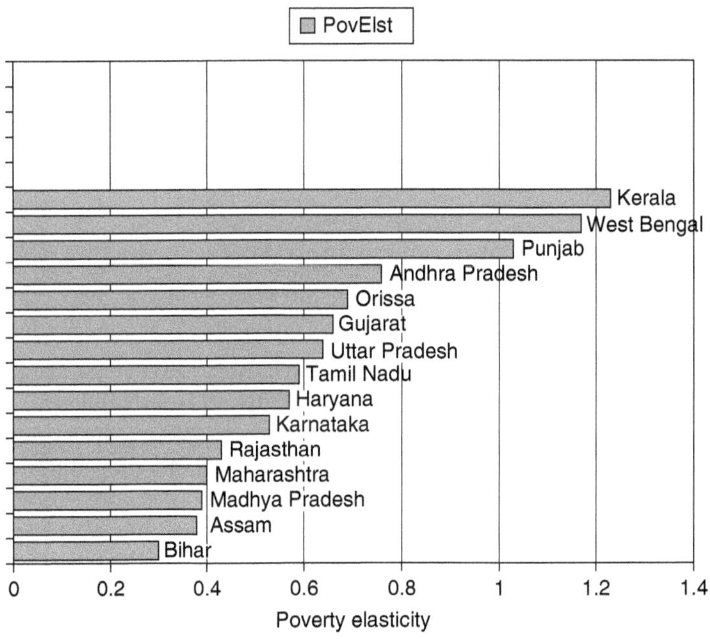

Figure 7.1 Capacity to reduce poverty in states

Source: Data on poverty elasticity is from from Besley, 2007, Figure 3.1. This data should only be treated as broadly indicative because, as a recent paper by Suryanaryana (2007) points out, there are significant measurement problems with pre-1980 consumption data in India on which these rankings are based. In addition, the issue of remittances from overseas complicates the calculation of the "growth elasticity of poverty" in some such cases as Kerala.

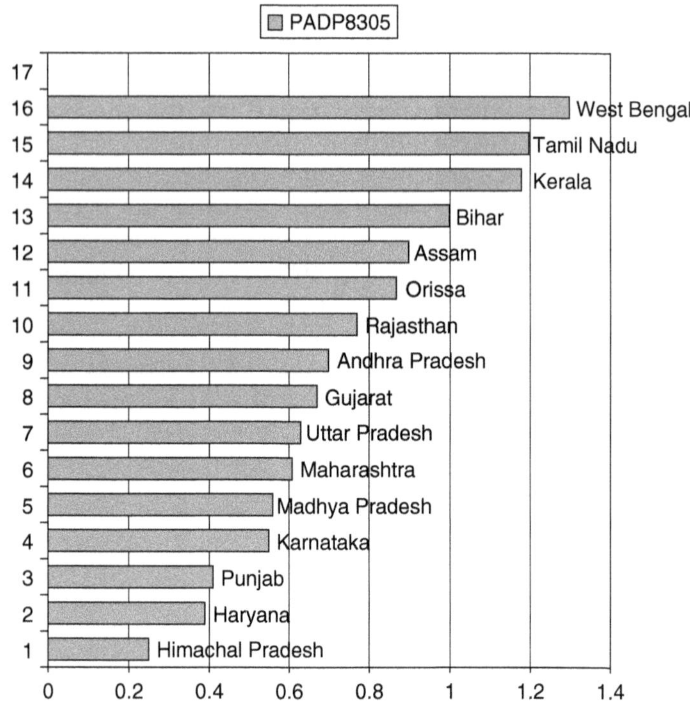

Figure 7.2 Decline in poverty in states (1983–2005)
Source: Data adapted from Mahendra Dev and Ravi (2007).

(–0.30 per cent and –0.39 per cent respectively) (Besley et al., 2007, Table 3.1). This suggests that Bihar and Madhya Pradesh will take some four times the growth rate of Kerala and West Bengal to reduce the same amount of poverty.[9] How does one best understand such differential capacity across Indian states to reduce poverty?

Some scholars – mostly economists associated with the World Bank – have sought to identify numerous proximate variables (for example, growth rate of farm yields, and such initial conditions as irrigation infrastructure or literacy (Datt and Ravallion, 1998); or access to finance or security of property rights, among others (Besley, et al., 2007) – that may help explain why growth is more poverty reducing in some states than in others. Other scholars – mostly political sociologists – have sought instead to go deeper into the causal chain to investigate how such more 'distant' variables as distribution of political and social power, and/or bureaucratic effectiveness, may mould redistributive outcomes

(Herring, 1983; Kohli, 1987; Echeverri-Gent, 1993 and Harriss, 2003).[10] Continuing in this tradition, several patterns are notable in Figures 7.1 and 7.2: the two states that reduced poverty the most, West Bengal and Kerala, have long had experience with left governments; three of the four southern states – Kerala, Andhra Pradesh (AP) and Tamil Nadu (TN) – are among the top half of those states that have reduced poverty the most (Figure 7.2) and have a high capacity to reduce poverty (Figure 7.1) (while Karnataka does not do so well on these measures, it is important to note that the percentage of the poor in Karnataka also remains below the Indian national average); by contrast, all the Hindi-heartland states – Bihar, Uttar Pradesh (UP) and MP (also Rajasthan) – are among the bottom half of the states, either on the dimension of capacity to reduce poverty or in terms of actual decline in poverty or both. How might one interpret these patterns?

The main hypothesis that best explains these patterns is that poverty has been reduced the most in states where effective governmental power rests on a broad political base; in such cases rulers have minimised the hold of upper classes on the state, successfully organised the middle and lower strata into an effective power bloc, and then used this power to channel resources to the poor.[11] While the ground level realities are a lot messier (they always are), on balance, I believe that this simple hypothesis survives an empirical scrutiny. Let me elaborate. First, let us consider the two left-leaning states of India. Much has been written on both Kerala and West Bengal. There is more of a consensus around the case of Kerala. Poverty in Kerala has been reduced sharply and its human development indicators are far superior to that of the rest of India. (Dreze and Sen, 2002). And all this was accomplished while economic growth rates in Kerala have been close to the all-India average. Underlying these redistributive achievements are complex historical roots, including the political mobilisation of lower castes and the classes well before independence.[12] This broadened political base then facilitated the rise of a well-organised, communist party to power. A more pro-poor regime interacted with a more efficacious citizenry, creating what Dreze and Sen (2002) have rightly called a 'virtuous' cycle. This created both a supply of and demand for a variety of successful pro-poor public policies, including land reforms, higher investments into and better implementation of education and health policies, and greater gender equality (Shah and Rani, 2003). The fact is that, when compared to other Indian states, by now the cultivated land in Kerala is distributed most evenly and wages of landless labourers are highest in India (Suryanarayana, 2007, *see* Table 3.2.6, p. 75 and Table 3.2.17, p. 90).[13]

The case of West Bengal has also been well-studied but the evidence is more mixed. It is clear by now (as seen in Figure 7.2) that poverty in West Bengal has come down significantly. The underlying determinants of this trend, however, are less clear. I argued two decades back that the communist government of West Bengal was relatively effective at pursuing tenancy reforms and promoting other anti-poverty programmes because of its superior party organisation and a broad political base of power; the ruling party excluded upper classes from direct access to state power, successfully incorporated middle and lower strata into a social democratic power bloc, and then utilised this cohesive power to pursue moderate redistribution (Kohli, 1987). Others subsequently disagreed (Mallick, 1994).[14] Yet others intervened in the debate and found supporting evidence for the CPI(M)'s redistributive capacities and/or for its superior capacity to implement anti-poverty programs in West Bengal (Lieten, 1992; Harriss, 1993; and Corbridge et al., 2003). The main dynamics of poverty alleviation again seem to be that a well-organised regime with a broad political base has been relatively effective at pursuing tenancy reform, helping push up minimum wages – though only somewhat – and implementing centrally sponsored anti-poverty programmes more effectively than other states. Land inequality in the countryside in West Bengal is also among the lowest in India by now, though wages of agricultural labourers are only marginally above the all-India average (*see* Suryanaryana, 2007, Table 3.2.6, p. 75 and Table 3.2.17, p. 90.) Some economists have also found evidence that tenancy reforms – via enhanced security and bargaining power – have helped agricultural productivity, thus, making the growth in West Bengal more inclusive (Banerjee, 2002).

If India's 'social democratic' states have effectively leveraged superior party organisation and a broad political base to pursue modest redistributive reforms, how does one interpret the fact that all of India's southern states are above average in their poverty-alleviation capacities? To begin with, one should not exaggerate the sense that all southern states are similar. They include Kerala at one extreme, and Karnataka and Andhra at the other, which at times do not fare much better than UP on some dimensions of poverty alleviation. And yet, it is the case that poverty in three of the four southern states has come down relatively rapidly (Figure 7.2) and the human development indicators of all of them are better than the all-India average (Dreze and Sen, 1997, Table 1, p. 38).[15] Economic growth rates across the southern states, though above average, vary quite a bit. So what other characteristics besides growth do they share that distinguishes them, say, from the Hindi-heartland states, and might help explain their superior capacity to alleviate poverty?

India's southern states share two sets of distinguishing political traits, one well researched and the other much in need of research. The well-established fact is that the narrow domination of brahmins was more effectively challenged in all the southern states relatively early in the twentieth century (Frankel and Rao, 1990). Since independence, the political base of power in these states has generally been middle castes and classes, and in some instances even lower classes (Harris, 2003, Table 4). This is quite distinct from the Hindi-heartland states, where brahmanical domination was only challenged relatively recently. The other fact is that the quality of state-level bureaucracy in the south has generally been superior. I hesitate in asserting this 'fact' because, to the best of my knowledge, it has not been documented by scholarly research; comparison of state-level bureaucracies across India is crying out for further research. I make this observation mainly on the basis of impressions gained, while conducting research in these states. During field work, I was repeatedly struck by a sharper sense of professionalism among state-level bureaucrats, especially in Tamil Nadu, more akin to the IAS than to prevailing practices in the Hindi-heartland. The roots of this may go back to the traditions of direct rule in the Madras Presidency.[16]

How might prolonged rule by governments with broader political base and more effective bureaucracy influence poverty alleviation? Leaving Kerala aside, land redistribution has not been very effective in the southern states. The main policy instruments of poverty alleviation have instead been somewhat different. Over the last several decades the southern states have invested more heavily in education and health than in the Hindi-heartland states (Singh, forthcoming, Chapter 4). John Harriss (2003, p. 225) also notes that, on the whole, southern states have benefited more from subsidised public distribution of wheat and rice; populist leaders and superior bureaucracy must get the credit. With a more effective bureaucracy, other poverty-alleviation programmes (such as a variety of employment generation programmes) have also been implemented better.

The contrast with Hindi-heartland states is striking. Of course, these states have also experienced low growth rates, underlining the point that, though higher growth rates do not assure better distribution or rapid poverty alleviation, low growth rates make the obstacles formidable. Nevertheless, growth rates are not the whole story; as already noted, it will take four times higher growth rate in a Bihar to reduce the same amount of poverty than in a Kerala. What factors help explain the poor capacities of Hindi-heartland states to improve the lot of the poor?

A number of relevant studies of UP and Bihar already exist (Dreze and Sen, 1997, Ch. 2; Corbridge et al., 2003; Witsoe, 2006; Pai, 2007). Based on these, as well as on my own earlier work on these states (Kohli, 1987; and 1991), it is not difficult to list the factors that help explain 'what is wrong with the Hindi-heartland'. Well into the late twentieth century, the main mode of politics in these states was Congress Party rule that rested on a narrow political base of upper castes and classes.[17] With patron–client ties as the key defining unit of the political society, factional bickering among the patrons was the core trait of state politics. This personalistic bickering detracted from any type of constructive use of state power, whether in promoting growth or distribution. With long traditions of zamindari or talukadari rule (forms of indirect rule), the quality of state-level bureaucracy that these regions inherited was also generally low. Virulent patronage politics politicised the bureaucracy in post-independence years, further diluting the state's developmental capacity. For some three to four decades following independence then, a narrow political base, personalistic factionalism and a less-than-professional state-level bureaucracy characterised the nature of state power in this region of India.

Land reforms were very poorly implemented in the Hindi-heartland states. With upper-caste landowners wielding considerable power – both in the state and in the society – and with a readily corruptible bureaucracy, this failure was not surprising. A variety of other state interventions that might have helped the poor were also ineffective. For example, I documented some two decades back the poor implementation of employment generation schemes in UP (Kohli, 1987). In recent decades, the political base of state power in all of these states has broadened, though social power of upper caste landowners remains significant. Over time, this broadening of state power may lead to some greater benefits to the poor, as has recently been evident in Madhya Pradesh; this of course, will remain in tension with the political developments at the national level, where redistributive policies are likely to remain on the backburner. Meanwhile, factional bickering and politicised bureaucracy have nearly been institutionalised in the Hindi-heartland areas, leading to policy ineffectiveness.[18] Thus, Dreze and Gazdar (in Dreze and Sen, 1997, Chapter 2) document with great care the continuing poor implementation of public services in UP, especially education. In a recent ground-level study of select districts of Bihar, Corbridge et al., (2003) similarly documented the relative ineffectiveness of lower-level governments in providing for the poor. Decades of malign neglect and policy ineffectiveness have thus accumulated in the Hindi-heartland, creating the largest concentration of the poor within India.

To wrap up the discussion on Indian states, I have continued to emphasise both the political base and the organisational effectiveness of governmental power as variables that help explain varying success in pursuing poverty-alleviation policies. States with a broad power base in society, well-organised ruling parties, competent bureaucracy and an activist citizenry – for example, in Kerala – have effectively implemented modest redistribution and direct attacks on poverty. India's southern states as a whole share some of these political traits of India's 'social democratic' states – a broad power base and competent bureaucracies – but not others – well-organised ruling parties and an activist citizenry – creating within them some capacity for poverty alleviation. Hindi-heartland states pretty well lack most of these traits, creating a political landscape in which repeated redistributive failures have by now become a norm.

7.5 The role of local governments in India

India's local governments have generally been quite ineffective at pursuing either redistributive policies or poverty-alleviation programmes. Of course, there has been some variation on this score, with some pockets of success, especially in states that have prioritised the welfare of the poor. On the whole, however, panchayats have not functioned very well because of the complicity of corrupt local politicians and bureaucrats on the one side, and the powerful among the upper castes and classes in the village society on the other side. A variety of distributive programmes sponsored in Delhi or in state capitals have thus failed to reach the intended beneficiaries. Future efforts to pursue such minimal poverty-alleviation programmes as public works employment generation or delivery of public health and education in the countryside will require more effective panchayats.

Panchayats have a long and chequered history in India; the details are readily available elsewhere (Mullen, 2011; Kumar, 2006; and Ghosh and Kumar, 2003). As the lowest rung of the Indian state, our interest in panchayats here is limited to their evolving role in redistributive development. Three issues need to be addressed: why did panchayats play a fairly limited redistributive role in the past; how does one best understand their limited success in some regions and in some time periods; and what is their likely role now that local elections have been constitutionally mandated (in 1992–3).

Most of India' poor live in villages. If government-sponsored programmes are to help the poor, they must somehow reach the poor.

That local governments should implement such programmes and policies is then clearly one viable option. Following independence, for several decades local governments in much of India were mainly administrative organisations in which lower-level bureaucrats sought to implement policies made at higher levels. Up until 1992, when they became the law, regularly elected panchayat governments were rare in India; Maharashtra and Gujarat have conducted regular elections since the 1960s and West Bengal since the 1970s. Off and on, Karnataka flirted with elected local governments. For the most part, however, state governments found local elected governments a constraint on their ability to create patronage chains, and thus, avoided them. The fact that it was political compulsion that led a few states to violate this norm – that is, to actually institutionalise locally elected governments – only underlines the general point (Ghosh and Kumar, 2003).

In much of India, government-sponsored programmes in villages were implemented by lower-level bureaucrats, say the block development officer, who worked closely with local politicians, say, the member of the legislative assembly, and a variety of local 'big' men. The story of how these local elites appropriated much of the little that was intended for the poor has been told so many times that it is too tedious to retell (for example, for my version of this story, see the chapter on UP in Kohli, 1987). The main point that is usefully reiterated is that, for some three decades following independence, most of India's rural poor were deeply embedded in a variety of patron–client relations dominated by propertied upper castes. This was not a fertile soil for social democratic interventions. Even if the commitment of the state elite to help the poor was genuine – which it often was not – prior preconditions for success were either mobilisation of the poor, or forceful public intervention via well-organised parties and responsive professional bureaucracy. For the most part, these conditions were absent in India. As a result, panchayats either did not function or functioned mainly as agents perpetuating the status quo.

What about the few instances in which elected panchayats actually came into being well before the constitutional amendment of 1992? Maharashtra and Gujarat have long had elected panchayats. However, local governments in these states were really not redistributive, either in intent or in outcome. Both of these states are India's economically advanced states, and in both the growing economic pie enabled the accommodation of intermediate groups. The regional dominant castes – Marathas in Maharashtra and the Patels in Gujarat – were the main beneficiaries of the well- functioning panchayats during the

1960s. With her populist rhetoric and intent, Indira Gandhi during the 1970s weakened panchayats in western India, channelling resources via the bureaucracy instead (*see* Ghosh and Kumar, 2003). For the most part, the lower-level bureaucrats during the Indira Gandhi phase were captured by local power structures and proved to be relatively inept as agents of redistributive development; a partial exception was Maharashtra's well-known employment guarantee scheme, though this functioned as a result of several unique conditions, and even then, there is a doubt whether the beneficiaries were the poorest of the poor (Bagchee, 2005).

Prior to 1992, the only state in which local governments effectively supported some redistribution and implementation of anti-poverty measures was West Bengal. The ruling communists in the state chose to penetrate the countryside by facilitating the election of 'red panchayats' and then by channelling resources to these bodies. Since the landed elite were effectively isolated at the lower rung of the state, the panchayats were used to implement tenancy reforms and to pursue effectively the centrally sponsored schemes for the poor (Kohli, 1987). The success was notable, but also partial. The power of Bengali communists in the countryside often rested on small landowners and tenant farmers rather than on the landless. This limited their redistributive intent; for example, they seldom pushed hard for higher wages for agricultural labourers, gains that would have undermined the income of their key supporters. Over time, moreover, new stake holders developed: school teachers, party functionaries, variety of white-collar employees, small landholders and tenants farmers whose security depended on the regime, all became part of West Bengal's 'new class' (Ghatak and Ghatak, 2002). While the power pyramid in the state was definitely truncated, quite a few poor were still left out of the power structure. For now, even in a 'communist'-run state, these poor must depend on a buoyant agrarian economy to improve their life chances.

Ever since the 73rd constitutional amendment that mandated elections for local governments, the issue that has again arisen is, can the dynamics of electoral politics be translated into gains for the poor? The few available studies of the subject are not overly encouraging. For example, there was much excitement among decentralisation enthusiasts about Digvijay Singh's experiment in MP. One recent study of the experiment concluded, however, that local governments in MP continued to exclude the lower strata and the level of interest in panchayats as agents of development was pretty low (Alsop, 2000). Another study found that the limited dynamism in MP depended nearly on a single leader, and a few 'mission' oriented participants – traits that are not likely to be institutionalised – and that the 'success' of most programmes was 'not too high' (Kumar, 2006, p. 85). In the case of Karnataka, at least one scholar found that the refurbished panchayats are working well for the poor, even better than in West Bengal (Mullen, 2011). Her underlying reasoning is that electoral competitiveness in Karnataka inclines political leaders to seek the support of the poor by channelling real gains to them; conversely, the near hegemonic hold of the communists in West Bengal has made them at least complacent, if not corrupt. If borne out by further evidence, such findings are encouraging, because electoral competition is more likely to increase than decrease in the future.

The results of other studies are distinctly less encouraging. Gaiha et al. (1998) analysed the effectiveness of panchayats in implementing the Jawahar Rozgar Yojana (a public works scheme intended to create employment for the rural poor in the lean season). Using state-wise data across India, they found that majority of the beneficiaries of this scheme were not the really poor. While the design of the scheme was in part to blame (wages were often set higher than prevailing local wages, attracting those less-than-destitute), captured and unaccountable panchayats were also to blame, especially in a state like UP. Another study analysed the role of panchayats in the post-1992 period in provision of primary education and health in select states (Kumar, 2006, Chapter 6). The results are definitely mixed. Even the 'red panchayats' of West Bengal have only recently made some efforts to improve literacy and health. Moreover, the 'model' that seems to attract politicians in both Madhya Pradesh and West Bengal – states in which there is some enthusiasm for panchayats – is the one that creates an alternate pathway for the really poor, opening up the possibility of a two-track system, one for the better off and the other for the downtrodden.

As one looks ahead, the types of redistributive programmes that will be pursued in India are likely to be less-than-radical. Neither asset redistribution nor a basic shift in the growth model towards greater labour intensity is in the cards. As discussed above, past failures and the emerging pattern of state–class alliance at the apex preclude these options. What is more likely is that greater investments may be made in improving education and health, and in helping the poorest of the poor by creating public works type of employment generating programmes. The example of the flagship programme of the Indian government to help India's poor, the NREGA, is relevant in this context.

In 2005, India launched a programme to provide 100 days of employment on demand on public works projects in rural India. Over time, this programme has spread to nearly all of India. If well implemented, with an income of nearly US$2 a day for 100 days, this programme has the potential to make a sharp dent into the worst of India's rural poverty. Unfortunately, the quality of implementation remains relatively poor. While the programme has been well implemented in a few states, such as Rajasthan and Andhra Pradesh, for the most part, implementation problems involve diversion of funds by local leaders and bureaucrats, poor quality projects, opposition by landowners who fear an upward pressure on local wages and a sense of inefficacy among the intended beneficiaries.[19] Local panchayats were often more a part of the corruption and waste nexus and less agents of effective policy implementation. While local power structures are hard to penetrate, one area where state elites can intervene directly to improve performance is to improve the quality of local bureaucracy. Poor quality local bureaucrats remain a major obstacle to implementing a variety of pro-poor schemes, not only NREGA, but also efforts to improve the delivery of health and education in India's villages.

A variety of new pro-poor programmes – that focus more on creating equality of opportunity and less on substantial equalities – are now being considered in India. These new efforts are mainly a product of political pressures, some from those who represent the interests of the poor, and others because investment in 'human capital' is deemed to be supportive of growth. The real issue with these limited, but significant new programmes is if they can be implemented properly. It is in this context that the role of panchayats becomes important. On the whole, the past performance of panchayats as agents of redistributive development has been discouraging. The factors that help explain poor performance in the past include the power of those with local influence, political and bureaucratic corruption and low levels of mobilisation among the really poor; none of these underlying variables is likely to change dramatically in the near future.

7.6 Conclusions

I have in this chapter provided a sweeping analysis of the state's role in India in pursuing redistribution and poverty alleviation. Many important topics were discussed only in haste, and others were necessarily ignored. While noting a few pockets of success, the thrust of the analysis above was to underline the limited redistributive capacities of the Indian state. These limitations are rooted in part in the nature of the society, but also in patterns of politics. The caste and class structure of Indian society, and the changing balance of class forces, especially the growing power of big capital, put definite limits on redistributive possibilities in India. However, politics also matters: ideology and organisation of rulers, quality of bureaucracy, mobilisation of the lower strata, and of course, pressures of democratic politics, all have some bearing on the extent of redistribution and poverty alleviation. The analytical task above was to trace how such variables interact at the national, state and local levels in India.

In conclusion, only three final set of comments are necessary. First, there remains an unresolved tension in my argument above concerning the extent to which I believe democratic politics can counter class power. While some of this tension is driven by the underlying analytics, it is also a real world tension. Advanced capitalist democracies, for example, vary anywhere from the more free market Anglo-American model, all the way to the social democratic Scandinavia. As a large, complex society and polity, India is not likely to evolve either along the Anglo-American pathway or the Scandinavian route. And yet, the broader question remains: can democratic forces in India moderate emerging class and other inequities? While my answer above has tended towards the negative, the evidence is also mixed, replete with tensions; the most significant tensions are worth underlining at the end. First, notice that, whereas India's main model of development is being driven by a close alliance of state and capital, in order to stay in power the current rulers need to accommodate broader social interests; hence, the renewed commitment of the Congress Party to 'inclusive growth'. Second, below the near-hegemony that is evident at the national centre, politics in state after state across India is moving in nearly the opposite direction; even in UP, a party of the lowest castes and classes has now been installed in power. And finally, whereas in the past members of the upper castes and classes readily controlled local governments, by now the process is a lot more complex, forcing the political and social elites to channel some resources to those below them to secure their political support.

A second concluding comment concerns prescriptive issues: given substantial constraints, where, if anywhere, is there room for policy intervention that may support redistribution and poverty alleviation in India? The most significant policy areas are two: modifying patterns of public investment, and reform of lower-level bureaucracy. Given rapid economic growth, the state will increasingly have more resources to spend. There is also much room for improving tax collection, both via more efficient collection and by covering newer areas, such as the service sector. With more resources, there is a desperate need to invest more public resources into agriculture and into the poorer states of India. Growing investments in infrastructure, education and health will also need to be continued. What is not being given sufficient attention, however, is how well these resources will be utilised. Here there is pressing need to further understand why bureaucratic capacities in some states are so low, and how to improve the quality of bureaucracy nearly everywhere in India at the lowest level.

Finally, we come to the core concern, namely, what does it take to successfully reduce poverty? An analysis of the Indian materials above strongly supports the view that poverty alleviation is a broad social and political process that goes to the heart of the issue of how state and class power in a society are organised. If one is genuinely concerned about poverty alleviation, one needs to go beyond palliative efforts that aim to channel a few crumbs to the targeted poor. Such palliatives are praiseworthy, but seldom enough. What is needed instead is a much broader programme that may combine elements of asset redistribution, altering the pattern of growth, building human capital and then providing some welfare. Policy regimes that have succeeded in pursuing such a programme have more often than not been social democratic.

Notes

*I would like to acknowledge the research help of Kanta Murali. An earlier draft of this chapter was presented at a UNRISD seminar held at the Indira Gandhi Institute of Development Research, Mumbai, India, 12–13 July 2007. Comments of seminar participants, especially those of Vivek Chibber, were helpful in revising an earlier draft. Final draft: 9 March 2010.

1. Thinking comparatively, it is worth noting that, when averaged over five decades (1950–2000), the economies of India and Brazil grew at a more or less similar pace, though with different patterns of fluctuations. An average growth rate of some four to five per cent situates these 'middling' performers well above sub-Saharan cases, but also behind East Asian cases of South Korea, China and Taiwan.
2. An incomplete list of some of the notable contributions might include (listed in no particular order), Frankel (2005), Nayar (1989), Bardhan (1984), Chibber (2003), Potter (1996), Pingle (1999) and Herring (1999). For further references *see* Kohli (2004), pp. 438–41.
3. One study that broadly supports this claim is Banerjee and Piketty, 2003.
4. The acronym BIMARU generally refers to the following four states: Bihar, Madhya Pradesh, Rajasthan and Uttar Pradesh.
5. A good essay that reviews the evidence on both declining poverty and growing inequalities discussed in this paragraph is Mahendra Dev and Ravi (2007).
6. The evidence here is also fairly clear. For example, my own calculations suggest that market capitalisation of the top ten private companies increased

from 2.2 per cent of the GDP in 1990 to 12.9 per cent in 2004 and sales of the top ten companies during the same period grew from 2.3 to 9.3 per cent of the GDP. These calculations are based on company data from *Business World*, 22 August, 1998 and 27 December, 2004 and the sales data were collected from www.valuenotes.com. As R. Nagaraj explained to me in an informal conversation, value added would be a better measure than sales; unfortunately, the figures on changes in value added by firms were not readily available.

7. I say 'partially' because it is important to not ignore marginal gains. For example, in the 2007 budget speech Chidambram (the then finance minister) promised greater outlays for education, health and rural infrastructure. If pursued effectively (a big 'if'), these are clearly steps in the right direction. The same is true of the National Rural Employment Guarantee Act of India, 2005, where concrete implementation so far has been less than satisfactory. More on this later.
8. For example, when decline in poverty between 1980 and 2005 is regressed on economic growth across Indian states, the R-Squared is 0.49 and is significant at 0.03 level; the results for the same in the post-1991 period are 0.7 and 0.01. These are my own quick calculations based on poverty data from Mahendra Dev and Ravi (2007) and the growth data that is readily available online at www.indiastats.com.
9. In light of this, it is notable that poverty in Bihar has come down significantly since the early 1980s (Figure 7.2). This is in part a function of the fact that what growth there is in Bihar is mainly in the countryside, where most of the poor live. Unfortunately, the result is mainly a function of how high poverty in Bihar was at the beginning of the period. Even after a significant decline, nearly 40 per cent of Biharis lived below the poverty line in 2004–5, a figure only surpassed by Orissa among India's major states.
10. Notice that, if the analysis is well done, the deeper political and social variables ought to be connected systematically with outcomes via some of the more proximate variables acting as intermediate variables. Thus, for example, it may be the case that broader-based, well-organised regimes end up alleviating poverty more 'efficiently' because they facilitate investments into irrigation, implement land reforms and secure property rights, and/or invest in human capital formation. I do not promise such a full, systematic analysis in this paper.
11. I would like to acknowledge the helpful comments of Vivek Chibber in sharpening this formulation.
12. The social and political side of the Kerala 'story' has been well told by others. The accounts that I find most compelling are those of Patrick Heller. *See* a variety of his writings (Heller, 1999; and Heller, 2000). Also *see* his Kerala chapter in Sandbrook, et al., 2007.
13. It is also the case, however, that Kerala at present has the highest consumption inequality among Indian states in 2004–5 (Mahendra Dev and Ravi, 2007, Tables 18 and 19). While why this is so requires further research, it is probably driven by the enormous remittances that flow into the state from Keralites working in the Middle East.
14. Another more recent study (Bardhan and Mookherjee, 2005) finds that the strength of the CPI(M) alone does not explain very well the success of land reforms in West Bengal; what is needed additionally are considerations of

electoral competition. While an interesting set of findings, the research design of the study – which compares villages within West Bengal – is really not suitable for isolating the impact of the CPI(M) on land reforms. This is because the areas in which Congress Party is influential locally, as well as areas in which the CPI(M) and Congress compete, are all operating in a political milieu dominated by the CPI(M). In order to isolate the significance of the CPI(M) then one would need to compare West Bengal to other states. Yet another critical study of the West Bengal experience under the 'communist' regime is Maharatna, 2007.

15. On this dimension Andhra Pradesh tends to be an underperformer compared to the other south Indian states. For example, the illiteracy rates in 2004–05 in Kerala, Tamil Nadu and Karnataka were 7.5, 22.6 and 29.5 per cent respectively while the rate in Andhra Pradesh was 36.1 per cent (the average for all other major states of India was 34.3 per cent). For data, see, National Family Health Survey (III), Chapter 2.
16. Of course, it is entirely possible that the differences I refer to (if real) are of more recent origin, with repeated governmental instability and intense politicisation of the bureaucracy the main culprit in the Hindi-heartland states. All this awaits further research.
17. The fact that the lowest castes also voted for the Congress in these states, say, up until the end of the 1960s, did not make Congress a broad-based party. Members of lowest castes often depended on members of upper castes and were entangled in a variety of patron–client relationships. In spite of an apparent broad social base, Congress's effective political base in these states was thus quite narrow.
18. In a recent interview with a senior IAS officer in Lucknow, he/she noted 'in my nearly two decades of service to various ministers I have hardly ever heard the word policy mentioned or discussed'. I conducted the interview in July 2007. Since the officer is still an active member of the new government in UP, I will not identify them by name or gender.
19. I noticed the problems in a field visit to villages in UP (near Lucknow) in January 2009 and presented my 'findings' to a seminar on NREGA organised by the Government of India, Ministry of Rural Development, New Delhi, January 21–23, 2009. Two good surveys of NREGA are Dreze and Khera (2009) and Ghate (2009).

References

Ahluwalia, Isher Judge (1985): *Industrial Growth in India*, New Delhi: Oxford University Press.

Alsop, Ruth, J. (2000): 'Inclusion and Local Elected Governments: The Panchayat Raj System in India', The World Bank (South Asia – Social Development Unit).

Appu, P.S. (1996): *Land Reforms in India*, New Delhi: Vikas Publishing.

Bagchee, Aruna (2005): 'Political and Administrative Realities of Employment Guarantee Scheme', *Economic and Political Weekly*, Vol. 40, No. 42 (October 15): 4531–37.

Banerjee, Abhijit (2002): 'Empowerment and Efficiency: Tenancy Reform in West Bengal', *Journal of Political Economy*, Vol. 110, No. 2: 239–79.

Banerjee, Abhijit, V. and Thomas Piketty (2003): 'Top Indian Incomes, 1956–2000', MIT Department of Economics Working Paper No 03–32. Available at SSRN: http://ssrn.com/abstract=444880 or doi:10.2139/ssrn.444880.

Bardhan, Pranab and Dilip Mookherjee (2005): 'Political Economy of Land Reforms in West Bengal, 1978–98', unpublished manuscript.

Bardhan, Pranab (1984): *The Political Economy of Development in India,* Oxford: Basil Blackwell.

Besley, Timothy, Robin Burgess and Berta Esteve-Volart (2007): 'The Policy Origins of Poverty and Growth in India', in Timothy Besley and Louise J. Cord (eds) *Delivering on the Promise of Pro-poor Growth,* Palgrave Macmillan and the World Bank, Washington, DC.

Bhagwati, Jagdish and Padma Desai (1970): *India: Planning and Industrialization,* New York: Oxford University Press.

Chakravarty, Sukhomoy (1988): *Development Planning:* the Indian Experience, New Delhi: Oxford University Press.

Chibber, Vivek (2003): *Locked in Place: State Building and Late Industrialization in India,* Princeton: Princeton University Press.

Corbridge, Stuart, Glyn Williams, Manoj Srivastava and Rene Veron (2003): 'Making Social Science Matter – I', *Economic and Political Weekly,* Vol. 38, No. 24 (June 12): 1237–47.

Datt, Gaurav and Martin Ravallion (2002): 'Is India's Economic Growth Leaving the Poor Behind?' *Policy Research Working Paper 2846,* Development Research Group, Poverty Team, Washington DC: The World Bank.

Datt, Gaurav and Martin Ravallion (1998): 'Why Have Some Indian States Done Better Than Others at Reducing Rural Poverty', *Economica,* Vol. 65, No. 257: 17–38.

Dreze, Jean and Reetika Khare (2009): 'Battle for Work', *Frontline,* 5. 26, No. 1 (January, 3–16).

Dreze, Jean and Amartya Sen (2002): *India: Development and Participation,* New Delhi: Oxford University Press.

Dreze, Jean and Amartya Sen (1997) (ed): *India: Selected Regional Perspectives,* New Delhi: Oxford University Press.

Echeverri-Gent, John (1993): *The State and the Poor: Public Policy and Political Development in India and the United States,* Berkeley: University of California Press.

Frankel, Francine (2005): *India's Political Economy 1947–2004: The Gradual Revolution,* Princeton: Princeton University Press.

Frankel, Francine and M.S.A. Rao (1990): *Dominance and State Power in Modern India, two volumes* (Vol. 1 was published in 1989), Delhi: Oxford University Press.

Gaiha, Raghav, P.D. Kaushik and Vani Kulkarni (1998): 'Jawhar Rozgar Yojana, Panchayats, and the Rural Poor in India', *Asian Survey,* Vol. 38, No. 10 (October): 928–49.

Ghatak, Maitreesh and Maitreya Ghatak (2002): 'Recent Reforms in the Panchayat System in West Bengal', *Economic and Political Weekly,* Vol. 37, No. 1 (January 5): 45–57.

Ghate, Prabhu (2009): 'A Quick Survey of NREGA Implementation Issues in Selected States', unpublished manuscript.

Ghosh, Buddhadeb and Girish Kumar (2003): *State Politics and Panchayats in India,* New Delhi: Manohar.

Harriss, John (2003): 'Do Political Regimes Matter: Poverty Reduction and Regime Difference Across India', in Peter P. Houtzager and Mick Moore (ed) *Changing Paths: International Development and the New Politics of Inclusion,* Ann Arbor: University of Michigan Press, 204–31.
Harriss, John (1993): 'What is Happening in Rural West Bengal', *Economic and Political Weekly,* Vol. 28, No. 24 (June 12): 1237–47.
Heller, Patrick (2000): 'Degrees of Democracy: Some Comparable Lessons from India', *World Politics,* Vol. 52, No. 4 (July), 484–519.
Heller, Patrick (1999): *The Labor of Development: Workers and the Transformation of Capitalism in Kerala, India,* Ithaca: Cornell University Press.
Herring, Ronald (1999): 'Embedded Particularism: India's Failed Developmental State', in Meredith Woo-Cummings (ed.) *The Developmental State,* Ithaca: Cornell University Press.
Herring, Ronald (1983): *Land to the Tiller: The Political Economy of Agrarian Reform in South Asia,* New Haven: Yale University Press.
Jalan, Bimal (1991): *India's Economic Crisis,* New Delhi: Oxford University Press.
Kohli Atul (2012): *Poverty Amid Plenty in the New India,* New York: Cambridge University Press.
Kohli, Atul (2004): *State-Directed Development: Political Power and Industrialization in the Global Periphery,* New York: Cambridge University Press.
Kohli, Atul (1994): 'Centralization and Powerlessness: India's Democracy in a Comparative Perspective', in Joel S. Migdal et al. (ed) *State Power and Social Forces,* New York: Cambridge University Press.
Kohli, Atul (1991): *Democracy and Discontent: India's Growing Crisis of Governability,* New York: Cambridge University Press.
Kohli, Atul (1989): 'Politics of Economic Liberalization in India', *World Development,* Vol. 17, No. 3 (March): 305–28.
Kohli, Atul (1987): *The State and Poverty in India,* Cambridge: Cambridge University Press.
Kumar, Girish (2006): *Local Democracy in India,* New Delhi: Sage Publications.
Mahendra Dev, S. and C. Ravi (2007): 'Poverty and Inequality: All-India and States, 1983–2005', *Economic and Political Weekly,* Vol. 41, No. 6 (February 10): 509–21.
Lieten, G.K. (1992): *Continuity and Change in Rural West Bengal,* Delhi: Sage Publications.
Mallick, Ross (1994): *Development Policy of a Communist Government since 1977,* Cambridge: Cambridge University Press.
Maharatna, Arup (2007): 'Population, Economy and Society in West Bengal since the 1970s', *Journal of Development Studies,* Vol. 43, No. 8, (November): 1381–422.
Mullen, Rani (2011): *Decentralization, Local Governance and Social Well Being in India,* London: Routledge.
Myrdal, Gunnar (1968): *Asian Drama: An Inquiry into the Poverty of Nations,* New York: Pantheon.
Nayar, Baldev Raj (1989): *India's Mixed Economy: the Role of Ideology and Interest in Its Development,* New Delhi: Popular Prakashan.
Nagaraj, R. (2000): 'Indian Economy since 1980: Virtuous Growth or Polarisation', *Economic and Political Weekly,* Vol. 35, No. 32 (August 5): 2831–39.
Pai, Sudha, (ed.) (2007): *Political Process in Uttar Pradesh,* Delhi: Pearson Longman.

Pingle, Vibha (1999): *Rethinking the Developmental State: India's Industry in Comparative Perspective,* New Delhi: Oxford University Press.

Potter, David (1996): *India's Political Administrators: from ICS to IAS,* New Delhi: Oxford University Press.

Rodrik, Dani and Arvind Subramanian (2004): 'From "Hindu Growth" to Productivity Surge: The Mystery of the Indian Growth Transition', unpublished manuscript.

Rudolph, Lloyd and Susanne Rudolph (1987): *In Pursuit of Lakshmi,* Chicago: University of Chicago Press.

Sandbrook, Richard, Marc Edelman, Patrick Heller and Judith Teichman (2007): *Social Democracy in the Global Periphery: Origins, Challenges, Prospects,* New York: Cambridge University Press.

Sen, Amartya, K. (1999): Development as Freedom, New York: Knopf.

Shah, Shekhar and Manju Rani (2003): 'Worlds Apart: Why are Kerala and Uttar Pradesh so Different in their Human Development Outcomes?', unpublished manuscript, Background paper for the World Development Report, 2004.

Singh, Prerna (Forthcoming): 'World's Apart: A Comparative Analysis of Social Development in India', doctoral dissertation in preparation, Princeton University.

Suryanaryana, M.H. (2007): 'Economic Development and Economic Inequalities: Indian Experience', paper presented at the UNRISD seminar on 'Poverty Reduction and Policy Regimes', Indira Gandhi Institute of Development Research, July 12–13, 2007 (Chapter 3 in the present volume).

Weiner, Myron (1991): *The Child and the State in India,* Princeton: Princeton University Press.

Weiner, Myron (1967): Party Building in a New Nation, Chicago: University of Chicago Press.

Witsoe, Jeffrey (2006): 'Social Justice and Stalled Development: Caste Empowerment and the Breakdown of Government in Bihar', *India in Transition,* Philadelphia: Centre for the Advanced Study of India, University of Pennsylvania.

Index